ONLY CHILD

By the same authors

IT'S MY DUTY, ISN'T IT?
The Plight of Carers in Our Society
by Jill Pitkeathley

AGE GAP RELATIONSHIPS:
The Attractions and Drawbacks of Choosing a
Partner Much Older or Younger Than Yourself
by Jill Pitkeathley and David Emerson

ONLY CHILD

How to Survive Being One

JILL PITKEATHLEY
and
DAVID EMERSON

SOUVENIR PRESS

First published 1994 by Souvenir Press Ltd,
43 Great Russell Street, London WC1B 3PA
and simultaneously in Canada

Reprinted 1994, 1997, 2005

ISBN 0 285 63182 9

Photoset by Rowland Phototypesetting Ltd,
Bury St Edmunds, Suffolk

Printed and bound in Great Britain by
Creative Print & Design (Wales) Ltd, Ebbw Vale

5/17
unique

ACKNOWLEDGEMENTS

We planned this book for some years, since David first thought of the idea. We are grateful to all those people who have since listened patiently, helped us with suggestions and given encouragement. We thank Simon and Rachel for all we've learned from them and our friends for letting us test out our ideas. Most of all, we want to record our deepest gratitude to all those only children who so generously shared their time and their feelings with us, and whose words we quote extensively. For the sake of anonymity their names have been changed, but we know who they are. We are extremely grateful to them all.

Since the book was first published we have received a number of moving letters. We said that we wanted to reach people who felt that 'the experience may be relevant to them and whom it may help to understand themselves better'.

I thought, as so many of your interviewees obviously did, that my feelings, responses and 'world-view' were a result of the unique condition of my upbringing. It has been a revelation and a liberation to discover that I do, at last, belong to a group which shares characteristics and experiences. Letter, 1996

This is what we have done – we are glad to know it did mean something to many who have read the book to date.

JILL PITKEATHLEY and DAVID EMERSON

A selection of comments from the many letters we have received since publication

'I have just finished reading *Only Child* which I found absolutely unputdownable. I was quite amazed how the analysis fitted my character and development on almost every score. Hours and hours of psychoanalysis could not have produced the self-revelation which your book has done.'

'I've just read your excellent book. The extent to which the descriptions apply to me as an only child is remarkable: if I was paranoid, I'd say that you'd been spying on me! I'm sure that the book will help me in overcoming problems that I face in my life.'

'I found your book a revelation. So many aspects of my personality and the way I am, which I previously thought were peculiar and problematic, turn out to be common among only children. You have explained me to myself and made me much more confident in stating my needs – now I know they are real needs (because of my upbringing) rather than oddities to be suppressed.'

'It was a brilliant book and I am sure I am not alone in saying that it has helped me to change my life. I recommend it to as many other only children as I can.'

'The sense of relief is enormous. I laughed aloud with recognition time after time . . . Your book is all so true. I shall recommend it to every only child I meet. I have read a number of self-help books. Yours is really outstanding and I congratulate and thank you for it. I feel quite normal, for the first time in my life.'

Writers' names and addresses withheld for reasons of privacy.

CONTENTS

Introduction

Only children are distinctively different from all other children. Not worse, not better, but different. This book describes those differences.

We believe this distinctiveness has not been set out before. The popular image of the spoilt, selfish, self-centred but successful only child is far from being the complete picture. Of course, first-born, middle and youngest children have their differences too, but this book isn't about them. This is, in fact, the first one to draw entirely on the experience of only children themselves, to analyse what it is like to be an only child, how it affects you and how you can use the experience more positively.

We have interviewed sixty-plus only children in depth about their background, childhood, schooling, relationships, careers and many other aspects of their lives. From this we now know that being an only child is most definitely a special and very different childhood experience. It has great gains – of parental love and attention amongst others – as well as great losses, especially absence of sharing with other children. And the only children we interviewed had strong views about it:

I get very irritated at the tired old stereotypes about only children. They are not necessarily doted on or spoilt any more than other children. Conversely, they are not freaks to be pitied. Nor is onlyness a reason for a youngster or an adult having behaviour problems. All the stereotypes are insulting assumptions. But our experience is different and that makes us special. I wish the world would realise that.

Childhood without siblings leaves a legacy of burdens which present themselves as 'problems' with far greater force in adult life than ever they do in childhood. As our interviews reveal, there are unique pressures and responsibilities for the adult only child. Most certainly, all is far from rosy behind the assured and confident exterior that only children usually present to the world.

But if it is so different, why hasn't the only-child experience been identified before? Perhaps because only children themselves have rarely recognised how much the way they behave in relationships, and socially, stems from being an 'only'. They tend to feel any odd behaviour as just part of their own identity – after all, they've never had a brother or sister against whom they could check out their reactions:

It's hard to explain the total ignorance of any other child in growing up.

And where behaviour is noticed by others, it's often defined in terms of the 'spoilt, selfish only child' image. Only as an adult will an only child spot another at a party, and perhaps laugh with him or her at a shared trait.

A constant feature throughout our interviews has been the surprise of interviewees that what they had just described to us as an individual experience from their own upbringing was one we had heard from many other single children. In having no other siblings with whom to share recollections of childhood, the only child has not been in a position to recognise a common experience:

If I had to live my life again I would not wish to come back as an only child. I'd never wish it on anybody. I'm not saying it's dreadful, because it wasn't. But I just wish I'd recognised earlier what the effect of being an only child is.

This book aims to help with that recognition. Early childhood is the most influential period of our lives, when fundamental character is set. Indeed, whatever your situation was at this time – whether a first-born, middle, youngest or only – it will have had an influence on your adult life. The issue is not *whether* that upbringing will have had any effects, but *what* those effects will have been. The book offers a chance of greater understanding and awareness of the many effects of the absence of brothers and sisters. Through this awareness it will give you, we hope, an opportunity to change, and to achieve more control over your life.

In Part 1 you will recognise, perhaps for the first time, the varied patterns of only-child behaviour, and spot in yourself patterns that may have been unconscious until now.

Using that awareness, in Part 2 we go on to show how to make those patterns work for you with friends and with your partner, and at work.

Part 3 is for the partners and for the new or prospective parents of only children. For partners, we point out some likely reactions of only children that may not mean they don't love or care about their partners' needs – just that they aren't used to having someone living so close to them. In turn, their partners' closeness and concern can easily seem overwhelming – only children aren't running away from their partners, but from the threatening sense of confinement. For the parents of only children, drawing on the suggestions made by our interviewees, we offer hints that may help in bringing up one child.

It is particularly timely that this book should appear now because there are more only children than ever before, and their numbers are increasing. A survey in 1993 showed that five times as many people are choosing to have only one child as compared with a decade ago. Only children were common during the years of the Great Depression and the Second World War, but were rarities in the years of the so-called baby boom. Now, for all kinds of reasons, including women having babies later in life and the increasing numbers who do not wish to take a break from their career for child-rearing, the situation is reversed. Though the UK figure still stands at 1.8, the average European family now consists of 1.4 children.

We are only children ourselves, and writing this book has unexpectedly proved to be for each of us a way of coming to terms with our own experience. We hope those who read it will feel the same.

The Only-child Identity

In claiming to identify the distinctive only-child experience, are we saying that all only children are the same? That there is a typical only child instantly recognisable to those who know the signs? No – we are not saying anything of the sort. There isn't one only-child experience, but there is a range of typical only-child characteristics. No one only child will exhibit all of them but, judging from our interviews, most will recognise in themselves perhaps two thirds of them. The probability is that any one only child will be more like another only child than like a child from a sibling family. Put another way, there is much more of an overlap between any two only children than there is between any two others. If you don't believe us, try this simple test next time you are in a group of people. Ask yourself who is

the most responsible person in the group?
the most organised?
the most serious?
the one who is rarely late?
the one who doesn't like arguments?
the self-possessed one?

The chances are that the one who is all these things will be the only child. It's not infallible, but it's pretty reliable as a test.

Of the characteristic only-child traits, how many are displayed by any one will depend on his or her individual upbringing, parental circumstances and parental attitudes.

Most of the people quoted in this book started their lives in a household with two parents. In spite of increasing divorce rates and the tendency of more women to have babies outside a permanent partnership, this is still the commonest situation in which to pass your childhood. As for the only children we interviewed who were from single-parent families, their only-child outlook was more diluted in significant ways, and it seems clear that the experience of having only one parent is much more dominant than that of having no siblings. This will have to be the topic of another book!

Who *Is* an Only Child?

'Just who is an only child?' you may be asking. Clearly, if you have no brothers or sisters at all you are one. But what if you have, say, a brother or sister ten years older or younger? Or, once into teenage or your twenties, you lost a sibling? We don't want to make precise definitions, as it is the childhood experience that's important. If you *feel* like an only child, as far as we are concerned you are! However, if you have or had siblings but still feel yourself to be an only child, for this book to be most useful to you – since not all of it may be equally relevant – one distinction may be helpful.

This distinction is that there are two senses in which you can be an only child. One is that, in having a childhood without siblings, you are likely to develop a particular outlook which will influence your behaviour. And if you have a much younger or older brother or sister, but were effectively brought up alone, then you may identify with these aspects of being an only child.

The second sense is that of having no one to share parental expectations with, and later, having all the responsibility of caring for your parents. This position may be shared by those brought up with another child or children but who lose them when young. If this is you, then while our description of single children's behaviour is unlikely to ring many bells with you, you may find their feelings of responsibility and living up to expectations familiar.

*   *   *

What you will read in this book are not our views but those of the only children who gave so freely of their time and their opinions. We have attempted to interpret what they told us so as to enable others to share in their insight. We are deeply grateful to all of them.

Part 1

About Being an Only Child

Of course I've always thought there should be an organisation for only children; I even thought of a name for it – AOKs!

'So what's the big deal about only children?' we can hear those who had a sibling childhood ask. 'Why on earth should they feel there could be a need for their own association? Haven't they always had the best deal, the best of everything – surely they can't want still more? What's so special about them, for goodness' sake? What sort of problems could there be for a group who, we all know, have had more than their fair share of parental attention and goodies?'

One of my friends was an only. You always knew she'd have the latest toy, the latest fad, and as we grew up, the latest fashion.

Well, having all those goodies, all that undiluted parental attention, not having to share with other siblings, missing out on the rough and tumble of a sibling childhood – and many more distinct experiences – does create in the only child someone special, someone with behaviour that can seem strange to those who have grown up amongst brothers and sisters.

Of course, we recognise that the pressures and rewards of being a first-born or a middle or youngest child all create distinct behavioural patterns too. We don't claim priority for only children. But the experience of growing up as a lone child in an otherwise adult household can produce distinctly different patterns of behaviour that get in the way of successful relationships, confuse partners, create problems at work and produce a permanent sense of isolation:

I shy from having friendships that are too close – I think I find it too claustrophobic when people come too close – it's a problem for me, but worse for my family.

Despite having been married for a long time my relationships have always suffered from the lack of social playfulness which a family can also engender, at best.

My education was heavily influenced by both parents' expressed wish for me to do well in it. I was 'expressed' through various streams at primary and junior school . . . and this created numerous problems in terms of my social development – which I probably still suffer from as a result!

These patterns of behaviour are recognised by others, too. 'Aren't their foibles so glaringly obvious?' asks the outsider. A counsellor comments:

I can spot an only child at twenty paces. It's something about the space they always need, the lack of ability really to engage with anyone else or to be able to share themselves.

And everyone knows that all only children are self-centred and spoiled . . . One woman described her ex-husband thus:

I always thought he was a classic only child – completely self-obsessed, only thinking of his own needs and really believing he is the centre of the universe.

It is a view so well held that it has long been reflected in literature:

Unfortunately, an only son (for many years an only child), I was spoiled by my parents.   Mr Darcy, in *Pride and Prejudice*

One is the indivisible number but one is lonely.   Erica Jong

For only children themselves, the reality may be very different from the image held by others. All those we have spoken to expressed strong negative feelings about some or all of the experience:

Of course it's a life sentence – it never gets better.

We have been able to group their reactions around five broad headings:

Being Everything;
Rough and Tumble;
Self-image;
Social Maturity;
Always Alone.

Our interviewees' reactions were not always negative: we heard about happy and positive experiences too. For the most part, though, they echo the words of the only child who said:

There hasn't been a day of my life when I haven't wished for a brother or a sister.

1   Being Everything

The intensity of the only-child experience is key – feeling you have to be everything.

I felt I was carrying all the responsibility a lot of the time – all the eggs in one basket, and I was the future. That is the key thing for me – the all-the-eggs-in-one-basket thing. That is, you know, the great nub of it.

This first chapter examines the strong senses of *responsibility*, *expectation* and *blame* felt by only children and frequently expressed by them as 'being everything'. We then look at the effects of being on the receiving end of *all the attention*, and getting *all the 'goodies'*.

Why are these feelings especially strong for only children?

In most societies, two people living together as partners are not the usual idea of a family. We don't hear a man saying, 'I'm a family man' when he only has a wife at home, or a woman saying she wants to give more time to her family if she just means her husband. Only when a baby, a third person, arrives does that unit become a family. As that third person, at a very early age the only child comes to realise that responsibility for being the family, for carrying on the family line, for making the change from 'couple' to 'family', rests with him.

With me it was the total investment syndrome. They knew they

weren't going to be able to have another, so everything got chan-
nelled into me: my mother's frustration with the marriage, my
father's frustration with himself. All hopes were pinned on me. I
was the Messiah child. Everything was going to be all right now
I was here.

The sense, experienced by many only children, that they
have to carry all the responsibility, all the expectations and
all the blame for the whole family means that they have to
perform a greater variety of roles in respect of the family.
They may find themselves acting as

mediator or arbitrator between the parents;
companion;
fulfiller of ambitions – in relation to career and main-
 taining the family line;
bringer of joy, and mood-maintainer; and
carer.

But it isn't just within the family – there are roles outside
too: as the family representative at school, in community
activities or at social events. And all these roles are taken
on because there is no one to share them, there is no one
else to make up 'the family'. As one interviewee, now in
his seventies, said of being an only child:

God, you wouldn't wish it on anyone – you have to be everything.

While few of our onlies felt as strongly as not to wish it
on anyone, almost all of them referred in some way to the
burden of 'being everything':

You're everything to your parents. You're their reason for being.
And I think it's very easy for parents of only children to exploit
that with the guilt trip.

Or they increasingly saw it as pressure:

There's a lot of pressure when all their hopes are pinned on you
– it's a big pressure. In a way I feel the pressure of being an only
child more now than as a child. As they get older I'll feel it even
more . . . I dread caring for them. As a child you don't know

*any better – as you get older the pressure grows, the guilt grows.
I feel a responsibility to my parents now – it's a role reversal.*

But being everything does include the positive as well as the negative: getting all the parental attention and all the material goods that are going – hence, perhaps, the myth of the spoilt brat.

Let's now look more closely at each of these themes.

All the Responsibility

Who is in charge? Who does the organising? Who makes the lists? Who takes the responsibility? The only child, of course. Everyone knows how serious and dependable they are – the repository of their parents' ambitions, the high achievers, the ones who are always correct.

Taking on board their pivotal role in creating the family makes only children very responsible people with a strong sense of having to behave properly, to be in charge:

I've always wanted to kick over the traces but never felt I could, somehow – always that sense of having to be 'sensible'.

I am very good at taking responsibility for my own actions – I believe too good, now. I think I set too high a standard for myself. But I now believe my parents did too.

The eldest child in a family will feel this too, as he is always asked to be responsible for siblings. As one woman said to her older brother:

When we were young I learned to be selfish, whereas you learned to be selfless.

We know that only children can feel this sense of responsibility more strongly than other children – as one woman of 33, whose brother died when she was 21, illustrates:

When my brother died I thought at first that the extra responsibility I felt for my parents and for just about everything was because of his death. Later I realised that it wouldn't go away as we adjusted to his not being there – it was now a permanent feature of my life – made worse by my having no other person of my blood to share these feelings with.

Only children take on the responsibility for being the leader, the one who completes the tasks, the one who is in charge. They can often recognise another only child in a group by their worried or serious look and the number of times they say 'Sorry':

I am very much a mother hen, even with friends. I'm concerned how they'll get home or if they are ill with drink, etc. Mother hen is linked to bossiness – but I do have a concern for others. And more than that, I feel responsible for them.

The responsibilities fall into two distinct categories.

1 RESPONSIBILITY FOR PARENTAL WELL-BEING

The only children we spoke to felt strongly the burden of being responsible for their parents' happiness and well-being. Do those with siblings feel this to the same extent?

I felt I had to be good all the time to keep my mother sweet. If she was in a good mood all was well and then it was bearable for us all.

My parents split up for a while when I was going to university. I felt a great weight of responsibility to Mum when Dad left. She was on her own and I was the only one. I spent a lot of time, coming down from college. I was the only one to do anything and feel a sense of responsibility towards her: it's only me. Dad did return but I worried at the time what would happen in the future. It was a worry.

Several were aware of weaknesses in their parents' marriages, as a result of which one parent, usually the mother, leant on the only child for support:

I believe my mother needed too much from me. I also feel strongly that this need is very different for mother/son and mother/daughter, but they are equally powerful.

I was always manipulated by Mother into being on her side. Father was scapegoated and blamed and I was required to recognise this and speak out against him, as the price for being supported by my mother.

I couldn't upset my parents and be responsible on my own. The slightest thing was always a problem, so it was anything for peace and quiet. You had to pussyfoot around and not upset anyone. And my parents had a three-way thing with my grandmother too, because she was very off with my father who wasn't good enough for my mother! And I was observing all this and really didn't want to throw any more grit in the works!

When Dad was ill I had to go up – I felt obliged to go up. Mother needed me – to talk to, take charge, etc. I wished she was as practical in a crisis as I was.

My father had a perforated ulcer and I remember having to go back and look after my mother while he was in hospital. She wasn't terribly good at coping on her own.

I felt an incredible sense of responsibility towards Mother. She was very possessive and quite weak and dependent on me – a role reversal. I can remember resenting the fact that I had to prop her up, and everything.

Of course, most offspring would feel a sense of responsibility at such times of crisis, but having no one to share it with, having always to carry it alone, was the real difficulty:

No one to whom you can say 'our mother', feeling it all devolves on you, that's what makes you feel overwhelmed.

This sense of responsibility can sometimes extend to trying to be the mediator in the parents' relationship. A surprising number of the people we talked to felt the need to be a go-between:

My parents rowed endlessly. I used to take bedclothes and sleep outside their door to try to stop them.

I am very conscious of very much being the mediator between my parents. If they argued I had to make things right. I knew I had the power to make things right. For the first year of the remarriage Mum often packed suitcases for her and me, and we'd drive off and I'd sit in the back of the car with my teddies and ask, 'Will Daddy be all right?' I was always the mediating factor.

If happiness is connected with happy families, as most of us learn at an early age, then as an only child you believe you hold the key to it:

There was also, I think, by that stage a feeling of a level of responsibility for my mother inasmuch as I was very much the centre of her life, and I think it was made quite clear to me that it was very important to her that I was not too far away . . . you know, if I had wanted to go to Edinburgh . . . ! So although I went away to university I went to Essex, so it was far enough that I wasn't living at home, but we both agreed that was a good thing.

There is this inherent guilt thing when you're an only child. Looking back . . . you are the focus, and with my father now being ill it is almost as if when I go there the entertainment has arrived. It's not quite as if you are the life and soul of the party, but almost as if you are duty-bound to support them with something.

Our interviewees often felt they were responsible for the success or failure of events such as Christmas or holidays – a perception that we encountered so frequently that we have given CELEBRATIONS a short chapter of its own (Chapter 11).

2 RESPONSIBILITY FOR THEIR OWN EXISTENCE

It was remarkable how many of the only children we talked to felt responsible for being an only child in the first place. This idea seems frequently to have been implanted by over-heard conversations:

My mother was always telling people that she was very badly knocked about giving birth to me.

I was always made to feel that the reason there were no more was because I was so difficult and my mother was so exhausted.

Or they were told directly:

There were problems with the birth, and I certainly got the message that it was my fault. My father still has that: he tells me it was a difficult birth, said Mum wouldn't like to have gone through that again – 'Once we had you we didn't want any more', etc. I didn't feel especially wanted, not wanted that much.

The idea is even sometimes fostered where it has no basis in fact:

Family mythology is that as a baby I caught mumps and passed it on to Dad, so that was why there were no more children. I didn't realise until I was grown up that I didn't have mumps until I was seven.

Some of these stories may be true, since there is a greater probability that only children will have had significant medical problems associated with their birth – that is, a proportion of them are only children *because of* such problems. But, for the child himself, such tales easily translated into guilt: 'You were such a lot of trouble', or 'You're so difficult', was the message that some only children picked up:

As a pregnancy and birth I was extraordinarily difficult. I don't know, I sometimes wonder, because my mother used to tell me this a lot – it's almost as if she needed me to know this – she used to say over and over again, 'Your father was given a choice: did he want to save me or the baby?' I think there was a factual element in that, I really do, but it was repeated a lot in late childhood.

Perhaps the guilt which later becomes such a significant part of the only-child experience starts here:

I think from what my mother said it wasn't a very pleasant experience, and I do have a certain sense of guilt. It was a hard birth and everything combined together and, what with their experience of me as a baby, deterred any further sort of forays, really! My father always said that my mother found the early years of upbringing difficult. I don't think it was planned that 'We're only going to have one.'

I was an enormous baby and called 'the elephant' by nurses, and presumably painful. Mother has made me feel guilty about this, as about everything. That's why I resent it so much.

In cases where the other sibling has died, the distress or thoughtlessness of the parents can instil a feeling of responsibility for the death of the sibling into the only child:

My mother had a baby boy who died after two weeks, when I was seven, and later a baby who died at birth. So I was an only child up to seven, when other children were imposed, but then they didn't exist. I had guilt when they died, perhaps wanting them to die. If you've been an only child for seven years and a brother arrives who I didn't especially want . . . Quite a long time after I felt quite guilty that I might have killed him.

Because my mother had lost this daughter, I have lots of memories of me as a child trying to play under the table, with mother in front of the fire, crying, with the lights off. I don't think she ever got over it, and she used to go on to me all the time: 'If your sister was alive she'd have kept you in your place.' I used to get that, which was deeply boring to me as a six-year-old boy, since a dead sister didn't mean anything to me. And she'd say, 'Your sister would have been 12 today.' So there was a lot of that going on which was an extra burden, and a reflection of my mother's pain, of course.

*   *   *

Only children take on these responsibilities in response to direct or indirect messages from parents and family. And they continue to accumulate responsibility earlier and faster than their peers, through a process which works like this:

—Being surrounded by adult company and being the centre of attention, the young only child quickly develops a larger vocabulary and models the behaviour he sees around him – adult behaviour.

—What the parents then see before them is a child behaving in a much more adult way than normal for his age. This may be especially so if the parents are not able to observe the child playing in a normal childish way with other children.

—The natural response is for the parents increasingly to relate to the child as an adult, and give him responsible tasks and involve him in decision-making about the house and family.

—In turn the only child becomes more grown up, the parents relate in a yet more adult way, and so on.

—The phenomenon of the 'little adult' has been created.

Because during my formative years it was just me, it made me grow up very quickly – I felt like an adult long before I'd have been classified as one. It has given me a sense of standing on my own two feet.

The consequences for the emotional development of the child are considerable. The small child is still there behind the apparently grown-up mask. (What this means we develop further in Chapter 4, SOCIAL MATURITY.) The parents, often unaware of this, may respond to the adult presentation of the child and start giving him responsibilities:

I was aware of money – awareness was shared with you – what could and could not be spent. I was very aware of what could be

*bought at Christmas – I asked once for something too expensive.
I was told it was about budgets; I was very aware of this and
how it worked, early on. Beyond my pocket money I worked from
very early on to get anything extra. Being part of the decision-
making, I was consulted early on when I was quite young.*

*I actually knew what my parents' financial situation was from a
very early age and would certainly never have nagged for things
or – well, we didn't have TV advertising – dragged them past a
toyshop saying, 'I want one of those . . .' If something could be
afforded I would have it.*

It may not just be her parents who recognise the apparent
maturity of the only child:

*I was always fairly old-headed, always grown up and responsible.
Other mothers would ask, 'Is Fiona going? All right, you can go
then.' I was an approved person.*

Giving the child responsibility or freedom may be a conscious decision by the parents to help the child, a deliberate
attempt to compensate for the dangers of overprotection,
which we describe later in this chapter under *All the
Attention*:

*Mum gave me more leeway than other kids, as she felt it important
I went out and was with other kids. Now I'm amazed the things
I was allowed to do – things that'd make my hair curl now!*

And, of course, having or being given this responsibility
has its own consequences both at the time and later:

*Through being involved in family decision-making so early, I soon
became aware of when I had power. I don't think it was two
adults with power – you don't tend to have two with power –
that's not how adults work. The major problem for the only child
is realising his power position: how much power they do have,
and they have the choice whether to exercise it or not.*

THE EFFECTS OF BEING TOO RESPONSIBLE

Being responsible is a positive trait, with benefits both for the only child and for society. But being a little *irresponsible* might not do some only children any harm, and most seem to have acquired rather too much of a sense of responsibility. They apply it to matters way beyond their control:

> *There are days when I just pack a suitcase into the car and just drive. I would go, but I always feel so responsible for everybody. I'm always rushing round looking after everybody. You know – I've got to keep everybody happy! And if I didn't? I'd be miserable.*

What effect does this overdeveloped feeling of responsibility have on the only child? Many of them felt they had had no proper childhood, that they became grown up too early:

> *I didn't feel I was ever allowed to be a child, carefree and unfettered by a sense of duty or responsibility.*

Later, in adolescence, awareness of what they saw as their accountability to parents inhibited any teenage rebellion:

> *I think only children don't have teenage rebellion in an overt way – I certainly didn't. You can't really, can you? It's too much of a responsibility. There's only you and it's too hard on them, really. So you find other ways. That's probably what it is.*

> *I had no rebellion. It wouldn't have been possible. I was always in at 10pm and I'm very angry when I see girls who are cheeky or play up. Why are they allowed?*

The feeling of bearing responsibility is carried on into adult life and may be expressed where it is not entirely appropriate – for instance, feeling responsible for the happiness or the situation of others where there are no possible logical grounds for doing so:

> *He is terribly over-responsible. I kept telling him – you cannot solve everyone's problems. If that is a trait of only children, then Charles is that 100 per cent. Once when I was low and asked him to stay in, he said he had a dinner engagement. It turned out*

he had taken his secretary out to dinner because she had been upset by breaking up with her boyfriend! I told him he couldn't take everyone out to dinner who was upset! He totally feels responsible for keeping the whole world happy.

This same sense of responsibility gives only children other qualities:

I have this great sense of fairness. I'll always fight for the underdog.

I hated bullying at school, and I was very protective to younger girls who were being bullied and I looked after them. It helped that I was quite tall by then, anyway. I would say, 'If you have any problems, tell me.' And every time they were bullied, I'd step in and say, 'Right, you can bully her, but you come through me because she's a friend of mine – OK?' I started looking after all the girls who were being bullied.

Again, this can usefully carry through into adult life:

I'm a strong and responsible person – almost to the point of neurosis, though. I feel guilty for other people, for their actions. This makes me a good advocate. When other people are bullied I go berserk inside.

I have a great need to cope for other people – desperately so. I take on lame ducks left, right and centre, and cope for them. I feel I can help, but I'm cementing over shaky foundations to make me feel better, because I've set myself up as a coper, and am putting myself in the position of the victim, so I can't easily ask for help when I need it. I have a strong sense of what is right – politics, everything. Like the Waterbabies, do as you would be done by. When I see that infringed I get desperately angry, and spend a great deal of vacuous anger getting angry about things I can do nothing about.

There's a fine line where responsibility dips over into guilt, which can damage the relationship between the child and one or both parents:

I resent all that guilt, and for all of it I sustain a deep loathing for my mother. I can't bear her. So now what I do is spend all my time and as much money as I can afford in paying her off; I see her as often as I can stand, and I give her things if I can afford them and take her out for Christmas lunch. It is a grotesquely cynical operation and I know absolutely what I'm doing, but she's not going to be able to say to me, 'We paid for you to go to school; we paid for you to go to college – what have you given us back?' She can't say that any more because I've paid her off, and more. So I am literally trying to buy off my guilt, quite cynically. Because I couldn't bear it. The alternative . . . leaving her . . . I can't bear that.

I feel strongly that I do not want my children to feel guilty about me as I do about my mother. Guilt is very important. My husband was an only child and from the day I met him I believe he felt guilt towards his mother – for leaving her, for putting someone else above her in importance. In fact he couldn't do this. Now I realise I too felt guilt towards my mother, although it was different. In both cases because of the shortcomings of the two fathers as husbands, the mothers needed too much from their only children.

We refer to the guilt of only children frequently, as it is a commonly felt emotion.

Developing a sense of responsibility in early life is not without its compensations. It can produce bonuses later:

Being an only child is an advantage in getting yourself motivated – you've got to sort out activities for yourself as a kid and this carries through into adulthood. That's why I can work at home happily. I don't mind doing things on my own – I prefer not having the restriction of someone else. It's a positive, being able to do things on your own.

If I have a goal, I'll really go for it. It takes a lot to get me off the track.

I've never missed a deadline in my life. It's unthinkable for me to do so. My message of doing what you've said you would is too strong.

I learned early on that failure to do something you were supposed to do was not permitted. The result of failing to deliver was my parents' wrath. No, not wrath exactly – that would have been easier to cope with. It was this disappointment thing . . . the feeling of letting them down. It was hell at the time, but I have to say the results have been good. I never miss a deadline, always deliver what I'm supposed to at the time I'm supposed to.

But the only child is also likely to be too hard on herself and too intolerant of others:

I'm terribly, terribly, terribly self-critical and set myself high standards, and I have high expectations of others. I can't tolerate sloppiness in others at work. And I do compete against myself terribly.

And only children are not always much fun. Many do seem to be over-serious and to have difficulty letting go and being irresponsible occasionally. In Part 2 we'll show how to deal with this sense of responsibility and make it work for and not against you.

Feeling such responsibility is connected with the next element of 'being everything' – being the recipient of all expectations.

All the Expectations

All families have hopes and aspirations for their children, not all of which will be fulfilled. For all offspring there is a greater or lesser feeling of tension between what they know or believe their parents want for them and what they want for themselves. This is a natural state of affairs to which the only-child family is no exception. Where it *is* different lies in the fact that the parents have only one hope of their ambitions being realised. Many of our interviewees expressed a tremendously strong sense of expectation being focused upon them, in two ways. There could be a *high level* of expectation to achieve, especially academically or in a career. There could also be a *wide range* of expectations – personal (marriage and grandchildren), cultural, academic and professional. The single child has to carry the burden of all such expectations from parents, grandparents and other close family members. 'Messiah child' is how the role has already been summarised by one interviewee. Most felt the pressures as a burden.

How the only children that we spoke to perceived the expectations and in turn reacted to them varied considerably. Some expressed the perception in a *general way*:

You are the seat of all your parents' hopes and expectations.

They wanted me to have the perfect upbringing. I was going to make up for their damaged childhoods. I was going to be perfect.

I now realise that I have spent so much of my life trying to conform – to be popular, to be 'as expected' – and failing, and blaming myself, that although I now am able to attempt to be me (whoever that is) it will never be perfect. I need a certain strength to persist with what I want to be, and even now it is not always easy or clear.

Others experienced parental expectations in more *specific ways*, for instance, as pressure during childhood:

I've always been their pride and joy. That's been a pressure. I know especially from my father that I'm always his 'shining star'. I've had pressure on me to do well academically and career-wise and to make good boyfriend choices.

or as stronger pressure, later:

When we bought a house in S. Manchester, my parents were in Blackpool and we pushed to get them nearer to us in Cheadle. Without doubt we felt pressured to do so.

or as a need to achieve:

If I'd have had a brother or sister I honestly think I wouldn't have bothered going to university. I never liked it really – it was always a waste of time for me. But there was this thing about having to achieve and there was no one to achieve but me.

or as a mixture of educational and personal demands:

I did have a lot of expectations on me, especially along the lines of education: what I was going to do and when, college, etc., and especially from Dad. My dad wants me to end up marrying the right type of person. He's not said that to my face, but I'd hear if they weren't good enough. I do get on better with Dad now but I still have some sense of expectation. But I'll be who I want, and if I want children now I'll do it. I feel he'd feel let down if I did that. It wouldn't stop me, but I'd feel it.

Or parental expectations might be felt in relation to one particular parent:

Well, I was everything for my mother, especially after she left father. I was her helpmeet as well as her child. I don't think my parents laid that kind of number on me, but even as I say that I realise that in fact I've fulfilled all my mother's expectations: I went to London University, I became a journalist as she'd done, and I've got two perfect sons. She's dead now, but she'd be pleased.

or in relation to the other parent:

I did fishing with my Dad – being the boy he wanted. He's very competitive. I've been told that if I'd been a boy, I'd have had a terrible time.

or in the recognition that they were the single opportunity for their parents:

Whatever happens to you, it is the only one of those experiences your parents have – like my wedding was not what my mother would have chosen, and she didn't have two or three others to make up for it for her.

One reaction to such pressure can be to express the frustration of not having a sibling to share the load:

When you are an only child everything is channelled into you. If you don't live up to expectations, they can't look at anyone else. I

used to say to them, 'I wish I had a sister who was perfect, and
a sister who had got all her O levels and been a perfect student,
and who would go off and get married etc., and then you'd be all
happy.'

Some expectations can have a selfless element, while
none the less remaining a pressure:

They wanted me to get married and have someone to look after
me. They always encouraged me to study – but also to find a
wonderful man who'd look after me.

Within this range of expectations, pressure may be most
strongly expressed in the parents' or family's *personal hopes*:

You are the repository for all your parents' hopes and ambitions.
I'm the only person who could have brought them grandchildren
and I've failed, and I'm the only person able to look after them.

The parental (and often grandparental) desire for children
is, not surprisingly, one of the most frequently expressed,
both for women:

Apart from the academic one, there was also the expectation to
get married and have a family, and I'm a source of great disappointment to her about that.

I feel guilty about not having a grandchild – not a child, if you
see the difference. It's the one thing I didn't do for her – I did
every other possible thing. She was worried about me not having
anybody, in the sense of not being looked after.

and for men:

There is a pressure for grandchildren. I'd be very pleased to manage
this before they die. I haven't done so and I'm getting on, at 35.
In their lifestyle it is very late. All their relations are grandparents,
and they are not. It would be a beautiful gift to them to be able
to present grandchildren – it would make them smile in their souls.

Both sexes had felt pressure about carrying on the family
name, or 'line':

As a child I was often told of the delight of great aunts etc. when *in their late thirties my parents finally had a child, and a boy at that, who would carry on the surname. My name was added to the family book and it did dawn on me that all those relatives were expecting me to carry on the line. 'You are the last of the Blackwoods, you know – we mustn't let the name die out.' Fortunately, I have male cousins now so I don't feel that pressure so much.*

When you marry, don't change your name or there will be no more Chiltons.

If the expectation isn't realised, guilt is usually the result:

Now I've split up with a man who was their ideal, I feel guilty at having spoilt their dream. That is quite recent.

This may happen even when the only child appreciates the impossibility of resolving conflicting expectations:

When Mum was on her last legs she said, 'I would love to have seen Jill married' and I felt SHIT – you can't just do it for the sake of someone else; you have your own life. And you can't always be what they want you to be.

For some parents it could be moral or behavioural codes that the only child would be expected to follow:

Mum and Dad are very churchy – Catholic. I was an altar boy, but as I grew up I started to question and rebel against going. My mother has a strong personality and sometimes I'd give in for a quiet life, but I burned with resentment and there was great bitterness – there still is. She is very upset that I'm not a practising Christian and finds it hard to take. I always think that if there'd been other children it would all have been less intense and there would have been less pressure on me.

My family were Mormons and when I got to college I left the Church – a hard thing to do. My parents were very upset, and various well-meaning people wrote to them and to me saying they should disown me etc. Really vitriolic letters.

My father had very strong moral convictions and he expected me to follow them: no alcohol in the house. The expectations were less of a scholastic nature than to do with my behaviour, which they disapproved of very strongly. In that sense I didn't live up to their expectations.

The pressure on the child to fulfil *high career or academic expectations* was frequently acutely felt:

There was pressure to achieve, especially from Father. He was always showing me off at British Legion dos and saying, 'She is going to get into Cambridge.' It was nice in a way, I was pleased and proud. It was very nice, but the implication was I felt pressured to do well.

This can translate into a particular career:

I went to be a teacher because my mother expected it – it's as simple as that.

I went into my father's business for the simple reason that I was the only child – if there'd been a son he'd have done it and I could have been a nurse, which is what I wanted in the first place.

The expectation was often explicit:

I didn't tend to mix very much with boys at school up until A levels, because my parents didn't want me to go out with anyone. What was all-important to mother was getting qualified – she wanted me to get a degree. (But they didn't want me to do anything with it except have a family!) The main thing was that she wanted me to do well academically. It was explicit – I was aware, oh yes – phew – I couldn't fail to be!

but not necessarily especially demanding:

My parents were very, very keen that I achieve academically. I never resented that. I love books and have a lot. Their expectations were not a problem, but it was very clear that that was what they wanted. They still want me to succeed and are very interested in every job or career move.

As with other expectations, they can be stronger from one parent:

I felt my mother's academic expectations at school. Mum was an only child and had been head of games, head of school etc. etc. She was the star pupil for everything and lived up to her parents' expectations, and she was bright. My father had won scholarships, got degrees and a doctorate very quickly, and he was also very good-looking and everything. Everyone loved him. Grandfather had been very bright too. It was not easy for me.

I was of the generation where all my father's frustrated academic ambitions rested on me because he hadn't had the opportunity of university education himself – he had to leave school at 15 and become a breadwinner. There was a lot of hope resting on me so I did feel a great deal of responsibility to do well, but at the same time I didn't find it terribly difficult to pick up all the eleven-plus, the O and A levels.

One child can find himself the subject of a split between the academic and the emotional desires of the parents:

At the age of eight I was taken round to look at boarding schools, to go away. My father was very keen for me to go; he was very much into education. My mother wasn't so keen – she didn't want me to go at all, really.

And the academic pressure is recalled early:

It was very important to them that I passed the eleven-plus, and I was made to take private tuition before then. I can remember the book clearly – Practise Your English: *a book with a red stripe and* Practise *with an S. I am still very consciously pedantic, even about grammar, especially 'different from'.*

Sometimes the academic pressure is acceptable, and shared by child and parents alike. Many of our interviewees came from a working-class background, and it had been the joint parental ambition to ensure that the child didn't have to work in a factory, like Father:

Relatively, they were still high expectations – their aim, or perhaps Mother's, was for me to be a teacher. For Father, for me to be able to read and write well was a good achievement, but in absolute terms this was not too demanding. Mother's self-knowledge pushed me into education, with father's backing. The pressure was copable: I was doing all right, even when I failed to get into art school first time because I didn't get good enough grades. After I'd got O levels the pressure was off, because I'd already done well.

My parents wanted me to do well, and were very good and self-sacrificing. They didn't want me to end up on the factory floor, like Dad. It was constantly frustrating for them that I was such a lousy scholar. I wouldn't cut the mustard, and just wanted to go out with my friends all the time.

I did only moderately well at school, which disappointed my parents. They were working-class and had got to the top level they could make. I was then expected to continue the climb up the social ladder. They were looking to get their success through me. Mother, for some reason, had the idea I should be an optician. They were devastated when I only managed to get into teacher training college.

The worst situation was where love for the child was – or appeared to be – conditional upon academic achievement:

Expectations from the parents were contradictory. My parents would tell me they loved me constantly and my mother obsessively. Then when I didn't do very well at school the love apparently vaporised.

Except for Mum's sudden concern once in mid-teenage, when I started saying something like 'Someone's got to come bottom in the class' or some such – I'd always said before that 'Someone has to come top', meaning me – I never remember them tying in love to success. But it's the clear message I've picked up. Achieve, be good – in every sense – and we'll love you. God, I hate that – it's been so destructive.

While most of our interviewees recalled some degree of academic expectation from parents, their response to it was variable. Sometimes the expectations were thwarted unintentionally:

> *Basically I wasn't interested in school; I didn't find it very interest-*
> *ing. My parents were both very bright, my father especially, and*
> *my grandfather had been two years ahead of his age year at school*
> *– it was a very bright family. And they have this one, demented,*
> *simple child – me.*

and sometimes intentionally:

> *I put quite a deal of effort into resisting what my father wanted*
> *me to do – he wanted me to major in sciences (I'd have been*
> *incapable of that). Having got my degree, he then wanted me to*
> *be a civil servant or tax inspector! He had a thing about figures*
> *which I couldn't share. So I suppose I made a point of doing my*
> *own thing. My mother just wanted me to get back to Scarborough*
> *to teach and be there again. I just couldn't. I never did go back.*

These kinds of expectation may be felt in many families,
but we were surprised by the number of only children who
felt themselves responsible for the *emotional tone* of the family:

> *There is this feeling that you have to be there on high days and*
> *holidays – you can't say to your sister, 'It's your turn this year.'*

> *It's as though you can't take any time off – you have to be reacting*
> *and interacting all the time – the spotlight is on you. I was never*
> *able to go off to my room and just be quiet – somehow, I always*
> *had to be having some kind of reaction. I feel where there is*
> *another child . . . I could have taken a little rest while my parents*
> *focused on someone else.*

> *You know how all children go through moody phases? I never felt*
> *I could, because then the whole household would be moody. You*
> *can't lose yourself and be ignored till you are feeling better, if you*
> *are an only child.*

Feeling responsible for the mood of the family gets worse
as time passes, since as parents grow older they can often
become more demanding of the only child. Special occasions and celebrations are naturally significant to them,
but of course it is always the same family member whose
presence is required. There aren't other siblings who can

provide the attention on an alternating or rota basis, as we'll see more in Chapter 11, CELEBRATIONS:

If I don't go and see my parents within 24 hours of my birthday it's a big deal. If I don't go to lunch on New Year's Day it's a big deal. The importance to them is enormous.

Not fulfilling the parental expectation has its emotional consequences for the only child, while the parent may be unaware of the greater commitment involved:

If I forget to phone her one week she barely speaks to me the next. She obviously feels she owns me – I'm an important part of her life – she's not an important part of mine – she's not filled her life with anything else. I'm going down for a week soon, but Hugh has to take a week off work to look after our dogs. So two people give up a week each of their holidays. My parents' dog is a substitute child which never goes into kennels. It happens to be a bitch – is that significant? Anything to keep my parents happy, because it's not worth the consequences.

Even when a parent has herself experienced unrealistic expectations as a child and is aware of them, it may not stop her making demands:

Mum (who was also an only child) has said that she refused to give me the guilt trip that her mother had laid on her – that she had to always go back and visit, etc. But in fact she just does it in a different way.

The early maturity and awareness of the only child can be an asset in dealing with these expectations:

When I was in my teens I became very conscious that my mother probably would eventually rely on me far too much if I wasn't careful, and I set out at about the age of 16 on a very definite campaign to get her to join things, because she hadn't. She wasn't really a very clubby lady, and with a certain amount of pushing and discussion and – once I had mentioned it – the active enthusiasm of my father, we got her interested in things like the WI, and she became very interested. I do remember the feeling that 'there's got

*to be something else for her to do other than me'. I think she may
have been going through a period when she was concentrating on
me overmuch.*

*My parents wanted me to go to university and were very impressed
that I was going to read classics and could read those Greek
squiggles. But my mother wanted me to go close by. She'd been
so dependent on me, and I'd begun to realise just how much she
manipulated me. I was determined to get away, and there was
the most enormous row about me going to Exeter. My parents
hated me going there and marrying Robert, of whom they disapproved, and they never let me forget that they hated both.*

Once again, such burdens aren't necessarily unbearable:

*My mother and I were extremely close – probably as much like
sisters, in some ways, as mother and daughter. I spent a lot of
time with her and got on well. My mother never worked; she was
always at home, and in some ways that was a burden because she
was always expecting me and I had to be there. I couldn't sort of
decide to go off and do something; I had to get home in case she
worried. But on the other hand I did enjoy her company.*

Nor are expectations of the only child confined to family
members:

*I remember when I had one of those interviews about the scholar-
ship. You know, one where the headmistress of the posh school
comes to see if you are up to snuff before she accepts you. She
asked me about my family and I saw her write down 'only child'
and underline it. Then she asked me what I wanted to be when
I grew up. I replied, as I'd been primed to by my parents, that I
wanted to be a doctor. 'Oh,' she said, 'that is an excellent ambition
to have, and quite possible since you are an only child.'*

*When I was caught up in a slightly disreputable gang of blokes
and in court one time for driving without a licence, the bloody
magistrate even pointed out that my parents would be particularly
upset because I was an only child.*

THE EFFECTS OF EXPECTATIONS ON RELATIONSHIPS

Responding to the expectations and emotional needs of parents, or anyone else, can inhibit the only child's development of a range of relationships:

> *I had no relationships with adults other than my parents. I did have a slight one with an unmarried aunt, but I didn't like her. It was because Mum would have died of jealousy if I'd have gone off even to the shops with another adult. It must have come hard to her when I made close relationships with other people.*

Only children tend to have too high expectations of others, both practically and emotionally. We'll look later at what this means for their own relationships, and how they can deal with it. And their tendency to feel always responsible for fulfilling expectations can become a central part of their personality, an unquestioned part of their make-up and behaviour. And if it remains unquestioned, it may create an overdeveloped sense of duty in adult life and relationships:

> *There never was anyone more into being dutiful than me. Moral obligation, feeling that I ought to – that's what I can't get away from. The question of whether I want to do it or not doesn't come into it. If I feel I should do something – I do it – end of story. I couldn't face the guilt if I didn't, I suppose.*

GUILT AND OBLIGATION

As we have seen, the pressure of all the expectations, with only you to achieve them, creates a strong sense of obligation in many aspects of only children's lives. This very easily translates into guilt. One of the enduring impressions left with us is that guilt is an indelible part of the only-child condition. As one interviewee said, 'There is this inherent guilt thing when you're an only child.' Sometimes it was expressed in very strong terms:

> *I wish I could get rid of all the guilt in my life. I'm guilty if I forget to call people back, if I leave the answering machine on,*

if I work with my feet up all afternoon, if I spend too long in the bath. I'm guilty all over from the little toe upwards. I hate it, I hate it. Guilt is the common denominator of only children. It encompasses everything.

It's like Sundays. I have to go every bloody week. The only way I can get time off is by inventing some event I have to go to which they'll accept. If I say I'm not going, Mother will say, 'Well, there is nothing to get up for then, is there?' She controls me through guilt. She stakes her claim to her day.

I suppose I've been a big disappointment to her – I'm overweight, not married, I've had a breakdown, a drink problem and I clean houses for a living. Enough?

NEVER ENOUGH

Clearly, some expectations were met and parents were happy – sometimes. Looking back over our interviews, we noted that more often than not only children still felt they hadn't achieved what was expected; or, when they apparently had, the goalposts were moved:

For my mother, whatever I did was never enough. I was pushed not just for university, but for Oxbridge. At college I then brought my first proper relationship home, and afterwards told Mum I was sleeping with him (Why did I do that? I wonder now), and she gave me a terrible time. I went back to college, had a nervous breakdown, took a year off and went to South America; came back, finished my degree and started working in this very difficult, very competitive area. But I made my mark and by 28 was quite successful. Mum then asked why was my career so important, what about a family? That really sums it up, doesn't it? I had a high-sailing career, but that wasn't enough. Her dying wish was a promise that I'd have a child. I asked her about the first relationship and she said that she didn't want me to get married and throw it all away. Mum wanted me to be the best.

'Never enough' is the resonant phrase. However hard they tried, only children rarely felt they had achieved as much as was expected of them. And what's the result of all this? Only children tend to be very hard indeed on themselves. Other's high expectations of them are nothing to what they expect of themselves. The hardest taskmaster for the only child is himself:

I've always felt the pressure to do not as well, but better than, anyone else.

At forty I think you get afflicted not by depression but by a form of stress or panic at not achieving enough and efficiently, but it may feel like panic.

I constantly take all the world on my shoulders.

I collapsed and was taken into casualty. It turned out they diagnosed stress – I had controlled my life for years, now it was all falling apart. I had even contemplated suicide.

EARLY ESCAPE

As we say elsewhere, a key aspect of being an only child is the intensity of the experience. Confined within this tiny family and under such adult pressure to achieve, the obvious means of relief may be to escape as soon as possible. Several interviewees recalled that they couldn't wait to get away from home – and not just away from home like many other teenagers do, but as far away from home as possible:

My first choice was the university furthest away, my second choice the second furthest – I was very clear I wanted to leave home because I wanted a different experience – I don't think I've ever been forgiven for that!

I couldn't wait to leave home. Mum didn't say it, but I think she felt 'After all I've done for you', etc.

There was a lot of pressure from my school to go to what they called a good girls' college, but I was having my own little rebellion by that time. I actually went for the largest college I could find and one with the highest percentage of males to females I could find! And I wanted to go well away – at that time Barrow was almost two days by car – it used to take ages and ages to drive up.

The further away I was from Mum the better – moving away was a bid for independence.

There is nothing wrong with having expectations of your children. All parents have them, and part of a healthy up-bringing is to be set appropriate targets for achievement. It is the range and level of achievement expected of only children that can become a life sentence. And it is the legacy of unmet expectations that is particularly disturbing – a legacy of guilt or stress or extreme self-criticism or acute awareness of never being enough. Perhaps worst of all is the belief that your own self-worth is tied to achieving suc-cessfully expectations that have been set by someone else.

All the Blame

Only children face a dilemma. On the one hand they are the centre of attention and get all the goodies, and if things go right in the family they can take the credit. *But* when anything goes wrong:

There is no one to blame but me.

After all, there's no one else around, so it has to be her fault, doesn't it?

There's normally a black sheep in a family who takes the venom away for others, but unfortunately you're the one carrying the black-sheepness.

It isn't just that there's no one else to be blamed, it's also that there is no one else who can point out that it's the parents who might be wrong and have made a mis-judgement:

If someone is angry with you, you are unlovable and it must be your fault. You only see anger as related to yourself. A sibling can dispassionately see the cause of it. If your parents get angry or show disapproval, they are the only people you see who do and it's always directed at you. I think this links to the fact that I'm sure the only child is late in recognising the fallibility of parents. My mother was very demanding and I didn't question it until very late.

Our interviews have made clear, then, that there are these two separate elements: (1) there is only you, so it must be your fault; (2) there is no sibling, and thus no one whose objectivity can show you that your parents could be wrong. The feeling of being to blame can arise from your own awareness of having failed to achieve expectations:

If you do something that is disappointing, then they come down on you doubly hard.

or from what your parents may tell you:

Literally I was my mother's image – she told me what I was. It conflicted with not so much my identity but what I thought and felt. But I believed her. Mother would say, 'You're a naughty boy', and I would stand there and think, 'Well, I must be a naughty boy then.'

Whereas many people seem to be quick to offload blame at the earliest possible opportunity, the average only child takes it on as a matter of course:

I'm always saying 'Sorry'. I didn't realise this for a long time, until it was pointed out to me. At a party recently I'd said 'Sorry' a couple of times and another only child (as it turned out) said to me, 'You must be an only child.' It's that obvious!

Only children never have the experience of saying what is second nature to most children with siblings, '*It wasn't me – it was him [or her].*' They may learn the technique with friends or playmates, but that's very different from being able to do it with the family all the time.

Neither is it usually possible to blame one of the parents for a misdemeanour. The imbalance of power between a child and his parents makes that a non-starter. On top of this, they never see anyone else being blamed in turn, so they may never acquire a sense of proportion about blame:

I'm simply hopeless – I always feel I've got to take it on – if the train is late, if the soup is cold, if the report isn't ready, I feel it has to be my fault. I watch people shifting the blame to others – either overtly or subtly – and I marvel at it.

I always remember being with my cousins at some Christmas do or other. There were four of them, all born close to each other. Somehow or other an ornament got knocked over as we were larking about. The noise brought the grown-ups rushing in and I was amazed how my cousins all automatically blamed me for the breakage. I don't think they were being malicious, they just blamed someone else as a matter of course and I was the nearest. The thing is, though, I took the blame – it didn't occur to me to deny it because I wasn't practised like they were.

But perhaps the only child also takes on the blame because, in early adulthood, it seems the responsible thing to do, or what the adults would expect – because blaming someone else is childish and irresponsible:

Even when I know someone else is to blame, I find it very hard to point the finger – that's immature, 'wrong', it's not what you do. I can sort of hear that parental voice and I just feel a baby, I suppose, when I do blame others.

So saying 'Sorry' becomes an instinctive reaction:

I'm always saying 'Sorry' – hundreds of times. Someone else knocks into me in the street and I say 'Sorry'. I always say 'Sorry'. Sorry for breathing . . . Someone bumps into me: 'Sorry'. Why do we apologise when we haven't done anything? My friends keep saying, 'What are you saying sorry for? – you haven't done anything.'

Why? Because it's our fault, isn't it? There's only us, so if anything goes wrong or anyone's to blame it has to be us, obviously:

Even if someone stamps on my foot here, I'd say 'Sorry' that my

*foot was in the way. It's bizarre. I adopted this to pacify my
mother, who was a great sulker. I'd go for a week without being
spoken to. If I didn't say 'Sorry' I'd be in shtuck. It goes back
to the anger thing, and if they are angry they don't love you – it's
your fault. Though, of course, it's probably something to do with
them having an off day or whatever, and you just happened to be
there in the way. It's not to do with you at all.*

But there is no one else to help you see that it isn't to do
with you:

We're the little oddballs with guilt on our shoulders.

And, given half a chance, only children take on blame for
the world:

*I feel to blame for ridiculous things. For example, I come from
the Isle of Man and people always used to be asking me what it
was like for a holiday. I'd tell them and sing its praises, because
I do think it's a lovely place. Then they'd book to go there and
I'd be in a welter of anxiety about the weather, the place they
were staying, even the punctuality of the ferry, for God's sake. If
they came back and they'd had a good time, then I felt great, but
if they had not enjoyed it, had been ripped off or had rotten
weather, I felt it was all my fault. I almost felt I had to refund
the cost of the bloody holiday.*

Some only children recognised what was missing:

*I always felt I was missing out. I wanted somebody there, someone
to share the blame with. I couldn't pass the blame – there was
only me.*

THE EFFECTS OF TAKING ALL THE BLAME

*You are the centre of the universe from the year dot onwards. So
when you're told off it's a catastrophe because you have no experience of anyone else in that small circle being told off. So it is the
absolute end of life. With a brother or sister, even if you don't
get on with them, you have seen other people in the house treated
in the same way, which gives you a sense that life metes out good
and bad to people. Because you're on your own in this kind of*

nuclear core, and you're told you are loved and that you are the apple of your parents' eye, when praise is lavished on you you feel you are the only person in the world to receive praise – there's nobody else that you see your parents give praise and love to. Then that's taken away and you're told off because you're naughty – it's the end of the world because you've got no understanding that life's like that; you don't witness it happening to other people in the same way. So calamity is always the corollary of joy – there's no sort of thing in the middle.

Because of these two extremes, the only child is vulnerable in several ways. He may be easily exploited, feel guilty a lot of the time, and be easily hurt by others, who are quicker at shifting the responsibility and the blame.

Only children are used to assuming that everyone else in their world will behave in a certain way – namely, in an adult and 'fair' way. So they can find themselves at a disadvantage in not being quick enough to respond or shout back at unfairness when others are not playing by the rules and are shifting blame. (It is the same sense of fairness that prompts only children to stop bullying when they see it happening.) They can develop defence mechanisms to protect themselves. These are not usually in response to an attack – only children are often not good at dealing with attacks, and fear conflict. Rather, they set up defence mechanisms in order to outflank an attacker, to guard against the possibility of attack, to protect themselves beforehand:

I don't take criticism well. In fact, in business a lot of my effort is to ensure that I won't be criticised, to guard against it. I'm a collector, a gleaner of things, bits of information and so on, which I can use in a defensive way if I'm threatened. My boss criticises in a devious way and it's hard to fight back, but I get strong feelings of 'It's not fair.'

My agenda comes from having learned as a child to cope with Mum's moods by saying 'Sorry', and it worked. Later I learned to take responsibility. In a group I want to take the heat out of

*situations, and if you do that you are unlikely to get criticism. If
I was around someone in a bad mood, I'd think it was my fault.
My agenda is around making everything nice and smooth; playing
happy families, like I grew up in.*

Only children may be quick to take on the blame themselves, but this doesn't mean they take criticism easily. On
the contrary, most felt that they were over-sensitive to it:

*I can't take criticism, of course. Because you have no experience
of sharing criticism with other people, you always feel it is cataclysmic. If your mother tells you off, it is the end of the world
because she loved you two minutes ago and you haven't observed
other people being meted out the same treatment. Everything is
absolute and everything is terribly personal, and it becomes
terribly important to avoid criticism. My mates used to laugh at
me 'cos I used to say jokingly that I couldn't kick a dog in case
it didn't like me. I had to make sure everybody liked me. I couldn't
bear the idea of them saying something cruel.*

One of the effects of being quick to take the blame yet
finding criticism difficult is that the only child can be a
confusing and difficult partner in relationships. He feels all
right if he is voluntarily shouldering the blame himself, but
unhappy when being criticised for his own actions. If he is
in control he is comfortable, but not otherwise. We return to
this need to be in control in Chapter 4, SOCIAL MATURITY.

One of the other effects frequently reported to us is that
only children feel a very strong message, a compulsion even,
to 'get it right' – whatever 'it' may be. They want to behave
right, act right and react right. They want to ask the right
questions and give the right answers. They want their
relationships, their families, their lives, to be 'right'. Of
course, the problem is that they often have not the slightest
idea of what 'right' is. They know only that they mustn't
be wrong. Because you are an only child carrying all the
responsibility, you know from experience that you get
blamed if things go wrong. Grace, for instance, knew that

a holiday had to be 'right', even though she wasn't sure what would make it so:

> *I haven't had a holiday for eight or nine years because I'd be so nervous it wouldn't be right that it is easier to stay at home. A weekend is OK, because it is not so important to get it right.*

Most people don't have any trouble offloading the blame for their holidays not being quite right, do they? It's the weather, or the tour operator, or something. Not so the only child: she has to get it right herself. It's the same if she has friends over to supper:

> *I do so want everything to be right. Yet I do silly things, like trying new recipes. Of course, they sometimes go wrong and then I'm depressed. If only I could be more relaxed about it.*

That certainly would be better, not only for the only child but also for her companions. The combination of wanting to get it right *and* needing to take all the blame makes you pretty intolerant, both of yourself and of others. You are not exactly a relaxed, laid-back companion. This is an example of where 'being everything' can be a disadvantage. But, as we said earlier, there are advantages too.

All the Attention

So far, 'being everything' could appear to be an unqualified liability! It often is, but that's not the whole picture. There are some huge compensations, some tremendous advantages for the only child. As many of our interviewees pointed out:

> *You get all the support; you get all the resources, including financially. You are not necessarily spoilt, but you get the chance to appreciate your own company and develop as a person.*

And their partners noticed those advantages too:

> *I'm immediately struck by the confidence that comes from him being the only and adored – a completely devoted and loving atmos-*

phere. George was never compared to anyone else, whereas I'm second of two daughters. There was never anyone else on the horizon; he never had to share anything. But he's not acquisitive at all, as people in large families can be – I think because of that. Also, he is hugely generous, always gives. But he had to be able to amuse himself and had no one to share the burden of being a child – the emotional burden of being loved by two people – and when his father died also the burden of his mother of forty-something on a boy of twenty.

Let's look at the undivided attention only children receive, and how that leaves them feeling:

I was privileged in having all my parents' attention lavished on me. You are their only chance – they're going to give you their best shot. As an only child you are able to absorb your own thoughts and cultivate your own resources to entertain yourself.

The parents of many of our interviewees had wanted more children, but couldn't have any. For them, their one child was very special, and the attention focused on her could make her feel at the centre of the universe:

One of the positives of being an only is being treated specially by parents and being aware of being something precious.

In the evening I was all my parents had to worry about.

I think for anyone it is very warming and encouraging to have sort of undivided loyalty and support from two adults who you know will be rooting for you, right or wrong. You would always know that you had that support.

Attention in the form of support in learning was frequently mentioned:

You get more attention – not just spoilt, but your parents can put more time and effort into you as far as learning, which Mother certainly did. Mainly just time, effort and input.

Some interviewees valued this attention because it had

enabled them to develop interests which, with siblings around, might not have been possible:

> *My father gave me the wonderful sense of inquiry. He also gave me a knowledge of gardening – I would spend hours on the allotment with him.*

It is probably difficult for the child to recognise that he is being treated differently, but some were aware of realising what a brother or sister might mean:

> *From an early age I've always seen the advantages of being an only – centre of attention and also of love and resources – quite something in a working-class family. Parents used to tease me and say they'd get me a baby brother, and I remember feeling very upset – there was no way I wanted an intruder.*

> *I'm not honestly sure if I'd have wanted a brother or sister, though I felt as a child that I should say I did. I just loved being the centre of attention – the only object of my parents' love.*

Being in the limelight for a few years is something first-born children may share with only children, and may explain some of their shared characteristics. But for the only child, of course, this focus is never shattered:

> *I'm still happiest when I'm the centre of attention. I suppose all first children have that period of being the apple of the eye and they are rudely awakened when the squawking baby arrives. We only children never get that – we always remain at the centre.*

What are the effects of all this attention? Some of them are positive:

> *For me one of the positives of being an only child is to do with the fact I had my parents' undivided attention. They encouraged me in anything I wanted to do – any hobbies. I liked art and they'd provide the stuff, the materials. They were concerned that I wouldn't get bored because there was only me; so they were keen to follow up any interest I expressed. That gave me a great sense of being valuable, important; for a child I had a very strong feeling of being precious – it has left me a lot of self-confidence.*

Having only the single child to worry about, parents tend to manage things in a way that, through lack of time, would probably be impossible in a larger family:

In childhood we planned all my social, non-school time – the summer holidays. There'd be a discussion with my parents, who would say, 'We've six weeks' summer holiday – let's plan it.'

The summer holidays were planned like a military operation, to keep me entertained.

And in lots of small ways, the greater time and attention available from a parent means the child's needs can be met fully and quickly:

Clothing was never a problem – you could get the clothes you wanted – even to mum making a white tie when they were in fashion. Everything was very immediate. If you wanted something done – cooked, ironed, mended – it was. The result now is that I like things to happen immediately. *I have a sense of immediacy. I hate waiting in queues. I do it but hate it, because I don't have the money. If I had money I'd bypass waiting for things. At my home things would happen with a degree of alacrity because my parents could do them now.*

The undivided attention of both parents means that whatever you say is likely to be heard:

But I wasn't perhaps aware until I went into other children's homes when I was older that I didn't have to compete for attention, and I think that's the chief thing. You are terribly aware, if there's a whole load of children clamouring round the parent when they go in, that that's not a situation you ever face. The moment your foot crosses the door there's a parent saying, 'Hello, how are you? Has it been a good day?' and 'What do you want for tea?' You know it is terribly spoilt – by the amount of attention I should say, not materially.

Or, as a sibling partner put it, interrupting an interview we were having with his wife:

Only children are used to people actually hearing what they say.

They grow up saying something and their parents respond, whereas in a multiple-child family you say something, and half is going to be ignored. So when Annette tells me you are coming round, she thinks I am listening, and I didn't hear!

But, although being the focus of attention can be a very good childhood experience, generating the self-confidence expressed by many only children, there were also negative aspects. The family of three creates an intensity to which we have already referred, and will again. The concentration of parental attention contributes to this:

Only children have had the number-one spotlight on them from the day they were born, and even parents who try hard not to do this inevitably do. If a child is crying and two others are beating each other to death with saucepans, the parent deals with the two first, not the one crying. With more children, the parents don't have the time to focus continually on the only child.

Because the focus is on you and you can't afford to put a foot wrong, you are on your guard more yourself as a child. If there's three or four the parents aren't looking all the time, and the odd slip can go unnoticed. When the focus is on you, every slip is noticed.

Total attention can generate a sense of claustrophobia, or of 'no escape':

I felt constrained by the form my mother's love has taken: 'Go ahead and do precisely as I say, and I'll love you.' For only children, there is less escape. I exclusively feel and exclusively resent that, as an only child.

I regret the over-possessiveness and claustrophobia of being just three of you, plus all the hidden agendas, some of which you knew and colluded with, some you didn't. I can look back now and see what they were, but as a child I couldn't.

Our only children certainly felt there were catches to being in the spotlight within the home. At its minimal:

Having all the attention is a disadvantage because you are the one who always has to wash up, do everything, look after Mum when she's ill.

Parents' undivided attention can be too demanding when it is coupled with their needs:

As far as my mother was concerned, there were times when I had to be everything in impossible ways . . . son/daughter/lover. Remember that marriage and motherhood was her total activity – it left lots of time for me. She demanded concrete expressions, tangible evidence of being everything. A sister would have taken some of the demands – still would take them. I learned early on that it was: meet Mother's needs, or else.

or when there are unresolved issues between the parents:

With my parents, I was always in the middle. The trouble with being an only child is that you get all the emotions put upon you, and there's nothing to deflect it. My father would always say, 'Don't answer your mother back' or 'Take that look off your face', etc., while mum would say, 'Don't upset your father', and you always felt as though you were the shuttlecock between the pair of them. If Dad sulked then Mum would share things – if Mum was upset with him she complained to me about it.

Outside the home, if not in it, only children realise that all this confidence-building attention does come with a price tag. As the centre of your parents' world, when they talk it is to you they are talking; questions, commands, expressions all naturally have you as their focus. No one else is involved, no one else's opinion or interjection has to be even thought about, let alone allowed for. Everything centres on you, and such unquestioning attention leaves the only child expecting a similar reception elsewhere:

We have a peculiar notion that we should be seen, recognised by others; that we have a God-given right to have our feelings recognised. We get our upsets picked up by our parents very quickly – even through body posture; they know us so well and recognise our body language. But it appears that only people who are demon-

strative about their feelings get noticed and get picked up on how they are feeling, and that doesn't seem right to us. When someone demonstrates their feelings in a big way (which they do naturally because of their large family where they had to shout for attention), they get recognised and even applauded. We're outraged because we think we have demonstrated our anger or feelings and not been noticed.

One of our failings is that we expect everyone else to know exactly how we feel – 'They should know.' That's the positive part of your parents adoring you without question.

But the world outside is not like the cosy world of home. For many of the only children we interviewed, there came a very rude awakening. They had to learn that they are not the centre of the universe, only the centre of their own small world. Soon they go to school, to work, to other relationships where people tell them to fight their own battles, to stand up for themselves, to share with others, to think of other people. All children go through this experience; it is not unique to onlies. But children with siblings have had some practice – they've tried it out a bit, this world outside the self. They have been through some rough and tumble and have learned gradually, perhaps less traumatically.

The concentrated attention that only children receive leaves them vulnerable to solipsism and lack of balance. They may not be spoilt, but many of them confess to being 'self-centred in my bones', as one put it:

My partner complains that when I hear about the problems of someone else, my first thought is how it will affect me. Like when I heard about the death of a friend's mother, my first thought is how will I get to the funeral? It really isn't that I am not concerned for my friend, just that that is my knee-jerk reaction.

I wanted to be loved and at school I liked the attention – I was sick of being on my own at home, so when I'd got an audience I'd just go off and have a great old time.

I don't remember school being difficult – I was quite a one for being the centre of attention at nursery school – there were just ten of us. It was probably because it was the first time I'd been at school.

When they play with other children, their lack of experience of joining in can hold them back and make them appear stand-offish. If they are at the same time expecting to be the centre of attention, they are likely to get short shrift from schoolmates:

I remember playing this game of football, and someone on our side scored. I shouted, 'Well done, I couldn't have done better myself', meaning it as a real compliment. I couldn't understand why everyone was so mocking. I thought it was a natural thing to say.

The parents' view of the specialness of the only child means that their attention can take a possessive, overprotective form, especially for daughters:

I didn't go to nursery. I was very isolated, smothered by Mother, who didn't want to let me out of sight, because I was so very precious to her. I remember all childhood feeling smothered.

And the terrible fear of my parents – it is incredible I didn't end up a nervous wreck. You know, every parent is anxious if a child is home late. My mother was more than anxious, and I was always a tomboy, very adventurous, and she would go absolutely spare when I would go climbing up things because she obviously had visions of . . . well, it's all the eggs again.

I think it may be worse for a woman only child. Fear – my mother is still so nervous about me – if we fly anywhere, it's major, she panics – I had that all through my childhood, it made me cautious. They were always afraid they'd lose me. I think I was much more cosseted; couldn't be late home.

But this overprotection may lead to a teenager leaving home less aware of the ways of the world than his peers, and certainly not streetwise:

And I was overprotected too, although I didn't appreciate it at the time. When I left home I think I was naïve about the world to a certain extent.

In later life the only child may continue to try to recreate, or place herself in, situations where she will be the focus:

I loved always being the centre of attention. I always want to be, and don't like it if I'm not. When I was younger, life used to revolve around me and what I wanted to do. Consequently, I expect to be the centre of attention and am quite disappointed when I'm not.

Only children have an unbalanced view of their importance in the scheme of things. Do only children want to be the centre of attention because, if you once were – for good or ill – you want to continue it?

My husband (an only child) only comes to life when he is in the spotlight.

The child may strive for the rest of his life to repeat that experience:

The incentive to shine: in a way it is never as easy to shine as it was as a child, because you were the focus of everything. As you get older you have to excel in order to shine, so you put a lot of pressure on yourself, and there are the feelings you get if you don't succeed.

THE NEED TO BE SPECIAL

Having been constantly in the spotlight, and seeing themselves as special, for partners in adult life only children look for people who are in some way special themselves, or who will let them stay feeling special:

If there is any pattern in my partners, it is aspirations to class and development. I like people who are different – I like people to be different and varied. I have always felt my mother to be different from her group – as she viewed herself . . . And romantically I want and have always wanted that special love. Kate is the youngest of three and quickly kicks me down – she has a lot more people to consider than just me. I want love to be a special, sacred thing of our own. I still long for a one-to-one specialness that no one else can interrupt or interact with. I can get too precious, and Kate keeps me in order.

Everyone I've had a relationship with I've seen as special or different. I've never been attracted to anyone who's bog-standard. We feel we've got to be perceived as being special by that other person. That was my ex's trademark: 'You're a one-off!'

Their responses may be excessive, or unbalanced:

As the centre of the world, in an adult relationship with a partner you become hypersensitive to criticism from the loved one, and if she turns round and says something critical, you think it is the end of the relationship. I've discussed this with other only children, who feel the same. I'm sure this goes back to the fact that you've never learnt that life deals out to everyone good and bad – there's no sense in that, to an only child.

You *can* learn not to constantly seek, demand or unduly expect. Most only children *do* learn this, however painfully. Yet, all their lives, that need to be at the centre will probably remain. It may account for the reported over-representation of only children in acting and other professions that offer the opportunity of being centre-stage. We shouldn't forget that Genghis Khan and Stalin were both only children!

All the Goodies

As if having all the attention wasn't enough, there's a tangible form that this being in the spotlight takes. Only children get all the goodies that are going:

You get presents, inheritance, the house, everything.

It is this which gives rise to the all too familiar epithet, 'spoilt only child'. As we point out in Chapter 13, HINTS

FOR NEW PARENTS OF AN ONLY CHILD, where being spoilt and the myth of the spoilt only child are discussed more fully, being spoilt is about a child's attitude to material goods themselves, not to the amount of them. Such an attitude arises from the parents' outlook.

There is no denying that a crucial bonus for only children is that any spare resources in the family are available for them:

> *You didn't really have to argue, certainly not nag for things. If something could be afforded, I would have it.*

> *My mother told me, 'We wouldn't have been able to do for more children what we did for you.'*

Many of our interviewees had been able to make considerable progress socially through a combination of parental attention to their education and financial support for study and training, which might not have been available had there been more children:

> *I was made to take private tuition before I took the eleven-plus exam, and my husband [also an only child] also had private tuition.*

> *I wanted to be a model, and had a concrete offer while I was still at school. My parents said, 'OK, as long as you've got your O levels, you can do it for a year and we'll back you, subsidise you.' And they did, and it started to take off and after a year I was making an income, so I was able to carry on.*

Subsidising one child may just be a possibility – subsidising more is usually financially limiting. Having to fight or work for things as a sibling may give you a competitive edge in life, but a touch of the silver spoon must be equally advantageous.

Clearly, only children are likely to have more chances to travel and see other parts of the world, to visit palaces of culture or to indulge in the more expensive hobbies, such as riding or skiing:

If I'd had a sibling, maybe I wouldn't have been able to do all the things I've done.

They took me to museums when I was ten or eleven once a month. I suspect with more children we might not have done it.

Once starting careers, only children have access to more parental resources – to cushion, support or subsidise the choices they make. This offers them a greater range of opportunities than might be open to those with siblings. Having more resources available is significant for the success of only children, as a group. So is the outlook that results from getting the goodies without having to share them:

I don't think I stand out as an only child, except to my girlfriends, and the way in which they spot me is by my chocolate. My Mars bar is mine – I do not share my chocolate. If you want some, I'll get you one, but my bar is my bar. *All these girlfriends say, 'You don't share your chocolate.' It is my manifestation of being an only child. My bar is mine, all of it. That's the way I expect it to be; and that's my plate, etc. If you want a bar of chocolate I'll get you one, but don't take mine. If I wanted half a bar of chocolate I'd have bought half a bar. If it is mine, I want all of it.*

This may have significant effects on their ability to share in later life:

I will always buy two bars and give one to my partner, or make sure I buy something that can be split into two. I don't want to share mine. I'd buy lots of other bars for other people, but a chocolate bar is person-sized.

If I've opened a packet of crisps and Tony puts his hand in, I'll say 'If you want some, there are plenty of other packets.' I'm quite happy to buy him more – I'm not ungenerous.

Note the distinction: this isn't about generosity – many partners told us that only children are generous people:

He is the most generous of men when you point out the need to him. It's just that he automatically thinks the last cake on the plate belongs to him.

When you see a person take the last slice of cake on the plate, rest assured that's the only child. They think it is theirs. They are not being malicious; they just never learned any other pattern. For them, in childhood at least, this is the natural pattern – that if there are any goodies going, the only gets them.

Through social training or politeness, they can learn not to take the last slice:

I think we are overly polite. I always cut and offer portions of food – I think I'm so conscious of possible selfishness I've gone the other way.

But it is a difficult lesson because of their previous experience:

For a long time as a child I was puzzled by how little other children seemed to get for Christmas, when their families seemed to be in the same sort of income group as us. I just didn't catch on for years that if there were three kids, you got only a third of the total.

I remember very clearly what made me want to become a social worker. It was just after Christmas and I was playing with one of the many toys I'd had. My parents weren't well off, but of course what they had they lavished on me. The paper boy came and while my mother was finding him his money, she asked him what he'd had for Christmas. His lip trembled and he said he'd had the puncture on his bike mended. I can remember still the wave of shame which came over me. It was the first time I'd realised that everyone didn't get what I did.

Believing in your right to all the goodies comes from the experience of most things belonging to you alone – no contest. It may be hard for other people to understand, too, that this isn't a defiant or angry shout at the world – it's a natural statement of an only child's rights: this is the way the world is. Whether it is treats, presents or extra food, it all comes to the only child. This may seem obvious, but it's essential to understanding only children. The absence of sharing is fundamental to the only-child experience:

> *A few friends would come on holiday with us, but these weren't the best holidays. I liked the idea in principle, but when it happened these weren't the best holidays because I felt restricted: there was someone you had to share the room with. I didn't appreciate sharing at all. I had a major problem with sharing, in all senses of the word: friends, time, material things – it didn't come naturally.*

> *I'm incapable of sharing anything – if there are six magazines in the room, you can guarantee that the one I want is the one Keith is reading!*

Their lack of skill and experience in this will follow them all their lives. We will look at sharing again, in relation to several other themes.

2   Rough and Tumble

I deal badly with the rough and tumble of relationships. I suppose it's because I never had all that sibling rough and tumble.

When we started our interviews, we soon encountered this description of an only child's feelings, but we paid it scant attention. As we talked to more and more, we were struck by how many times the phrase reappeared, quite unprompted, in our conversations:

I simply couldn't cope with the rough and tumble of family life, like seeing two boys fighting. I couldn't bear it.

It was obviously very significant to only children. So we began to ask why this was so, and how it came about? And what was meant by the phrase?

The meaning became apparent as our interviews progressed. We have defined it as the sorts of exchange that are normal and natural in sibling families, but seem to be rare in the families of only children. These are the touching, pushing and shoving, both overt and covert, that are normal between siblings, as well as the fighting and the affectionate physical contact which most people experience within their families:

Do you realise that as an only child you don't often have the sort of physical contact which most people take for granted? I always occupied the back seat of our family car alone, always sat at one side of the dinner table alone. I only squashed up next to someone at the Sunday school picnic, and I hated that.

But crucially, too, it refers to emotional rough and tumble. And what on earth is that? It's the emotional equivalent of the physical jostling – it's about having the edges knocked off you, being teased, being laughed at, being brought down to size, made to keep a sense of proportion. It is also what enables you to cope with anger and conflict because you have experienced it as a normal part of your life:

A disadvantage of being an only child is with emotional growth – not being able to bounce off someone your own age. No one there to play with. Even if you've got the best toys in the world, you've no one to play with or share with or fight with.

You miss out on the competitive cut and thrust of being with siblings.

The absence of the physical contacts and emotional jostling that most other children have to deal with has a significant effect on only children's development. This has been reported to us time and again. Even where the actual words 'rough and tumble' were not used, the lack of this 'cut and thrust' and its effects were felt keenly.

WHY IS IT SIGNIFICANT?

In short, because it seems to be the mechanism by which children learn about how to relate in a balanced way to other people in adult life. They gain a realistic picture of themselves by trying themselves out against others. Of course, from their first schoolday onwards only children relate to other children, and learn from that. But the importance of rough and tumble is that it involves learning relationships with people of the same generation, if not of the same age, living under approximately the same constraints – and *not* with adults – their peers. It also means learning about these relationships within an environment from which you cannot walk away, but have to make some sort of accommodation or achieve resolution. The rough-and-tumble experience teaches you *what* accommodation, *what* resolution.

As we have already noted, by living exclusively with adults the only child misses out on some of the experiences that other children have, and this gives him his only-child distinctiveness. The absence of rough and tumble is at the heart of the only-child experience, and it is a most significant absence. Our interviews suggest that only children recognise that others gain the full set of social and emotional skills through their rough-and-tumble experiences, while they themselves have to make up for it later:

> *Siblings learn how to live, to have relationships and not take arguments to heart too much in a safe environment where the parents are referees. In a single-child environment they have to learn these things in an unsafe way, outside the family. Often they don't learn at all, or very late or even too late, and there is no referee.*

Only children are usually well into adulthood before they realise that they don't seem to have all these skills. It is then that they make the connection that it must have been the constant cut and thrust in the families of other children that helped them learn the skills that they themselves are lacking. Our interviewees realised that many of the difficulties they had in later life were attributable to this absence in their own earlier lives.

We don't want you to be left with the impression of only children as a group of hugely disadvantaged social misfits. That isn't a correct picture at all. Greater exposure to adults often gives them well advanced social skills, as we point out in Chapter 4, SOCIAL MATURITY. And they do mostly catch up with the emotional skills in later life. The point is that it can be well into mid-life before they do:

> *I mostly mixed with children who were older. The only problem*

I had was sharing, in the sense of emotional sharing. Kids go through phases of saying, 'Oh, you're my best friend and she's not', and all that is part of working everything through. I suppose I didn't, because I think in a sense I opted out. I wasn't going to compete, if I couldn't be someone's best friend. If I couldn't be that, it wasn't worth competing for! There didn't seem much point to me, so I didn't bother. Later on, of course, you have to because you've got to learn the skills anyway. But I did it at a much older age.

And some don't – ever.

'So what?' you may be thinking. 'Does it really matter?' Yes, it does. The only children we interviewed believed it affected their behaviour in ways that were likely to make life quite tricky, not only for them but for those they love and live with. They felt that this lack of physical and emotional rough and tumble gave them an overdeveloped need for personal space (physical and emotional) and problems with sharing space and possessions, and made them both secretive and subject to illusion in relationships. As if that weren't bad enough, most of them felt it also gave them problems with handling conflict in later life.

We'll now see what our only children said about each of these in turn, starting with the most frequently reported: space and sharing.

The Need for Space

Almost all only children have this need. Certainly, everyone we interviewed spoke of some degree of need for space:

I need my own space, and people don't always understand that. I need to be here in the house when it's empty sometimes. If I don't get enough, I make it. Even on holiday with friends, I'll potter on my own.

I like everything in its place. I like my privacy. I found sharing rooms at college with four other girls difficult. We had our own bed, wardrobe and cabinet and that was it. I came home every weekend for my own space. I really needed that space. At home I would then move things round to get my own roots, my own space back. It was all sort of competition. Sometimes getting back at weekends I'd not talk to Mum for several hours, to get my own space.

The personal compartment is bigger with only children. I love being in the car on my own. I thought it hadn't affected me. Till you mentioned it, I have never thought of it. But of course I need space – room and car. Our need is greater than yours. I've suddenly identified that.

Many only children find ways of escape from others, and of getting time or space alone. Travelling was very much part of the pattern with some only children who contacted a counselling organisation, for example:

It is a way to get time alone.

Only children have a need for private time and they find travelling a way of getting it.

And of course, you don't always have to get away to get away. One person spent years building a boat, for example.

I like time for me, for myself to do what I want. If we go on holiday together we both make a break for a couple of hours in an afternoon – it's never been discussed, it just happens.

I need personal space, though I love having people around. My room is my cocoon when I live with people. I'll retire and hide away just to get my own space. My preferred evening is in my own room on my own, surrounded by my things.

But recognition and acceptance of this need can take a long time:

I only recently came to terms with being happy on my own – going home and pulling up the drawbridge. The greatest invention is the answerphone you can monitor! I used to feel that being on my own was being selfish, being spoilt, and I'd invent illnesses to be on my own. It's abnormal – but that's part of me and the way I operate. Now I realise I'm much better off going out twice a week and for the rest of the week doing what I want, often on my own.

We look at the consequences for partners and for friends in Chapters 7 and 8 respectively – but here are some examples:

I work from home and do get territorial about the office – if he's left things there I go berserk and scoop them all up and dump them in his drawers. We have separate bathrooms, and woe betide him if he cleans his teeth in my bathroom when I want to clean mine. But, of course, I do have the house all day.

The need for space is straightforward to describe. It also appears fairly simple in its origins. Space in the shape of their own room, or sufficient rooms around the home to do what they want when they want, is what most only children are brought up with in the absence of any sibling competition. So they are used to having that space as a matter of course, without having to compete for it in any way.

Watch a group of children run to a park bench or a swing. Watch how they immediately try to establish which is their bit, how much of that space is theirs, where the boundary of their territory is. See that one hanging back, being pushed out, not staking her claim? Guess who that is! Only children just haven't been used to the jostling and bumping up against each other that are common among other children.

Their space may well be filled with possessions that belong solely to them. What happens to those possessions happens only with their consent. There are no brothers or sisters to borrow or move things. Only children can retain a burning resentment at other people's thoughtless re-arrangement of this territory:

You do want to control what belongs to you. I don't like people touching my books. When people come to the flat I don't mind what they do. They can eff and blind but what will upset me is them moving my things – that's reorganising and invading my space.

If the need for space were confined to the physical it would not be too much of a problem, because there are usually practical ways of dealing with it. But the need for space extends to emotional space also.

What do we mean by emotional space? It's the need that the only child expresses in keeping some bits of himself private; the reluctance to open up; the unwillingness to trust people with his innermost thoughts:

I don't like anyone knowing what I'm doing all the time.

I need an awful lot of space, and only recently have I not blamed myself. I've been bad at making other people understand I need space. I've made myself a victim – denying my needs. I haven't said or recognised what I need. It's the opposite of being spoilt – you go to the opposite extreme of being unspoilt, and hurt yourself.

It is a strongly held need for most only children, and we return to it time and again in this book. In the context of rough and tumble we believe it comes from the lack of opportunities for testing out your emotional reactions. If your parents are the only focus and all their attention is on you, it is not likely you are going to take many risks. You want to please them, so you want to get it right. If you can't get it right, keep it to yourself. You develop protective mechanisms at an early age and these remain with you as you grow up, inhibiting your ability to be really intimate with anyone else. This is a problem for partners, as we shall see in Part 3, but it can be even more of a problem for the only child herself:

I do like my own space. I need it, as well. Very much so. Whether for an hour or so or for a couple of days. I want it as well in relationships. A guy I went out with recently, he wanted to be with me all the time. It lasted a month – he wasn't trying to be heavy, but I needed to be alone. He wanted to be with me all the time. I couldn't stand it, even though I wanted him very much.

The lack of rough and tumble can lead to other problems.

Problems with Sharing

How do most children learn to share? By playing with siblings and learning that you have to reach an accommodation with them. You may not want your brother to ride your bike, but you learn that unless you let him, he'll hit you or at best report you to Mother, who'll be cross. You also learn that if you let him ride your bike, he'll let you have a go with his train set, which you covet. You learn, too, that you can't guarantee that your things will be left untouched when you go out of the room or when you are away.

Only children don't ever learn these things at home. Even when other children come to play, the only child is still on home territory and can be in control. When he goes to another child's house he is on someone else's territory, but he always has the bolt-hole of his own place where there are no other children to disturb his plans. There can be no blame attached to this. Yet, only children are very aware of it, and are often shamefaced about it. They do like to control their possessions:

I couldn't share toys. Now, sharing machines, resources – I'm absolutely hopeless.

What I can't stand is anyone moving the place of things – tools in the shed or garage particularly. I'll lend them to anyone, but finding the hoe's been used and put back anyhow or the secateurs are left in the wrong place – borrowing without asking and putting them in the wrong place makes me really see red.

Naturally, partners have views on this trait:

If I want to borrow something she says: 'Oh, you want to wear my jumper – I thought I might want to wear it later.' As a sibling, I was always trained not to ask or take without permission, but only children are very protective of their possessions and don't like sharing at all.

And the only child's response:

You feel as an only child you have the right to say 'No'. If they ask to borrow you feel they've intruded on you.

Sometimes the reluctance to share is very practical:

If I offer my bar of chocolate, it is up to me, but I don't like being taken for granted. As soon as that happens I put up a front and step back five paces.

Rough and tumble with your siblings makes you able to share, because, perforce, you have had to. It may well be that the widely held image of only children as selfish has its origins in their lack of sharing experience. Branding them *selfish* is an easy connection to make for those who have been on the receiving end of what one only child called 'my complete and utter ineptitude at this sharing business'. Being inexperienced at sharing is not the same as actively not wanting anyone to have any part of your possessions. Only children may see others sharing and want to do the same. But they have to learn how to do it, as they have not absorbed the give and take, the rules of sharing, which are natural in a larger family. It clearly isn't an easy task, but for some of the women we interviewed their own children helped:

A single child does not have to share. I believe my husband (also an only child), as a man, never did manage this. I as a woman with children did learn less selfishness, a more giving nature, by necessity. However, I do think now that even though I can give or take (giving is more easy, natural), sharing is difficult for me also.

As well as leading them to need space and giving them problems with sharing, lack of rough and tumble may make only children secretive. Those looking to be pejorative may call it 'deceitful'.

Keeping Secrets

We're very private people. I think you'll find only children keep ourselves to ourselves much more.

I'm aware of being self-contained. Some of my friends have commented that I'm insular. There is an inner bit that I keep to myself. I need not be forthcoming. I suppose it's the classic only child?

I find people with brothers and sisters are much better at being honest.

It may also be not having the experience of being measured against someone else or facing competition that leads only children to be secretive. In sibling families there is more scope for each child to keep the odd secret from the parents, to find a way of not having the attention focused on her, to behave for a while without being observed. The only child may have to develop devices and strategies that permit her to take that kind of privacy for herself, as the normal family situation does not offer it to her as a matter of course.

Because my mother's attention was always on me and I could never hide anything, I learned at an early age that if I was going to win at all I had to become deceitful. I lied and pretended. My father guessed. I suppose we both colluded in a kind of lie.

As an only child you have to be more secretive about things – devious – not in a horrible way, but there are just things you need to hide, and as an only child it's more difficult to hide things because they have their attention on you all the time.

I always hid things from them, and I burned with resentment about it.

Of course, we do not know whether these only children did have to hide things from their parents, but clearly they *felt* that they did, and that is the important thing. It may be because everything takes on an extra significance when there is no leavening or dilution provided by siblings. If only children feel isolated or under threat at school, this may harden their tendency to keep to themselves:

> *I was very shy and very insecure, although I had those loving parents. I really was very unsure of other children – I was pathetic as a child, I really was. I don't wonder they didn't take much notice of me. I just kept to myself.*

> *I went to an all-boys grammar. On top of being an only child, that gave me all sorts of hang-ups. There was no way to find out about girls. No easy way, like others had. I was very lonely, very vulnerable, felt very different because I was Chapel and an only child. I never talked about anything, and especially not with someone of my own age or status.*

This tendency to be secretive may exacerbate the problems with sharing:

> *I think things through a lot, to myself. Rather than talk to a colleague I work it through for myself – I think too much, maybe. If I've a problem I don't necessarily share that. In friendships I try and stay on my own two feet – try and solve the problem, work it through myself.*

Self-containedness is most likely to surface in partner relationships:

> *When she is in tears, for example, she wants me to be protective, but I cope by not letting it get to me. I keep a bit aloof.*

and can give rise to unrealistic expectations:

> *I don't ask for help – 'You should know how I'm feeling,' I say to my husband!*

unless you have an understanding partner . . . or you team up with another only child, so that you can happily deceive each other!

Teasing, Gullibility and Illusions

We were surprised at how aware the only children were about their difficulties with teasing, their lack of experience in judging whether people were being serious or not, and the effects this had on them:

> *I'm not good at being teased. I find it very difficult. I always take it seriously, and get hurt by it. But looking at it dispassionately, it's the greatest compliment one can have if they like you enough to tease you.*

Some saw it as contributing to difficulties at school:

> *I was never happy at school – I never felt I fitted in. I never went into why, but I never felt I fitted. I lacked confidence. I couldn't cope with any sort of teasing and I think that's to do with being an only child, because I wasn't used to it. My parents didn't even tease me – there wasn't that sort of banter between us.*

> *I'm not sure when people are teasing – I'm not sure whether they are doing it or not.*

Many only children actively continue, as adults, to apply their imagination to situations where others would rely on knowledge gleaned from interplay with their peers, and find that not having anyone else to challenge or laugh at their dafter ideas means they are very vulnerable to making misjudgements in relationships:

> *I remember being completely obsessed by this girl, and I actually used to meet her off the bus on a Sunday night when she came back from having spent the weekend with another guy. I mean, what a mug!*

> *I'm very susceptible to illusion in relationships.*

They also tend to nurture inappropriate aspirations:

> *My ideas were always too big, too large, too exciting to ever really achieve. Silly, really.*

Their tendency to misjudge can make them gullible, too:

I'm the perfect target for any con as I can rarely tell when people are trying it on, and they seem to be able to spot me a mile off. Some of the things I've fallen for make me wince in embarrassment. Now, of course, I am always sceptical until things are proved otherwise, which means I end up offending people by doubting perfectly genuine stories.

I am definitely gullible – oh God, yes. I had two assistants on one job, and the whole relationship was one of them joshing each other. I thought it got nasty between them, was aware of all this lacking in me, and it got to me. But it turned out they were very good friends – just like brother and sister – but I thought they weren't getting on.

Only children also have illusions about how others are going to react to them because they have never had the experience of knowing just what you can and cannot expect from others. You expect, until you learn differently, that your parents will love you no matter what. Mostly they do, and when they don't you grow accustomed to it as you get older. It is from your brothers and sisters that you learn the realistic expectations.

One of the most problematic effects of the absence of rough and tumble, as reported to us, was the problems that only children experience in handling conflict.

Conflict and Resolution

Many only children referred to their inability to handle conflict and their difficulties in resolving disagreements. Many of them seemed to find conflict of any kind very difficult:

I'm bad at fighting and at handling anger.

I was always a spectator at other people's anger, never a participant. I simply never learned that squabbling, arguing and making-up bit which I later observed (and found difficult to cope with) in my own children.

Some had rarely witnessed or experienced anger:

There was never a raised voice or a thrown plate in our house.

Not being able to handle anger is a pretty serious problem for a grown-up person, whether it be in yourself, in others, or within an intimate relationship. It is not that only children don't feel it, or that they don't become angry. Of course they do! Rather, it is that they are often unable to deal with anger in a light-hearted or non-threatening way because they have never had the 'squabbling, bickering and then forgetting it all' experience that most children in a sibling family have virtually every day of their early lives:

I learned through my children that people can be awful to each other without it meaning they hate each other, and that the relationship can still remain intact, but I can still not relate this properly to myself.

Of course, most siblings don't have serious rows every day, but it would be a rare day in childhood when there wasn't at least a little contretemps, as any parent of more than one child will know. With your siblings you can 'practise' anger in a fairly safe way. But the single child has no one to practise with except his parents, and they are too risky because if he is angry with them they may stop loving him.

For only children as parents, this lack of practice in fighting can be particularly difficult:

The children fighting did get to me: the fact that they fought. It did get to me much more than it did to Bob. That made it even worse, and they would do it to wind me up because it was a sure way. They'd be as good as gold if I wasn't around.

What happens if you can't express anger? Does it matter? Yes, it does, if it means you can't be open and honest about your feelings, and if it means you channel the anger in different ways, possibly destructive. One only child expressed it like this:

I find it OK to be angry with inanimate things – the tap which won't stop dripping, the paper which won't go in the folder. When it comes to people, though, I am snide and really rather nasty in my reactions, because I seem only to know how to be resentful, not angry, with people.

And if you can't cope with anger and don't know how to clear the air with a good row, issues and feelings can be left unresolved. Most of the only children we spoke to felt they were bad at resolving emotional situations. They tended to retreat from them, not confront them. Of course, sometimes this is much the most sensible thing to do. At other times, though, the inability to resolve a situation causes difficulties – for instance, in the workplace:

I had this really difficult woman working for me – she was pretty hopeless at her job, actually. But she was marvellous at getting the better of me in ways which I now see were because I was an only child, whereas she had a lot of experience of protecting her back. Every time I tried to tackle the problems she would become aggressive, which immediately made me back off, and then she would somehow turn things round to make me feel it was my fault she hadn't met her targets or had screwed up the assignment. Being an only child, I was only too quick to take on the blame, so we never got any improvement. I am ashamed to say that I had to wait for another manager to take her over before we got any progress, one who wasn't afraid of confronting her and could cope with her reactions.

In your personal life, such an inability to confront a situation and resolve it can get you into even deeper trouble:

I'd been living with this American chap for a couple of years, but it didn't work out as far as I was concerned. He was still in love with me and wanted us to marry, whereas I knew that was the last thing I wanted. Yet somehow I just couldn't say that, or I did so obliquely, hoping he'd pick up my drift. I did start to have it out with him once but he got upset and angry, which I couldn't stand. Although he moved out, because I hadn't been clear I'd left him with the idea that I might still be interested. He came to me a couple of months later because his work permit was due to expire and he needed to marry to stay in the country. And I actually agreed to do it – I know I felt guilty that I'd let him down and that it was somehow all my fault that he was here in the first place. I knew it was foolish, but I just couldn't face him and say 'No'. The wedding was planned and he was all happy because, of course, it was what he wanted. The week before the wedding I told a friend, and he made me see that what I was doing was madness, tying myself to a man I didn't love, sharing all my worldly goods with him . . . just because I couldn't really end the relationship. I pulled out, and caused far worse chaos and distress than if I'd said 'No' in the first place.

So, in summary, what is the significance, for only children, of a lack of rough and tumble?

1 They haven't had experience of learning various important and profound emotional lessons in a safe environment, through watching siblings and through daily interacting with them.
2 They have had no challenges against which to defend themselves, no assaults to repel, no opportunity for illusions to be shattered.

This amounts to emotional immaturity, often disguised, as we explain in Chapter 4, by a heavy veneer of social maturity.

Many siblings envy only children their privileged position. Many say that since they don't get on with their brothers and sisters, a multi-sibling upbringing is far from being the ideal family that many other children suppose it to be. This may be true but, however well or badly siblings relate to each other, their very presence is a learning experience for the others. Relating to brothers or sisters and having to accommodate them, however reluctantly, is an invaluable training for later life. Sure, you can get by without it. Sure, you can often catch up on experience later, as many only children do. Sure, not having to think about others leaves you freer to achieve academically, to take on adult responsibilities earlier. But what siblings do provide is an emotional training for life that is difficult, if not impossible, to replicate:

> You can't seek commiseration over an injustice, for instance, so if you are unjustly punished by your parents because they've had a bad day you can't commiserate with a sibling – you have to carry this, and you have to carry it in life. People say, when I carp occasionally about being an only one, 'Oh, it's terrible having a sister [or whatever], we used to fight all the time.' But that's not the point – even if you don't get on, you're learning about inter-related actions, and that's the key thing. That's why I suspect it interferes with your ability to relate to other people.

Only children do not have this learning experience, for the most part, and many that we interviewed recognised that they were, as a result, ill equipped to deal with life.

If all this has made you feel down-hearted, don't be. While it is true that you cannot entirely make up for the lack of rough and tumble, having missed it in childhood does not mean you have to be the victim of that absence all your life. The key to changing is understanding. With the perceptions of our interviewees, we have illustrated the ways in which the absence of constant cut and thrust may affect the only child's personality. We hope that their insights may have passed on to you some of that understanding.

3 Self-image

The first thing I feel that's odd about being an only child is that you don't realise you're an only child, really, until you realise you're a lonely adult. It wasn't until I was in my thirties that I started getting insights into my childhood; it's only once I got into my thirties and early forties that I started to learn how to relate to people properly. And so all through my thirties I started getting these strange insights into this child who I'd always assumed was a normal child being brought up like everyone else – but you've got no yardstick, there being no one else to compare yourself with. I suddenly see this appallingly lonely child. I see myself sitting on a wall outside school, or trying to play on my own in the house with my mother in front of the fire. Extraordinary, lonely glimpses.

One of the strongest impressions gained from our interviews is the enormous contrast between the confident outward image of the only child and the uncertain, doubting and troubled reality. The confidence they so often portray hides a morass of personal doubts, and the only children we talked to confessed to continual internal tension. Many recognised that, while their public image was confident and assured, they knew that they were confused when it came to the skills that others around them seemed to display – skills that they themselves often felt unable to grasp, in either concept or practice:

Somehow I never seemed to know for sure how to react, when people were teasing or not. Everyone else seemed to know. Why didn't I?

Their uncertainty of how to bridge the gap between the reality and the image led them to adopt defensive poses and attitudes in order to cope in the world, as we saw under *All the Blame*, in Chapter 1. One described this as her 'chameleon-like' adaptation to any circumstances:

> *I am good at appeasing people – you're on your own and you either fight and dominate by power or you dominate by affability, by being a chameleon and adapting to different people – the chameleon way. I go into many situations and have to adapt with different people. Siblings have the chance to stay in a group, if they want: 'We are the Browns and we do this and talk like this and that's us.' And they have a defined group and background. I'll go anywhere and fit in very quickly and be happy doing it for quite a while. But it raises questions of who and what you are, because of that adaptability. If you are a Brown, you are a Brown – it's easy. For us, we have to get used to adapting – in that chameleon way.*

In Chapters 7 and 8 we discuss the problems for partners and friends who find the only child as a private person less emotionally skilled than his or her public presentation had led them to expect. In this chapter we look more generally at how only children see themselves. Many of our interviewees felt their self-image of earlier years had been very inaccurate, and that this had been a disadvantage. Only children probably catch up and learn to judge themselves better later on in life, but not before the false image has had a profound effect on choices and decision-making.

Because only children have no siblings to help shape a realistic view, the way they see themselves in relation to the world can be quite unrealistic. This then affects the way they function:

> *I was always being pushed by friends into doing XYZ or taking*

the lead – I never felt happy, never sure how I really appeared to them.

People always suggested I should apply for these 'leadership' jobs, but I never felt I could do them – always felt lots of others would be better. Now I've a lot more experience, I get frustrated by incompetents in high-powered jobs and I realise how I really did have those abilities and would have been good, but I've missed the chances to get on those ladders now. I also think if I'd have had, say, a sibling or close friend to whom I'd have been able to talk I might have been persuaded otherwise. I might even have persuaded myself otherwise!

People develop a self-image from what is reflected back to them, and especially from the 'mirror' of their immediate family. We believe that in having a sibling-free mirror only children share common factors in the development of their own image. These can be very different from images held by children from a multi-sibling family. So what are these common factors?

Rather Late in the Day

For people who go on to have a highly developed sense of self, it is odd that only children start with very little self-awareness. Many don't realise until adulthood that they may differ psychologically from other children:

It's only recently I have looked back and wondered if it's the repercussions of being an only child that have made me this way.

Having trouble with joining in at school, the only child just thinks he has a problem, and won't necessarily make connections with his upbringing or be able to change the way he sees himself:

The weird thing is, you know, that I don't feel as if I had a self-image: I just was, like Topsy. It wasn't until I started relating with my peers in the big wide world and had some sort of yardstick that I then started to have some sense of myself.

I'm not terribly sure you can recognise being an only child until you're older. You are just getting on with your life. It's not until you're at work or with a family and you go home and think, 'Oh, this is lonely.' It's something you have to discover yourself.

Several interviewees echoed this sense of coming comparatively late to an understanding of their 'state':

The whole problem of being an only child is that you don't know whether you are typical or not. That's the problem. Probably everyone feels abnormal, but I do feel very different, and the significance of it – and this is the most surprising thing of all – didn't dawn on me until quite late in my life. It took years for me to actually work out what was wrong.

The terrible embarrassment with which some of our interviewees recalled incidents in their childhood or adolescence was more than the usual cringe that people have when they recall that period of their lives. They were recalling how totally unequipped they felt for situations that others seemed to find quite normal:

I just couldn't react fast enough, somehow. I had no way of sort of instantly defending myself or having those sort of comebacks which seemed normal to the other kids. Once my mother and I were out on our bikes along a country lane. It was getting dark and we had no lights. A man came along riding his bike in the opposite direction, also without lights. He yelled out, 'Where's your lights?' To my amazement my mother instantly yelled back, 'Where's yours?' I just couldn't react like that . . . the quickness amazed me. My first reaction was to get off the bike!

Not knowing how typical you are does feel a problem to only children. When we asked interviewees to compare their situation with those of others, the most frequent reply was to the effect 'How should I know? I've nothing to compare myself with.'

Through Parents' Eyes Only

As is clear from Chapter 1, only children commonly feel not just valued by their parents as most babies do, but something special:

I thought I was quite special because they just had me. Mum said I was very special to her, and clearly I was because it was all she had.

Since people develop much of their self-image from what is reflected back to them from the 'mirror' of their families, only children, with no siblings to provide such a reflection, are much more dependent on their parents to provide it:

The only sense I had of myself was the image painted by my parents. So I was either a nice boy or a naughty boy or a clever boy who didn't try harder, or whatever ... I was all sorts of boys, but they were always images created of me by my parents. I never had a sense of what I was myself. With two or three children you've got more reflections of yourself.

My self-image was what my parents told me it was, to a large extent. I suspect I modelled myself on my father because he was the one who, in a sense, achieved. He used to say, 'If you don't tell people how good you are no one will know.' It was very important to please him, and I spent the whole of my youth trying to achieve things that Dad set up for me.

When the projected image is of success and of 'How clever you are!', only children can have the advantage of confidence and a strong belief in their abilities. But the flip side can be doubly hard. *All the Expectations*, in Chapter 1, showed how trying to fulfil parental wishes led many into powerful feelings of guilt. If you believe that you are what your parents say you are, then fail to achieve their expectations, this can generate an image of yourself as a failure. 'I'm feeling guilty *and* I'm a failure!'

First of all it was scholarship, then O levels, and then there was one anatomy exam I failed at the start of nursing. Dad never spoke or mentioned it except to say, 'It was entirely your own fault – if you'd have studied you'd have got it.' No 'Sorry you didn't get it' or anything like that – as far as he was concerned I'd failed, and that was all there was to it.

If the 'special' only child doesn't behave in the way the parents expect, it's not comparisons with a sibling that are made – he or she may be compared negatively with the parents:

I'm not sure what my own image was, but I think I was almost frightened of other people. I was painfully shy and it was almost held against me. I was always frightened of saying the wrong thing, putting a foot wrong. I couldn't take comment, I suppose. I don't think I was ever really told I could do something or achieve anything, so I didn't believe I could. Grandma was always comparing me to Mum: 'Why aren't you like your mother? Everyone called her Smiler – they wouldn't call you Smiler.'

Only children can feel that they must be a credit to their parents. As a partner saw it:

The parents will always try to organise the life of the only child. With several children, you stand back and become interested in how they all are. With an only child, parents feel it is a test of you, the parent; it's a huge responsibility, and it affects you as you feel the child reflects the parents, so you want it to talk properly, behave well, etc.

So only children take on the image of themselves as the reflection of the family, and this may stay with them:

You don't want your children to do anything that will reflect on you as a bad thing.

A partner commented:

He's very conscious . . . about the way the boys look.

When only children have their first experiences of relationships outside the family, these may be influenced by the image previously established by the parents:

I did feel an outsider at school – I was initially in a comprehensive school in East London. The children, my mother told me, were 'not my type', so I had this instilled in me that I didn't fit in. It was a really rough place and I was immaculately dressed in little white socks – turned out as the bee's knees. I must have been an awful pain. I cringe when I think of it now. I took an awful lot of stick.

Most parents try to give their children confidence and encouragement. For the only child this can be a great bonus, as we saw in Chapter 1, under *All the Attention*. For female onlies who were not competing with a male sibling, such encouragement could give particular confidence:

I think I'm quite assertive. My husband spends his life in the kitchen – that's what he'd tell you! I know things would have been very different with a boy, because of my parents' cultural background. I would have been in the kitchen with Mum. Because that wasn't the case I ended up in the study with Dad. It was all to do with there being no son.

I've always been able to solve problems, sort things out, and also do handy things, decoration, etc. Possibly someone with a brother wouldn't – Dad showed me how to do practical things, like wiring a plug.

Thus, in response to parental attention girls may develop a sense of themselves as powerful and capable – arguably a more appropriate self-image than that learnt by some girls with brothers.

Many interviewees had abandoned a 'little girl' image early on:

I was a real tomboy – mucking in with the jobs, plus the horses. Then, going to school, you haven't got older siblings to help you – you've got to do your own thing or it won't happen. That's probably why I'm bossy now – I know I am. Probably why I've gone out and done things, because I know if I didn't no one else would.

I was a tomboy. Perhaps I was a split personality because I had dolls, but I was a tomboy. I remember going through a long period just wishing I was a boy. I remember even crying that I'd been born a girl. I was very much into cowboys and Indians.

When young I was always treated like one of the lads, and I had to muck in. That I was the only girl was irrelevant – I wouldn't be put down by them.

It may be that the effect of parental behaviour is more dominant on a single child. For example, the role model of a strong mother may be adopted:

My assertiveness comes from my mother, who is terribly dominating of Dad. He does everything he's told, so my assertiveness is probably a parental thing which gave me a female role model of strong women. This meant I had all preconceived ideas of what women should do in a marriage, some of which I have carried on and some of which I've dropped. Because my father cleaned all the shoes in the house I thought that was what husbands did – Keith soon put me right on that!

Or it may be more generally the family or school situation that encourages an early independence:

I do think being an only child is significant. The fact that I'm more assertive is because I have had to cope on my own.

For women, there may be some distinct benefits in being an only child. Where all expectations fall upon them, they may gain from the undivided parental attention. More 'masculine' expectations might have been diverted to a brother, had there been one. Their parents may not project so strongly the societal patterns of deference to men and of traditional roles for women. An absence of male competition may ensure that early on they find their own strength and a belief in their abilities:

At college I actually learned to meet people and to make friends, and learned about men, met them for the first time – all the things one is supposed to learn well before one is 18! It was the first time I had really been with men, studied with them. I didn't know all these nice things, like girls don't compete with men, girls give way when they talk, and all the rest of it. And I didn't do that because I had never learnt it, and it is far too late to learn things like that when you have got to 18. I was a highly competitive individual.

I didn't really learn those lessons about being deferential to men. Then I trained in psychiatric nursing where one of their cultures was that nurses were as good as anyone else, so you didn't actually defer to consultants or psychologists – you treated them the same as anyone else. Nurses there were taught to be assertive, although I didn't realise it at the time, except that it fitted in with how I felt about things. It wasn't until I did general nursing and you were supposed to defer and do as you were told and salute the consultant. I didn't understand why they were so special – they were no different from psychiatrists, in my view. I'd adopted a culture, while I was doing psychiatry, which reinforced what I already thought. Then afterwards, of course, I had to look at it. It never occurred to me that my opinion might not be as good as anyone else's. As far as I was concerned, I couldn't see anything special about criticising a consultant, but people were horrified!

Difficulties in Evaluating

You can't observe your parents being parents to another. You can't judge or keep a sense of proportion. It's too much responsibility for one person.

It's difficult not having siblings to confide in for a problem or for a second opinion – like when buying a dress for a special occasion. I don't feel confident in my own judgement.

We see our image by self-reflection, by what is reflected back to us – only children don't have a peer or someone to provide such a measure.

When my father was ill I feel I was very naïve, but I didn't have any experience on which to base my judgement. There was no one else I could turn to who could say, 'You were right' or 'You did it for the right reasons.' My husband is supportive, but you can't actually check it out with a husband as you can with siblings.

The trouble with reflecting yourself only, is that you have no way to assess this reflection: for only children it is absolute. Furthermore, if it is based on what their parents say or do, then it surely must be right. There is no sibling to help question the parental assessment. This is a third common factor – the lack of opportunity to measure or judge oneself:

I think that was the bloody trouble – because there was nobody to put me right or wrong on anything, somehow. It's a strange feeling of there being nobody there; up to the age of 15 or 16 it never occurred to me to question myself or look at myself as an individual in that way. I was just me, fighting the world, fighting the odds. I didn't have a sense of self. Otherwise, I wouldn't have behaved in the way I did, if I had had some sense of the way I was behaving – which wasn't very well.

Other children are in a position to observe how their parents interrelate with another child or children:

With a brother or sister, even if you don't get on with them, you have seen other people in the house treated in the same way, which gives you a sense that life metes out good and bad to people.

By watching your siblings and your parents, you learn to judge through your knowledge of both parties the rightness or otherwise of the parents' actions, and can come to a realistic judgement of the parents' fallibility:

They are not always right – therefore their judgements about me are not always right – therefore I am not always wrong.

The only child is not in a position to understand this until he has gained some experience outside the family:

I remember vividly going to a party when I was 14 or 15 with a girl called Annabelle who lived up the lane and I'd always thought was a bit of all right, but I never knew what on earth to do. We were thrown together for some dance – it makes me shudder to even think – I didn't know what to wear. I was in a complete state as to what was to happen anyway, and I was put into my school suit, a pink nylon shirt I will never forget, a tie and matching handkerchief my mother had found which she thought was trendy with terrible flowers, and my father's patent leather dancing pumps. And my grandmother was in the drawing-room saying, 'I think he looks very nice. Now go off and have a nice time', and I remember thinking, 'I am not at all sure that this is it – I'm not sure that I am going to be the life and soul of the party dressed like this', and having a terrible crisis of confidence. We went off and, hey presto, needless to say she left her bag in the other room – metaphorically speaking – and was never seen again. The feeling of hurt and isolation, and almost the feeling that I'd been set up for a fall, was terrible. And I think these things probably are scars.

Such experiences can be much more painful than learning within the family. Siblings learn

in a 'safe' environment where the parents are referees. In a single-child environment, they have to learn . . . in an 'unsafe' way – outside the family, and often they don't learn at all, or very late, even too late – there is no referee.

Unless you have learned that your parents are fallible, you cannot make an assessment of the rightness or otherwise of their actions. Only children acquire a self-image closely correlated with whatever image the parents hold, because they learn about that fallibility only later:

If you are an only, the way to make the best of it is to observe other people's way of life, become an observer of others, because you have nothing at home by which to judge standards of behaviour or what to expect.

As mentioned earlier, the parents of only children tend to exert a far more dominant influence than do those of other children. This can be implicitly through their behaviour:

*Most of the things only children learn we learn from our parents,
and carry them with us through life. The definition of growing
up is being able to reject those things. Mum had an inferiority
complex and I've only recently realised that my own inferiority
complex was learned from her.*

Or parents may exert their influence more directly:

*When first married we lived near my parents, and I saw my
husband as the obstacle stopping me from doing what I wanted.
Once we moved and I was removed from Mother, I gradually
developed my own life and was more able to attempt to realise my
own identity. It is only now, when my mother lives very near me
again, that I can understand that it was she who was stopping
me.*

The only child's assessment, both of herself and of her
parents, is off-beam because she lacks siblings to measure
by. She therefore often lacks a sense of proportion about
her own image. The home is the single most important
influence on character development. Yet all the interactions
the only child can observe and judge here are interactions
between adults. Having no experience of seeing her parents
relate to another child is very significant for the only child.
We continue to explore this in Chapter 6, which sums up
Part 1.

As an only child you are really defined by other people.

so that having the approval of other people becomes especially important:

I've gone through life possessed by other people.

You Mean I'm *Not* the Centre of the World?

All babies think they are the centre of world; when you
have siblings, you get disabused of the idea pretty quickly.
For only children this does not happen until they come into
contact with the outside world, which is likely to be less
kind to them than home has been. The shock is therefore

bigger for them when they learn that the world does not revolve around them:

> *Being an only child certainly affects the way you define yourself. I think it is probably true that we see ourselves as the centre of the universe. It's at a sort of gut and non-thinking level – something to do with your relative importance in a family, or how much your presence or absence matters. It's like everything goes your way, and nothing goes parallel.*

> *You are a one-off.*

As nothing can quite live up to the undiluted attention of two adults in his childhood, the rest of the only child's life can be spent trying to come to terms with this early and quite unrealistic self-image that places him firmly at the centre of the universe. As with much else, the experience of our interviewees was that they mostly got their view of the world and their place in it into perspective at some stage after childhood, and may have made some inappropriate decisions along the way.

Certainly, they may have spent a lot of time or effort trying to preserve this privileged, if illusory, position, in the various ways outlined under *All the Attention* Chapter 1. They may do this through the sort of partners they seek. Because only children see themselves as special they may look for partners who are in some way special themselves, or who will recognise their specialness: for example, 'martyrs' who will let them stay feeling special or play needy people who allow them to be the rescuer. This may lead to difficulties – if the only child is not made to feel special enough, or when the martyrdom wears off for the partner, or where the partner is not so much special as peculiar:

> *I've never been out with anyone normal in my life.*

> *I really feel that I always went for the peculiar people.*

> *Only children do see themselves as special. I've been out with several only children and there has always been a particular reason*

why my partners have chosen me. Problems have occurred when they've later realised there's not anything special about me – or not in the way they originally thought.

The rude awakening of finding out that the rest of the world doesn't think you are so special can also shake your belief in yourself and lead to your being extremely sensitive to criticism. As we saw in Chapter 2 (ROUGH AND TUMBLE), you have had no experience of hearing criticism and learning to judge it as siblings do, as part of their daily lives. Perhaps only children are no more sensitive to criticism than are other people, but they certainly seem to think that they are:

I certainly hate criticism of myself or my work. I'm much better at doling it out!

I don't like criticism . . . it's definitely not being loved; I see it as a massive rejection, and somehow you have failed. It suggests you have fallen off the pedestal.

Much of their response derives from the lack of evaluation of themselves in childhood, and from their habit of taking all the blame:

I simply can't cope with criticism at a personal level. In fact, until about five years ago if anyone criticised me I'd go into a complete sulk. I'd be completely demoralised because I'd believe every word was true. I've worked on it and my partner has helped but, it's still bloody hard for me.

If someone criticises me I'll fight my corner, but I'm very easily dis-chuffed if someone is horrid about my looks or my attitudes. I know I have such a need to be liked that I play for popularity shamelessly, and that's why criticism hurts so much . . . you feel unloved.

Not being sure about their self-image means that only children can become over-anxious about what other people think of them:

I have an insecurity thing – if I hear people laughing or saying something I assume they are doing it about me, and they usually aren't. People say things and I assume instinctively that they are about me.

I have a persecution complex!

Not for them the happy-go-lucky approach of some later-born children, unbothered about what others think. The only child *always* cares.

Teenage Rebellion

Most people find their teens a period in which they can experiment with their self-image, test themselves against parents and generally rebel a little. Not so, apparently, with only children. It was quite remarkable how little evidence of teenage rebellion there seems to have been among our respondents. As a marriage counsellor says:

To be able to rebel and to find their own personality children need strong parents. Where the marriage is rocky, one parent is ill, if too much is invested in the child or where parents are so indulgent there is nothing to rebel against, the teenager may not rebel.

When you have expectations, you feel it is your duty to do well and behave the best. Only children never go through the phase of being diabolical – only children never have the free time to go through that phase until they are let off the hook a bit at 18 or 19. We all need time to go through phases when parents have someone else to be worried about. Only children don't want to let their parents down. And as an only child you know your parents are all you have got.

Several of our respondents identified with the notion of 'too much [being] invested'. Many felt that they became little adults too early in life, and they bore the weight of responsibility very intensely:

Teenage rebellion? What's that? Only children can't have it in an overt way. You can't really, can you? It's too much of a responsibility. There is only you and it would be too hard on your parents – so you find other ways.

If any kind of independence did begin to surface, the power of the parents may have been able to control it, or snuff it out:

For a phase I thought it was dead clever to be rude to my mother. She sat me down and said I was turning into a spoilt only child, and that made me think and feel terribly chastened and mortified. I only once overstepped the mark ever again.

'Don't argue with your mother.' That phrase still rings in my ears. I now realise my father had confused any kind of 'intellectual' questioning with all types of dissent, and he was so anxious, I think, that I should be seen as well brought up (or perhaps so scared of losing control) that I wasn't allowed to question anything and felt there was no way I could oppose this, and I never did. I suppose I've remained outwardly good ever since. What I realise now that I did was to sulk and be sullen, which I still do – a bloody anti-social pattern to be left with.

Although the parents of the single child may be in a better position to control any dissent, we suspect that the rarity of teenage rebellion amongst our interviewees may have been to do with the fact that they weren't trying to rebel, and that this may have derived from the image they had of themselves in teenage:

I didn't rebel. I've always behaved in a conventional way and I didn't kick over the traces. I didn't actively do anything against my parents – I still conformed.

I wouldn't have dared have a teenage rebellion. I never wanted to upset anyone – never ever. The few boyfriends I had, my father would be standing on the doorstep when I got back.

But rebellions may be waiting to happen whether you acknowledge them or not, and our interviewees found other ways of asserting themselves. Only children's form of teenage rebellion may be to do nothing. They may learn to use passive aggression as a subtle way of controlling people – a habit that may persist into adult life. Or they may divert into less overt ways of doing the same thing:

I was anorexic – it wasn't recognised at the time, but looking back it is quite clear I was, and I did get very silly about not eating, particularly. Because of that things were very difficult at home – they just wanted to force-feed me, really, which made it all worse and worse. I did pull myself together in the end. I still can't analyse why, why exactly it was. It was obviously my form of rebellion.

I didn't have a teenage rebellion but I chose as my best friend one of the naughtiest girls in the school, although I was always the passive one. Attraction of opposites?

I rebelled in a way that was acceptable, by going out with older men, e.g. I rebelled by being different, by doing things that weren't the norm. Because they weren't anti-social they weren't disapproved of.

An unsuitable partner could provide a powerful way of asserting identity, though:

After always being the model, conforming only daughter, I found my way of breaking out by falling madly in love with a man my parents thought was beyond the pale. From their point of view I suppose he was – he had a record, even. I'd have grown tired of him if they'd left me alone, but they had me made a ward of court so as to keep me away from him. Bloody stupid, because of course that ensured I had to elope with him.

For several, the rebellion translated into a great drive to leave home, perhaps at an unusually early age, as we saw in Chapter 1, BEING EVERYTHING:

I was ready to leave home at 16. There was no mega split – as I matured between 13 and 16 I found home suffocating and was ready to go. I moved in with my boyfriend at 16.

Mum never knew I smoked – that was my other bid for rebellion. By 17 or 18 I was very conscious I wanted to get away. I could

*never have rebelled personally, which is why I went along with
their demands – I could only do it by going away, and the farther
away I was from my mother the better.*

*A trip was arranged through school to stay for the summer with
a family in France they had links with. To me it was a normal
progression, but for my mother it was excruciating. It was the
longest I'd been away from home – absolutely. I just knew I had
to make that wrench, and in some ways it was trying to make it
easier for when I did go away. I just had to be cruel to be kind,
really – to make that break.*

And with some, perhaps, there was an implicit recognition
of the element of rebellion:

*I couldn't wait to leave home. Mum didn't say it, but I think she
felt 'After all I've done for you', etc.*

Others were able to reflect back on the significance of missing that rebellion:

*I've a very poor relationship with my parents. I didn't have a
teenage rebellion and I still feel I haven't broken away. I can't
relate to them at all. I'm always very envious of friends who get
on with their parents.*

Teenage rebellion is more possible when you have siblings – either through shared sibling power, or as a result
of the divided attentions of the parents, who have more
offspring to control. The link with missing siblings was
made by some:

*To me personally I don't think it helped, me being an only child,
but then I haven't anything to compare with – that's part of the
problem of being an only child. I feel if I'd had a brother or
sister, she might not have been stronger-willed than me but together
we might have rebelled a bit more. I couldn't do it on my own.*

It was as though these children could not have a 'normal'
rebellion, but had to find other ways of making acceptable
the changes they wanted to make. Some had achieved a
specific and often calculated change of image, in a sudden

and quite dramatic way. So dramatic, in fact, that we refer
to these changes as transformations.

Transformations

Most only children adapted the view they held of themselves through adulthood until they seemed to reach an
image just as realistic – or otherwise – as most people. For
some, the process of reconciling the image with the reality
of the person was marked by a more calculated process of
change:

> *I certainly didn't have a teenage rebellion, because looking back
> I was barely a teenager. I am not sure I was ever quite a teenager
> – not in the spirit of the thing. Fifteen years on, I was absolutely
> trying to find my own identity. It was adolescence all over again.
> It embraced lots of things that were different, even music – I took
> an interest in different sorts other than classical. I drank more. I
> went from Renault 4 to two-litre Cortina cars! I almost forced
> my wife to swap her car for an Alfa Romeo – an old classic.
> There were things bursting out! I was also influenced by people,
> like an extrovert neighbour who previously I'd never wanted to be
> interested in and now I was emulating his interest in car racing.
> I even joined a wine-tasting club.*

One interviewee referred to his own 'metamorphosis'.

> *In my late twenties there were some sensations going on inside me
> that were a bit . . . not quite straight and narrow. I had got to
> know this woman in the office, and the inevitable happened one
> Christmas – it's always Christmas dos, isn't it? I had a bit to
> drink, she had a bit to drink, she sat on my lap and she virtually
> said to me, 'Do you fancy being unfaithful?' I think that must
> have been about the most outrageous thing that had ever happened
> to me up to then. And that was it – I went into two years of
> having an affair with her. Life was never going to be the same
> again. It challenged all my understanding of what life was about,
> and I can remember even as early as a few weeks after the affair*

started having some thoughts that were terribly unsettling. Thoughts like 'If I wanted to get away from my family, would I?' It was stupid, because it was never that scenario – it was sex and it was exciting. But, I mean, why did I have those early thoughts after just a few weeks of an affair? It can only be because somehow I wasn't really believing that the life I was in was the life I could stay in.

And I started a process of changing every single part of my life. It was a bit like the caterpillar-to-butterfly job, although I don't say I'm a butterfly. I remember saying to my wife, 'I think I shouldn't work at the steelworks – I think I need to test my ability in other sorts of lines – I'm going to go and be a salesman.' I had just been promoted to the point where I was the most senior guy of my age amongst two thousand people, and a week later I walked in to my boss and said, 'Thanks for the promotion last week, but I'm resigning.' And he couldn't believe me. I was exactly thirty. I also changed everything else – my entire appearance. I got rid of my beard and felt suddenly that I looked much better. And I started to go out and buy different sorts of clothes. I'd never really been the sort of person that was interested in buying their own clothes. But I got one of these credit cards in one of these fairly trendy men's shops and started buying clothes which were probably never me. I didn't get it right, then, but the extreme change, from being very frumpy . . .

I began another affair and was starting to live dangerously and to live on a certain amount of adrenalin and ego. This is an awful indictment, but I got a thrill out of juggling all this life change. Having three women – none knowing about the others – and suddenly I had power and experience which my childhood, my adolescence, had completely passed by.

The changing job bit – I'm not even sure I completely understand it. Part of it was quite rational, in that I really didn't believe I could stay there for ever. It's the sort of place where you become institutionalised, and I think all these changing spirits in me couldn't cope with that. Eventually I moved up here, and the change had become complete: I had a new appearance, a new job; I had a new location, I had a new partner. I had no friends from before – all were loyal to my wife to the point of completely alienating or ostracising me.

There was a sense of inevitability felt by these only children, and those close to them, about the impending changes. It was that sense of an accident waiting to happen – that the conflict between the opposing forces of fulfilling parental expectation and asserting one's own needs and identity had to be resolved eventually. One wife commented:

You cannot keep up being the perfect child. Some go round the world, into drugs, come out, or whatever. Everyone has a certain form of rebellion within them and if they can get over it early, so much the better. For only children the spotlight's got to turn off at some stage. For Charles, the Cambridge episode was inevitably going to happen.

Charles' view is much the same as his wife's:

I suffered terribly when I first went to Cambridge. The other students saw me as a fish out of water because I was too good, too law-abiding. I wore a collar and tie, I got my work in on time, was so conventional. I deliberately sought out people I felt comfortable with, who spoke with the right accents and had good table manners. But they were richer and grander than me, so my rebellion was getting into debt, drinking too much and living a sub-Evelyn Waugh existence. I got into terrible trouble for not working and running up huge debts. In fact, I developed a serious drink problem. My father told me I was killing my mother with worry. He couldn't understand why I was turning into a monster. My mother wrote me a letter hoping I'd soon turn back into the boy they knew. I really screwed up magnificently, and neither they nor I could really understand this huge change.

It is probably significant that, though teenage rebellions did take place in the presence of parents, what we have called 'transformations' erupted well outside the parental orbit. Soon after being freed of parental expectation and control the only child could rebel, but not before:

I was very much a conformist – it was only in my adult life that I became non-conforming.

When I got to college I made a conscious decision to depart the old life. I sat in the car park before I went and decided I'd start a new life. I thought it all out, clinically. I'd be called Ed, not Edward. I'd leave the Church, and thus my parents, behind. College was a real watershed for me.

The changes weren't simply a matter of overturning parental expectations. They could also be testing the alternatives:

Towards the end of school a big change happened. Father was not well, and they decided to sell up and move to Devon to be a housekeeper and gardener. I was to stay in Cheshire and do exams. But I thought otherwise. On my own without their stability, I discovered motor bikes and dances and drinking. Most of all I discovered sex. I was staying with my mother's brother and his much younger wife, and I started having sex with my auntie! I had a wild time with, as I thought, the best of all worlds – a home where I was looked after but not restricted, good times with my mates, a motor bike, and masses of sex with auntie when uncle was out of the way. It was very exciting, but of course school work went out the window. I left and got a job, and the wild time continued. Then I ran short of money and auntie started to worry that uncle would find out. Actually, he must have known, because we took great risks . . . having sex in the house when he was digging the garden, for example. So I went to live with my parents and literally started a new life. I decided I'd let my parents down and that now I'd settle down and study and become a model of good behaviour, and I did. For five years I worked hard in the day and at night to get exams, and was almost devoid of friends. It was as though I had to make up for all the wasted years and become good again. I felt I had to prove myself to my parents.

The transformation could be helped along by someone else:

I had a very important relationship with a girl when I was twenty, which transformed my life, really. I actually look back at her and think in many ways she saved me. She gave me a sense of myself and a sense of purpose, and a sense of being able to control one's own destiny to a degree – or at least that you can think things out for yourself and operate on it. She was very beneficial. My mother hated her. She was 17 but she was exceptionally clever, a genius, a one-off; a wildly eccentric exhibitionist with an enormous brain, and she just blew all my bourgeois anxieties out of the window. She revealed that all my secret thoughts were the right ones, and it was very good for me.

But transformation could also happen out of the blue, and cause great distress to partners:

He married me at 23 – perhaps an escape from home. There had been pressure all his life to go along a route he didn't want to go, and he followed his father into shipping and into the company, which he shouldn't have done. He was being driven along a route which his father had decided, and he never questioned this at all. In mid-life he suddenly stopped and brought himself up short. He wanted to go and leave us all and live in a hut in Ireland, and we couldn't work out what this was all about. He said, 'It's my life, and I've never lived it the way I want.' He felt he had always been trying to please someone, and didn't want to do this at all. Out of this he then chose to be totally, totally alone, and if he could he would be preferably without a telephone.

* * *

A confused self-image and coming late to any awareness of how you are perceived by others makes for muddle and difficulty. But remember: if you have ever been thought of as special and the centre of the world, this gives you great emotional advantages on which you can learn to capitalise. As well as understanding that you have some making-up to do, you have to cherish that experience and the good it did you.

4　Social Maturity

I see only children as well advanced in the social graces; maybe in their emotions they are not. It feels now at last at 35 I'm coming out of adolescence. Emotionally you are very young for your age – otherwise you're old. It's only just come, though, to me.

Being an only has shaped my whole life, if I'm honest, because during my formative years it was just me. It made me grow up very quickly – I felt like an adult long before I'd been classified as one. It has given me a sense of standing on my own two feet. Career-wise I've tried to get on and so support myself. But although I grew up very quickly because I was responding to all the adult stuff, behind that all the usual childish things were going on. I could and knew how to behave sensibly, but a great chunk of me wanted to be a child.

None of us have unerring social skills and complete emotional competence. We all have weaknesses and insecurities in the ways we deal with the world. But for most people there are reasonable trade-offs – perhaps not being so able in public situations, but good at handling one-to-one relationships. Most people manage a fair balance between various aspects of their lives. Most, but not all. We suspect that many who do not are those only children who appear so well balanced:

An only child through adult company quickly becomes skilled well above average in group situations – but can be quite the opposite in one-to-one situations. They often cannot handle close personal relationships at all. Externally, only children can appear, and be, very able. It is internally that they are screwed up.

I'm pretty immature emotionally, but thank God I found myself a partner who can cope with it. I certainly come over as grown up, though at a pretty superficial level.

Many counsellors report that only children seek help in numbers disproportionate to the rest of the population, and the reason may be that they are not nearly so well developed in the emotions department as their outward appearance would have you believe. Through our interviews, one of the clearest patterns to emerge was that of the confident and socially gifted only child who finds handling his own emotions difficult and experiences close relationships or living with partners as threatening and overwhelming. We see this uneven balance as a tussle between social maturity and emotional immaturity. If we wanted to be more judgemental, we could term it 'public adequacy versus domestic inadequacy'. One only child put it even more explicitly: 'exterior control covering interior turmoil'.

Typically, the person in question deals more skilfully and comfortably with professional, practical and social situations than her peers, but proves relatively inexperienced, inept even, when faced with emotional demands:

I had this insecurity about being in big groups of people, yet I always had lots of confidence in taking control, from very early on. I always wanted to be the story-teller at school, and I used to stand up in front of all these kids, most of whom I wouldn't dream of playing with in the playground, and I wouldn't necessarily read a story, I'd make one up, on the fly in front of thirty kids in the class, and I did it over and over and over again and was really happy with it. At senior school when I was still – even more so – worried about the way I got on with other kids, somebody only had to say, 'There's a debating competition' or 'There's a chance to be chairman of this or sec of that', then I was there, though I used to go through sheer hell in terms of whether I could cope with it. Yet, given a chance to have a chat with half a dozen in the playground, I'd say, 'No thanks – can I go inside and do some reading?' I've never understood that paradox in me.

It *is* a paradox, but also an imbalance, and one we foreshadowed in Chapter 2, ROUGH AND TUMBLE, where we dealt with the effects of not experiencing the cut and thrust sibling competition. The absence of this kind of sibling interaction, we believe, is one of the main mechanisms behind this imbalance, but it is not the only one. This chapter looks at the other contributing factors, as well as at the pattern itself. In contrast to the early experiences of the first child of two or more, those of the only child are never countered by the arrival of siblings who, though they bring competition, also offer alliances against the adult world of the parents.

The Process

PARENTAL INFLUENCE AND ADULT COMPANY:
How does this imbalance arise? Answer: The only child receives an overdose of parental teaching, while being starved of the chance for emotional expression and understanding because of relatively little interaction with peers:

Without siblings you have no reflecting view, no sounding board, no 'Look at what John or Sylvia or whoever have done' – none of that kind of system of domestic checks and balances which I'm sure are hugely important. Nor have you the ability to mix in with or get to know sisters' relationships with other girls. So you have a house that's pretty Spartan, in the sense that you have a mother, a father and me and two old grandparents, and this sort of 'You're going to a party but your father will pick you up at six.' But it wasn't clothes everywhere, screaming girls, parties, 'Not her

*watching that ghastly TV programme again!' and fighting your
own corner. There is a view, and I think it's a fair view, that
that constitutes to a greater extent what we describe as normality.
Not surprisingly, I came to view normality as what I was used
to – my version of normality. The shock of finding that it left me
short-changed in a number of areas . . . I didn't actually know
what to do and I was frightened.*

The fact that the only child spends a great deal of time
in the early years with adults, together with missing out on
rough and tumble with siblings, explains how she gets put
on the fast track to adulthood:

*Mum was a real, total companion. I don't think she actually
played with me a lot but I give her great credit for developing me
– I could read quite a lot before I went to school, and so school
wasn't a trauma. It was 'Oh great, here's a chance to do some
learning and get some encouragement.'*

*Dad would spend hours playing with me – whenever he was at
home I was the centre of his life. He gave me an interest in
astronomy – I don't know many other girls with that interest. He
talked of life with interest.*

*Mum felt badly that I was an only child, and tried to compensate
by being a companion.*

We got the impression that for many of our interviewees
a very large proportion of their time – much greater than
for children with siblings – was spent in adult company or
playing alone. And even when playing with other children,
only children may experience more adult participation:

*Mum was very good and I used to have lots of friends back, but
there was a fundamental difference when I went to friends' houses
and when they came to mine. If I stayed with a friend, if they
weren't an only child, we were sent off to play in a separate room
– we weren't sociable with the parents. But if they came to my
house the expectation was that there'd be a communal element
involving my parents; we'd not go off to a separate room to play.*

*When my parents had friends round, it was just the case that I
expected to be involved with them.*

The most intimate relationships we ever have are with
our families. A person's family exerts more influence on
him than any other experience. For an only child the largest
proportion of what he is experiencing is of the adult world
and he learns from this, picking up adult vocabulary and
adult norms of behaviour:

*I always felt I couldn't live as a child, always adult company.
There was lots of it, as people from the sect came in. There were
lots of board games in which I sometimes joined, sometimes not.
I have strong memories of having to listen to endless hours of
adult conversation. Or having to play quiet games on my own.
There was no TV in those days.*

Through this exposure, the child becomes adept at integrating with adult company, at reacting in an adult way,
at presenting himself in a manner acceptable to parents
and to other adults:

*I don't think parents of only children tend to treat them as children,
somehow – it's just a third person in the house. Not so much
adults' and children's areas. I was always involved with what
my parents were doing.*

*I think in general only children are more mature in certain ways
than when you've got the sharing and rough and tumble of the
family. Often only children seem to be like little adults, when you
observe them. You might not see it in yourself so much, except for
the feeling of always being responsible, which probably gives you
that feeling of being rather adult.*

There may be some confusion over the adult/child roles:

*I was expected to play different roles – when other children were
around I had to be a normal child with them. It was different
when there were adults about. It was one hell of a shock to play
with hooligans you don't want to be with, when you are used to
adult company.*

So the only child may begin to prefer the adult context:

As a child I was always surrounded by adults, and I didn't always want to play with other kids when it was suggested. I was happy with my own company, and didn't always share adult expectations that I should play with other kids.

A few friends came on holiday with us, and these weren't the best holidays. If you have a friend around, then you are in that role – you're consigned to the 'child' role. On your own, you are treated with more respect.

The result is that the only child seems to be more adult than other children of the same age. Much greater exposure to adult company means many have difficulties in relating to their peers, in childhood and later. They may become more comfortable with either older or younger companions:

Now I have some difficulty making new relationships. It is something I didn't learn to do as a child, and it is always harder to learn to do those things as an adult. We are better at making relationships with older or younger. I felt more confident with teachers because teachers liked me because I was clever – I was a good pupil, a good student. I did find it fairly easy to relate to them, although it was always task-orientated.

At a later stage of life, feeling more comfortable with older or younger people may find expression in the choice of partner (see Chapter 12).

The adult behaviour is emphasised because the parents see before them someone operating in a more grown-up way. Naturally they may react to that image, rather than to the child behind it, by giving him more responsibility and expecting more of him:

From an early age I was always more comfortable with grown-ups. You seemed to be able to predict their reactions more. They gave you attention without you having to demand it, and they were always praising you. I can remember my mother swelling with pride when her friends admired how grown-up I was. 'Quite the little adult,' they used to say. 'What a grown-up little chap.'

Socially I was, and am, very mature. I went to the WI very early with Mum, and was in the WI panto. Mum could always take me anywhere, as I knew how to behave.

Being with adults becomes increasingly more comfortable because it doesn't involve the child emotionally in the way that playmates and friends do. An opposite process may follow. Inexperienced in social contact with peers, the only child finds it difficult to participate in games and play, and withdraws or joins a few similar 'oddballs'. Now outside that learning arena, she feels increasingly unskilled or unsure. This may not be reflected outwardly. One study of only children suggested that at school they appear little different in skills and attitudes from any other children, and may be above average in attainments. From our interviews, it appears that social poise may be gained at the expense of emotional growth, but as we suggest in Chapter 5, ALWAYS ALONE, they may become adept at avoiding situations where their lack of skill discomforts them.

In sibling families the child reinforces his learning by playing with other children as well as by observing them in relation to each other and to the parents. But for the only child, adult behaviour is not balanced in this way. The 'grown-up little chap' quoted above, though probably pleasing his mother and friends, is not experiencing play and interaction with others to anything like the same degree as other children. He may lack the opportunity, gained through contact with children in the same family, to measure and judge himself and to be, in turn, measured and judged by them. He won't be testing his emotions out in a safe, non-threatening environment.

School does offer more social contact, but only after five years of adult programming. For many of our interviewees, nursery schools had not been available and other children had been few and far between:

My parents were quite old and had a very limited circle of friends who were almost all adults, as old or older than themselves, who had almost no children present. So from birth up to school there were probably no children in my life at all. I never had a playmate as neighbour or friend, and none of my Dad's family had children my age.

The only child can arrive at school with an outlook already adult:

I'm quite a conformist. I don't know whether you can be at five, but I think you can, especially when you've lived with adults and you start life almost from day one in a calm, controlled, placid relationship.

And, as we have already observed, she may well be inexperienced in relating to other children:

In childhood I didn't have very good experiences with children, for not only was I alone in the sense of being one in the family, I was alone in the sense of not understanding true childhood peers and friends. So my first experience of other children around me was going to school at five. There had been no nursery school or anything like that.

I was not good with others of my type, not wanting to indulge in the playground rough and tumble, but I managed always from quite early on to develop one or two quite good friends who were quite like me. But I think the majority of the other kids were not quite like me, so I think I was always part of a, you know, a small group of 'they're quite odd' sort of kids, which later on hurt a lot. There was a lot of pain at senior school over that.

By secondary school, the only child may be uncertain of contacts with those of his own age, suspicious of them, seeking a few friends apart from the group or choosing them from amongst other only children. He can appear stand-offish in play, because he finds protective strategies or ways of avoiding extensive exposure to the group.

They used to call me 'teacher's pet' because I always offered to help with tasks like sorting books or tidying the stationery cupboard, so the teachers liked me. But really I was just trying to find a way of avoiding being with the other kids, because I wasn't sure how to behave with them. I knew what the teachers expected.

The result is the uneasy spectacle of a child more comfortable with adults than with children:

At school I always had better relationships with the adults, with the teachers, than anyone else.

My parents' friends probably thought I was ever so precocious – I would have fought that description then to the hilt; I was just very adult for my age.

Older parents, too

Our respondents tended to have older parents, for two reasons. One is that several were children of parents whose childbearing years had been interrupted by the Second World War and for whom the only child was often a late, last chance. Secondly, several interviewees were only children because of medical problems involving difficulty in conceiving or childbearing. By the time the child came along, it was often neither advisable nor practical to have a further child. In both cases, such older parents may have interacted less playfully with a young child and have contributed to a home more focused around the two adults:

Having social graces can also be to do with elderly parents – older parents are less likely to 'goo-goo' a child and more likely to treat you as an adult. I was always treated as an adult. Being allowed not to be responsible doesn't happen with an only child.

*   *   *

Our interviewees told us that their childhood experiences left them with the appearance of social maturity while, in the view of many, having missed out on aspects of emotional development and consequently feeling emotionally immature:

At 18 I had the clear feeling of being slightly superior and above the age of my peers. I was very developed socially. But looking back now, I would think definitely emotionally retarded.

The Pattern

SOCIALLY MATURE . . .

Completing the fast track to adulthood gives a lot of advantages – in the adult world. Look at the successful record which so many only children show in their careers and in their social interactions. They chair meetings well, take the lead, appear confident at the party and the presentation, and on the platform:

Socially I've always been mature, and everyone at work thinks I'm much older than I am.

Charles is one of the few people you could put next to a dustman or a duke, someone aged 12 or 60, and he would talk to them equally and easily.

I know several only children and am always amazed the way they go off travelling or around the world on their own. I could, but just wouldn't want to on my own. But they seem quite happy to. I think it is something very distinctive – there's a girl at work who has just gone off to Australia for six weeks on her own.

The benefits of growing up serving the drinks at parties, and getting into the habit of being able to hold my own from the age of 11 or 12 onwards in adult conversation, always being dressed in quite a grown-up way, liking to dress that way, and becoming quickly accepted as part of an adult scene makes me now at the age of 37 one of the youngest senior practitioners in this industry, and able to go about my business with an extraordinary degree of inner confidence.

The only children recognised the value of these experiences, and often praised their parents for them. At the same time, though, painful emotional experiences had made them realise that there was a downside:

> *I'm on first-name terms with Cabinet ministers and was at dinner last night with six Footsie 100 leaders. I can talk to them, and vice versa, as naturally as I'm talking to you. I think that gives pretty high marks for my upbringing and all the things inside me which enable me to operate as a confident, mature adviser, and a man who is fundamentally happy in himself though suffers unhappiness. But my propensity to be hurt very easily, to not take much criticism, to be a bit self-orientated (not quite self-obsessed but a bit emotionally self-indulgent) – I think those things are qualities from a life like I've led which I think you'd find are typical of an only child.*

Such outward confidence and skills enable the only child to mask inner turmoil:

> *I have a sort of worldly-wise manner which belies the fact that I'm shit-scared about 120 things and worry like a drain all the time.*

It is the maturity or sense of responsibility that to most people is apparent in only children from an early age:

> *I was always old-headed, always grown up and responsible. Other mothers would ask, 'Is Fiona going . . . All right, you can go then.'*

Physical maturity may be linked to social maturity. Of the few statistics about only children, one that has been known for over twenty years is that girls who are only children are more likely to start menstruation earlier than those who have siblings. Yet why this is so is apparently still unresolved. Perhaps only children's advanced social maturity could be a contributory factor, since the lowering of the age of menarche in society as a whole over recent history is generally attributed to social development. The close proximity and greater time spent with her own mother may also physically influence the daughter.

One of the great bonuses, then, of being an only child is an advanced grasp of adult social behaviour and a security in taking on responsibility and leadership which frequently gives his or her career a flying start.

... But emotionally immature

So what's the catch? Where's the imbalance? In childhood time isn't infinite, and if all your effort has gone into rapidly becoming an adult you don't have long enough for, spend enough time developing, your emotional side. You may have trouble enough keeping pace with your social development. In the process of focusing on being a 'good' adult so soon, some of our only children felt their childhood almost passed them by:

When I look back now I'm not actually sure whether I've had a childhood or not – if that's not a too extreme thing to say. I suppose I did, but looking at my own two children I think I probably missed out substantial bits of it as well. That's not all to do with being an only child – it's to do with social circumstances and my parents' personality as well . . . a mixture. I sometimes think I'll have my childhood later, or I'm still having it, or maybe I'm even just starting it. It's taken me all this time to actually feel relaxed. I feel better about life now – and perhaps ready to have some fun – than I did when I was very young. Looking back I realise I was very uptight for a number of years and only now am I beginning to relax. My husband says I'm still a very serious person, although I actually think I'm a very frivolous person.

As this interviewee said, 'It's to do with . . . my parents' personality as well'. For an only child the parental example is likely to have a far stronger influence than where their dominance is diluted over several offspring:

I am not sure I was ever quite a teenager – not in the spirit of the thing. If you look at pictures of me, I went straight from being a child to an adult. I didn't look a very comfortable adult.

I had a very old head on me at 18 – I was older through my twenties than I am now, much older. I could never think of myself as being frivolous or doing anything frivolous. Now I am totally frivolous most of the time. And now I am starting to have my teenage years: not in a rebellious way – just the fun and stuff I didn't have.

In a way it's always been like that – trying to find the adolescence I didn't have.

The lasting result for many only children is that underneath that socially confident, grown-up exterior there lurks an infant mewling and puking:

I can be very childish sometimes.

I'm very immature, really, for my age. I can be terribly childish.

I do revert to childish behaviour. I'm very often childish – it has to surface.

And missing out on important stages of emotional development leaves you with some pretty confusing expectations. Other people expect you to be grown up, sensible and in control of your personal life – after all, that's how you appear to them. Yet the reality of your emotions is a different matter entirely. Somehow, you don't seem to have the skills to manage one-to-one partner or other emotional relationships in the same way that you handle professional and public ones. As one only child who had been through some very difficult times put it:

After a breakdown and psychotherapy, I am still waiting for my emotions to catch up with my grown-up exterior. I remember what someone said about that politician who went off the rails – that he was an adult waiting for adolescence to happen. Well, that's me.

I can be sensible in some ways, but I'm very childish. My emotions are behind, totally – I'm a sort of retard. Why do you think I'm on my own? Why do I walk away from everything? I've walked away from every relationship – no one's ever left me. And I'm not

*being big-headed, I don't mean that, I'm saying it against myself.
I've walked away from everybody.*

This state is summed up by one observer of only children,
a teacher:

*They have had such an intense relationship with the two adults
who are their parents. Superficially they appear more adult – they
have a better vocabulary, speak in a more grown-up way, but
beneath the surface they find it very hard.*

This is true of only children as they arrive at school, and
it is still true of them in teenage. As another teacher told
us:

*Superficially they appear very mature, especially in their vocabu-
lary, but underneath they are actually less capable in a lot of ways
because they haven't had close contact with siblings, or peers to
chat with and get streetwise.*

And a school counsellor commented:

*Only children hide their emotional immaturity quite well. But
they look at you very suspiciously if you try to show some interest
in them. They do hide their emotions well – the one who cries is
a rare exception.*

*Externally I can cope, but internally . . . it's part of my insecurity.
I do not show my feelings – I can put on a nice façade.*

This maturity – this, as one partner put it, 'apparent
calm and sanity' – is particularly deceptive because the
only child presents this false front while being very needy
and quite childlike in her expectations of other people and
of relationships:

*When I married for the first time, it must have been terribly
confusing for my husband. There I was, very confident socially,
never at a loss on any occasion for the right word, the right
behaviour. Emotionally, though, a different story. I was obsessively jealous, had no idea how to express my needs – certainly not
in a position to offer him support or understand his needs. I am*

sure he would never have married me if he'd known the depth of my insecurity, but it was impossible to know that, when I appeared to be so secure and together. I only realised this myself years later, through counselling.

Although I know I present as being very mature, I'm very possessive with friendships – I get jealous quite easily in all relationships. I did mix with other children, but I'm jealous even with friends. When I was younger I was used to Mum being there to look after me.

He is emotionally very dependent – he needs *someone to be there, has a need for friends, a need to have people. His emotional needs are much greater than everyone else's. When our marriage broke up he had someone else immediately, and if his present relationship ended I'm sure he'd have someone else quickly.*

In adult life, this imbalance between their socially mature presentation and their emotional immaturity means that only children have problems trying to achieve equilibrium. The lack of balance shows itself in several areas, which we examine in the last five sections of this chapter.

COMMITMENT VERSUS FREEDOM

On the one hand, only children want the closest possible relationships with partners, friends. On the other, they want to retain their space and detachment. This can lead to difficulties with commitment, which have been reported to us often. If you simply have to 'get it right' – the message, remember, that only children learn early on – perhaps it isn't any wonder you are worried about making a long-term commitment that you may not be able to get out of!

I'd like someone to be there when I come home at night – but only when I want them – not all the time.

The thought of being committed for ever to this person . . . I don't want to be pregnant – the thought of giving birth is a nightmare. Then, being tied worries me – once I've started this damn thing,

I can't stop it. I can't say, 'Well, it's been lovely, but the lease has run out' . . . it's for ever.

But:

There's a side of only children that really wants to commit, to have what they never had, which is someone or a family around them. They want to commit but they are frightened to.

though hitherto they had not all related it to being an only child:

I'd never thought before that the way I behave in relationships had anything to do with my childhood. It never crossed my mind. I just thought, I'm a free spirit; I don't want to commit myself.

Only children's difficulties with commitment in relationships were expressed thus by one partner:

There is a fear of being beholden, so whether they are loving and giving or not it's very hard for only children to accept something without knowing they are going to give something back – it has to be a two-way thing, or it's no deal. Even if it's five years later, they have to be able to give it back. They also have a fear of someone else giving more love than them – it has to be matched, and if they can't give back immediately it becomes a threat. Only children can't be given love and just accept that someone can love them in a different way from them. They can't accept the difference and feel 'OK, that's not the way it is for me but that's OK', and just let it happen. They have to feel they love back the same way, or it's panic. It is an immediate comparison – everything has to be as an equal.

For the lone child, who has had to carry all the expectations, all the responsibility and most importantly all the blame, failure may not easily be contemplated. If you remain detached, if you don't commit yourself, you don't have to face failure. Because you have not had the experience of seeing siblings make mistakes, get told off and yet live with the consequences of their behaviour, you have not learned that it is possible to survive such experiences, not only intact, but also still loved and not permanently hurt:

> *Why am I still single in my late thirties? Because we won't take second-best. Maybe the right person hasn't come along; maybe they have and we were too frightened at the time. Or does he exist? And that's what I'm beginning to think now. Now what? Should I start to be more realistic? For me the whole thing now is about the only-child effect on men, marriage and children.*

MAKING CHOICES

Only children tend to choose carefully what they participate in, to ensure it's something in which they will succeed. Where that outcome can't be certain, they are less keen to engage.

At the simplest level, most decisions involving a choice call for a small commitment, which only children can find tricky. In the home the only child may have had a great deal more choice than other children. He wasn't constrained by siblings, whose needs and wishes also had to be accommodated. The availability of more parental time may have meant support for whatever interests or activities he pursued. There were more parental resources available for the one child, which meant more options for those activities, for holidays or for toys:.

> *Although you can never be totally master of your own destiny, I like to have the choices and the freedom; I like the freedom.*

Does this make committing oneself to a single choice difficult for the only child? We certainly picked up hints of some people wanting to maximise choice and avoiding commitment in adult life:

> *I love having choices. For example, I can legally live in the UK or USA, but there are things I can't stand about each – I can't make up my mind where I want to be. And I can be having a wonderful time, say, in New York and I'll be thinking, 'Oh, there's a party on this weekend in Chiswick and I'm not there.' I want to be everywhere: Star Trek – beam me up! I don't want*

to miss anything, and I will run myself into the ground with nervous exhaustion to try and do three things in a night, and then come home and work on something else. I hate to miss out on anything.

To choose one thing means jettisoning the alternatives. Part of emotional maturity is a recognition that you cannot have everything – a lesson you learn when you have to share with siblings. This wasn't so for only children, who may now be over-conscious of what is being missed when a choice has to be made. They may indeed want to be everywhere, as well as have everything.

Some onlies appear unable to make up their minds what to order in a restaurant. Menus can epitomise the difficulties of making choices, as one partner related:

With Simon, every time we went out to eat, he would pick the wrong thing on the menu. It's a big decision – it's got to be right. And when it comes, does it live up to expectations? Everyone else's does live up to expectations – but not his. It was the pattern every time. And if I was ever to choose the same as him, he'd say, 'You can't have that.' The truth is that nothing lives up to expectations if you feel like that. The fear is that someone around you is going to have something better. I always chose the better meal with Simon, in his opinion – I couldn't win; even if I chose the most unusual item on the menu it would still be the best, to him.

If you're an only child you only have one choice – if you choose it, you've got to make the correct decision. I've never been able to go to a restaurant and say, 'I'd like to taste a bit of that' to a brother. You know the choice – the dilemma is choosing and, well, I've got to eat what's mine. I can't say I'll trade a bit.

I find menus difficult: I want a bit of everything – that's why I like Chinese.

Wanting everything yet being unable to make up your mind seems to be a common characteristic. With menus it is not too serious, but in relationships it is something every only child needs to guard against.

OVER-INTENSITY VERSUS OVER-DETACHMENT

Another conflict in their behaviour reported to us by both our interviewees and their partners was their lack of a sense of proportion in relationships. Because they often have no idea how to judge the rightness of their actions, as we have seen elsewhere, they often lack the ability to make sensible decisions about relationships. Several reported that this had led them to be too intense in inappropriate relationships, especially early in their lives:

> *You wouldn't believe how screwed up I got about my first relationship. I realise now I scared her witless. I just never had the chance to see brothers and sisters go through all that, or be teased by them in a way which would keep your feet on the ground.*

> *My first girlfriend Dorothy . . . I fell for her totally . . . no sense of proportion at all. I completely scared her off, of course.*

> *I think that is the problem for only children – nothing to measure against, no standards to judge by.*

This tendency to be too intense and too demanding of those who love them may persist throughout life, and is in direct conflict with another driving force felt by only children – the need to keep a certain amount of detachment. Time and again their need for personal space, both physical and emotional, has been reiterated to us. The coexistence of these two forces is confusing both for the only child and for his partners. One explanation lies in his attitude to control.

'I LIKE CONTROL, BUT ONLY IF I'M DOING THE CONTROLLING'

Does this sound familiar?

> *I need to be in control. Not necessarily in charge, but I need to be in control of things I do. If plans are disrupted . . . ! I like to plan, to know in advance. I don't like people dropping in at two minutes' notice. I'm sociable, but it has to be in my context. It's to do with being in control of emotions – this links in with it.*

The sense of controlling or being in control is very important to many only children. They grew up with the experience of feeling powerless beside their parents, of being controlled by them. Here was one small person versus two large and well equipped ones. This was a familiar pattern – which they may well have resented – and it seems to have left its mark on very many. So it is not surprising that they want to repeat it – but now roles are reversed:

Wanting to control? Oh yes. I'll tell you my greatest fear in life – it's a contract that goes on for a year. My terror is getting a West End show, because it means that my life is f***ing well predestined; I've got no control over it. I can handle relatively short contracts because I can grasp the end, and now I'm older a year is not such a long time. But when I first started work, before I was an actor, I got an office job in the computer industry. As far as I knew then, that was a job for life, and I had to go to the doctor because I was so stressed. I didn't know then why, though I do now – it was because I couldn't bear my life being prescribed for me. The idea of doing one job for ever just panicked me. That's why I like rep, because at the end of every year you can go or stay. If someone said, 'Here's a five-year option', I really don't think I'd fancy that at all.

Despite their early experience, wanting to be in control is in many ways a positive force that has given them leadership and organisational skills. However, it isn't always appropriate in relationships, and in this context is not always easy to escape in later life – within families:

I can't seem to help it, I need to know where everyone is all the time. It's probably because I'm feeling protective – that's the good bit of it, anyway. The other side is it's just because I'm nosy and want to be in charge. If I ask where one of the children is and am told my husband doesn't know, I get furious. I think, 'Well, you bloody well should know.' But of course I don't want everyone to know where I am, do I, because I want to be in control of my own situation.

– or within the home:

> With Felix the cat, before we got a cat-flap we thought we might
> have to do a cat-tray every day, and it panicked me completely.
> Even at 38 I panicked because I thought, 'I can't handle doing
> that every day of my life.' Of course I could, but the thought of
> it – that I've lost that control, that freedom not to do it if I don't
> want to – panicked me. That is very strong in me.

– or outside it:

> Oh, how I need to be in control! Parameters are very important
> to me. I like structure. I like to have the feeling that in the next
> few weeks I am doing so and so, in the medium term something
> is happening. I like that. I like to have something to look forward
> to, a project going on. I need control. I'm not very good in planes,
> lifts or trains. I've had counselling to try to get rid of this, and
> I know it is the control mechanism in me not liking the lack of
> control in these circumstances which puts me in difficulty. I've
> managed just about to cope with it now. If you can train yourself
> to let go of the controlling element, to let go, it makes it easier
> for yourself. I caused myself pain by trying to control my children.
> I realise I can't, but the controlling element in me is very strong.

Only children want to be in control, to be close, to be
very involved – but on their terms, not someone else's:

> It really appeals to me – the idea of open house – but I have
> difficulty with people calling unannounced. Give me ten minutes
> and fine – but ring first.

> I need time to myself, but it's my choice when I have it, and if
> someone else – my partner – chooses to do something in the time
> I've set aside, I feel a fear of loss.

> When I chose to go and spend Boxing Day with a friend, [my
> partner] felt rejected even though he wants the space and wouldn't
> want to go and visit this friend. It was because he hadn't made
> the choice, and wasn't involved.

But wanting a strong element of control doesn't have to

equate with dominating the relationship – only children aren't all looking for wimps as partners!

> *You get these people who want you to be dominant – they want you to run their lives for them because they see you as being dominant. I hate those people who are so pathetic and who want you to sort their lives out and can't control their own lives. I want to be with people with whom you can be more of an equal.*

The only child wants to control the contact, how much there is and where it is directed, and not to be the victim of it. From what partners have said to us, it seems this anxiety of only children and their inexperience of close involvement in shared activity can make them insensitive to partners' feelings:

> *With Richard we'd, say, discuss a film and agree we'd both go and see it one day, and then he'd phone and say he'd seen such and such a film on his own – i.e., the film in question – and when challenged would just say, 'Oh, I decided to see it.' But if I planned something at the weekend not involving him he'd say, 'Aren't I included in this, then?' or 'Where do I fit in?'*

Yet another indicator of a possible lack of balance that the only children noted was that they were confused about whether they wanted to be dependent or independent within their relationships.

DEPENDENCE VERSUS INDEPENDENCE

Only children have had a close relationship only with those on whom they are dependent, their parents. They may have tried to exert independence from them and found it a difficult task because the parents' power was so much greater than their own. This means that the only child may be confused about whether he is seeking a relationship in which he is dependent, or one in which he is independent. He is often unaware that the best kind of relationships are those in which dependency switches around, where the people involved alternate roles:

Only children have this tendency to think the world revolves around them, because in their early life it probably did. At the same time they want to get it right, because that was also a message they learned early on. Yet intellectually they know that self-centred people are not seen as being lovable. That is the conflict, between your natural tendency to solipsism and your belief that it will make you unloved. You want to be the centre of attention, but fear the consequences. Your grown-up side leads people to think that you are not very needy emotionally, while your childlike side is screaming for attention.

And a counsellor observed:

A frequent problem for only children is an inability to place themselves appropriately on the dependency/independency continuum. They are either very dependent on partner or parents, or so controlling that their partner has no independence ... They often had very controlling parents, perhaps who worried too much about their child getting it right (not when it was right for the child).

Only children want to repeat the pattern of being dependent as they were with their parents, yet resent the loss of autonomy that results. They want the closeness, but fear the effect it will have on them.

Having lacked opportunities for rough and tumble, lone children often have conflicting messages about where they sit on that 'dependency/independency continuum', which persist into adult life:

The trouble with my first husband was that I never knew if he was going to react in a childlike way and want me to take all the responsibility, or whether he really was going to live up to the image he presented to the world and be all grown-up and in control. At first I found this exciting, but after a bit you grow weary of it. I used to think, 'Well, if he makes the outside world think of him as together and in charge, why have I got to go through all these emotional crises with him all the time?'

This heartfelt lament from the former partner of an only

child found echoes among the only children themselves, most of whom felt that these crises had been precipitated by their lack of emotional maturity. 'Big deal,' you may say, 'so are most crises.' Yes, but they're made worse for the only child because the expectations of other people and of themselves are that they can cope. It is not the emotional immaturity that is the problem, but its juxtaposition with the social maturity.

Being grown up is a major preoccupation for only children as it is for first-born children, all their lives. This leads to feelings of pressure. In America the majority of people who seek counselling help are first-borns or onlies. Although statistics are not yet available in the UK, there is no reason to suppose it is radically different here. This suggests that the pressure of being socially mature leads to problems in later life. We should not forget, though, that being socially mature at an early age has its compensations:

> *The good things are that that confidence and sense of self-worth, and that sense of coming from a background that had given me stability and security, have paid infinitely more dividends than the down side.*

In fact, most of the only children to whom we spoke, though aware that the price of social maturity was often the emotional immaturity that had created problems for them and their partners, were also grateful for it because it had given them self-confidence and enabled them to make progress in their careers.

5   Always Alone

Being an outsider is always with you. Without making too much of a tragedy about it, it is the only-child loner thing.

I've never been part of a group. I always felt a little bit on the edge, the outside. I wasn't rejected by groups, but I consciously stayed on the outside. I do sometimes want to be part of a group, but I generally feel more on the edge of things. I'm just not quite in there . . . possibly that's where I feel more comfortable. I just don't want the closeness of being inside. I want to feel being able to be withdrawn when I want to be.

If, as is said, it is true that all human beings are, in the final analysis, alone, then only children are even more alone than most. Of all the experiences that they shared with us, the feeling of being in some sense apart and separate was one of the most common and most deeply held. During the course of our interviews we learned to recognise the subject they were moving on to through their body language – the look in their eyes, the sighing – as they overwhelmingly echoed each other in acknowledging that in some sense only children are always alone:

God, yes, always alone, even in the midst of a crowd.

I wish I'd known before that there were so many only children out there feeling as I do.

If you are an only child there is a sense in which you are always alone. Being the outsider is where only children naturally find themselves – although not comfortable, it is still the more comfortable situation to put yourself in because it is familiar.

More significant to me is the image of the lone figure – always alone. The need *to be alone.*

There is a sense in which I do always feel alone. I'm conscious from an early age I always wanted a brother or sister.

For me it is the one big advantage – that you are the only one . . . there is just nobody else.

Retaining a small secret place in your inner heart or soul may be part of the human condition, but it seems to be felt more strongly and passionately by only children:

I have always felt alone. Totally. If I've been upset, and even though I've got a partner, I still feel a bit that it's all inside of me. I can't let go – it doesn't seem natural to me.

I'm aware of being self-contained. I need my own space, and people don't always understand that. I need to be here in the house when it's empty, sometimes. If I don't get enough, I make it. Some of my friends have commented that I'm insular. Even on holiday with friends, I'll potter on my own. There is an inner bit that I keep to myself. I tend not to be forthcoming.

WHAT DO WE MEAN BY 'ALWAYS ALONE'?

Not a collection of hermits. Nor dozens of lonely onlies. 'Alone' does not necessarily mean lonely:

I do feel very much alone – but not very often lonely. I believe there is a great difference.

As an only child I do know the difference between alone and lonely – there's a chasm of distinction . . . If I was put into solitary confinement I'd have the best possible time out of it – playing blow football with balls of fluff . . . I would not sit around all the time.

While being 'always alone' can be confused with being

lonely, and may have its origins in experience of loneliness, essentially it is more about BEING APART than about being lonely. What is the difference? Alone is something you feel even when you are in company. It is that sense of separateness, of never quite being engaged with others – put very succinctly by one only child:

It is the room inside me where I retreat to. I can close the door and be self-contained from others and the world.

It is not necessarily negative, either. Some of our interviewees cherished their apartness, sought it gladly:

To come in at night and find no one there, no one I have to speak to or inquire about . . . what bliss!

I quite like being on my own. A bonus in marriage, actually, is if you get a day to yourself, or if someone isn't there.

I do remember being quite a solitary sort of person, but clearly when it came to it I did make friends and I've still got schoolfriends I'm in touch with. It's just that I quite liked being on my own.

Most only children require periods of aloneness to enjoy their own space, with which they are so accustomed.

When Do Only Children Feel Alone?

Always. Nevertheless, only children seem conscious of it more at particular points in their lives.

AS A CHILD, AT HOME

Always alone is a comparative feeling – you need to know other people's situations to realise that you feel differently. Since all children believe their family is normal at first, the sense of being alone in childhood was mostly reported as feeling THE OUTSIDER, particularly when there was a close relationship between the parents:

My parents were very much a couple. Although they had friends, they tended to live in a very private bubble of their own. I could never become part of their private world and felt there was just me alone with this couple.

or when there was a close relationship between other relations:

Although I had a lot of family on my mother's side and both my grandparents, I always felt on the outside slightly.

Being the outsider with parents may mean that the only child becomes more of an observer than a participant:

Going to the fair with my parents I never liked, because I knew these rough fairground men were robbing my parents – they were just there to take money off us, and it used to make me uncomfortable. When my parents asked me if I wanted to go on things, all my instincts would say, 'No, I don't want to give that horrible man money because they are all conning you.' I saw through all that, even when I was six. If I'd been with friends, there'd have been a sense that we were together as peers enjoying it. I could see that my parents were doing it because they genuinely wanted to please me, but I could also see that this man was cynically taking the two shillings off them which I knew was a lot for them. If I'd just been there with a mate, I'd probably never have thought about it. There is something going on with the only child.

It seems that even where the child cannot be aware of the processes operating, the sense of being alone is altering her consciousness from birth. It will develop and stay with her, influencing her decisions, her relationships, her choice of work and her behaviour generally.

We have been given graphic descriptions by only children of feeling apart from the rest of the world throughout their childhood:

There's a sense in which I've always felt alone. I can remember as a smallish child half my bedroom was always very, very dark and the other half had a stream of light from the landing, and I could only sleep if I could see that stream of light. I always woke up facing the door, and there was always that terrible feeling that there was only me in that room.

I lived in a terraced house between two other families with siblings, and can well remember the feelings of jealousy when I heard them long after it was dark, long after the doors were shut and I was fastened in with my parents. Even then I felt deprived, without question . . . those long evenings.

For many interviewees who may have had other children to play with during the week, a particularly strong memory of aloneness centred on Sunday afternoons:

Sunday afternoons were symptomatic of being on your own with one or other or both parents. The relatives came in to high tea later . . . yuk . . . in my memory there is the firelight, clock ticking, tea and tea-cakes and 'Oh, I'm so bored.' That for me was the worst of it – awareness of no one else to play with. A slight shudder at the memory of it. For the most part my parents were good at getting people in to play, but somehow this didn't work on Sundays, so it was always the worst day of my week.

I hated Sunday afternoons! Simply hated them. Because with my friend Mary that was very often family time for them. Invariably I was on my own then because my parents, after a busy lunchtime, were exhausted and put their feet up and had a snooze, so it was 'Occupy yourself with something and be quiet.' That's often when I'd take the dog for a walk. Sunday afternoons I was nearly always on my own, and I used to dread them.

For one, though, such was the isolation and boredom of the rest of the week that Sundays seemed a positive highlight:

I was aware of being lonely and bored in the holidays and week-ends. My parents used to take me out in the car and walk in the country on Sundays, so I always had that to look forward to. My mother and father are the most crashingly boring people.

Many onlies had particular moments that encapsulated their sense of aloneness in childhood. Others reported some deeper sense than just feeling apart – that of being unsupported and without allies:

An ally within the family was something I never had. You grow aware that it just isn't something you can expect.

The aloneness feeling might come from the constant absence of siblings or other playmates:

There was just nobody else – no one to squabble with, even. I don't necessarily think you to have to get on with a brother or sister, but the fact that you haven't got anyone not to get on with or get on with makes it twice as bad.

I used to get fed up with people always saying how fortunate you were, because I felt really deprived. I wanted in some ways brothers and sisters because there would always be something to do with them.

But even the presence of other children might not alter the inner feeling:

I was very lonely as a child. I had two or three friends and was always allowed people in, but even with them I felt alone, sort of apart. I carry that feeling with me still. I still feel isolated.

As many of our interviewees emphasised, though, even a strong feeling of being apart as a child didn't necessarily mean unhappiness, although the feeling of being apart was strong:

That hour when you were put to bed after playing in the street – put to bed and had an hour in the room before falling asleep. I looked out on to a factory wall and there is this broken pane of glass and it's completely embedded in my memory. I can recall it and have drawn it – it is the focus of being on my own. It wasn't unpleasant, but there was no one to talk with or ask, 'Are you asleep?' The atmosphere of that hour is very strong.

But don't run away with the idea that all the only children told us they had lonely childhoods. For many they were happy times, when only did not necessarily mean lonely:

I'm not conscious of being lonely in childhood. I enjoyed being on my own. I was quite happy playing with my toys – I didn't need other people there all the time.

There was no sense of being lonely or missing brothers or sisters . . . none at all. Quite self-sufficient, really, and not unhappy.

AT SCHOOL

School creates an ambivalent response. The shock of being exposed to many children after the secure and sheltered world of home can knock the confidence of an only child, as we reported in Chapter 3, SELF-IMAGE. For others, the desire for company and the chance to be the centre of attention in a larger group makes school an attractive option.

When they go to school only children usually learn to mix with others, but for many the feeling of being outside, on the edge, was not mitigated by this company – indeed, it might be made worse:

I didn't make friends very easily. I always felt on the outside, you know, I never felt complete. The only time I felt more complete at school was when I moved into my secondary school, where my cousin was, who was six months older. And then, because we had the same surname, if I got into scrapes or was bullied I could always call on him and it was somebody. We weren't that close, but it was somebody.

I felt an outsider at school after Marion left. I always felt a bit of an outsider with the other two – unable to break into their friendship. The last place I worked, I felt outside the clique too.

I always felt on the outside of groups at school. I was on the edge of the catchment area so I was the only one to come all the way back – not many others came my way, which reinforced the isolation. I couldn't bring any friends back from school because it was too far, and I found it quite difficult to fit in with them.

I've never been envious of other people, or anything like that. The only thing is that I would have liked a brother or sister. I did feel lonely at school at times. Most of the class there had either a lot of one family at the school or else there was an older brother further up in the school or perhaps a younger sister. I was always conscious of the fact that if I got into a fight I couldn't call on a brother. There was nobody who could back me up. That went through all my schooling, and I felt I couldn't quarrel with anybody. Even with a brother or sister you don't necessarily have to get on with someone, but there is someone there.

At school without a sibling there, only children, then, like first children, have to operate without support and develop an independence and self-sufficiency. What is not held in common with first children – except in the case of first children who are much older than their siblings – is a lack of outlet for expression at home after school:

An only child can't come home and let off steam to a brother or sister.

All the traumas faced at school or Scouts – there was no one else to relate these to, so I related it to my parents, and they gave you the business there and then.

But because the coping is done via parents alone, the pattern of dependency on the parents may be reinforced.

IN ADULT LIFE

The sense that being alone is somehow the normal state for you arises out of such experiences, and continues:

All at school I was an outsider. I occasionally feel it now. For example, I had one very close friend – we met at dancing school at age three – I was very much part of their family and we've been close ever since. But she died last year and it has absolutely knocked me sideways, because she was the nearest thing I've ever had to a sister. At her funeral they asked me into family pews, and that meant so much. I really felt part of that family. I felt part of something, whereas most of the time I feel outside it.

The feeling that it is natural to be alone leads to the instinctive feeling in adult life, as in childhood, that the

natural place to be in relation to groups is on the edge, just
outside:

> *I'm like a ghost observing, I don't feel part of it. Even in a group
> where I share interests with them, I'm always feeling I'm the
> fattest or the oldest and that no one will talk to me.*

> *I'm a bit of a loner. The odd thing is that I think people see me
> as part of a group and a participant, but I don't feel like that.
> I'm fine in a group and often end up facilitating it; I'm fine
> professionally; but I don't feel necessarily belonging.*

This may even apply to one's own family:

> *My own experiences forced me not to interfere in my own children's
> relationships, not to 'need' or 'expect' too much, but now I wonder
> if I have gone too far. My eldest son is married and I have two
> grandchildren. I love them all – but am distanced. Does my son
> know* how much *I love him and my grandchildren?*

The feeling of aloneness doesn't prevent the only child
recognising social obligations or appropriate social behaviour. However, his feelings may be very different from
his outward behaviour:

> *There are very few people I feel at home with. I'm very aware
> that I like being with myself, of feeling more lonely with other
> people than on my own. Which is not to say that I'm not gregarious,
> though. But I'm not good at large parties. I'll be a great joker
> and teller of stories; good at listening and making people feel at
> ease, I think. But I am better at a dinner party of four to six
> than a party of forty or fifty – at the latter I'll go home. I always
> feel vaguely inferior – 'Why am I forcing myself to be here?'*

> *I'm a little of the outsider – often happy in a tube train watching
> faces – and find people fascinating, watching behaviour. I do
> appreciate the importance of being gregarious and can do it happily
> when required – play the party games, be the egotist and then
> make way for someone else. But sometimes I just want all the din
> to go away.*

As they grow older, these people become more aware of

the difference between their own family and those of friends and contemporaries:

I've noticed being an only child more since I've been living away from home. Most people I know have sisters and brothers and they seem to have an extra social life.

When I got to college, because I hadn't played around as a teenager and was always attracted to older people rather than boys of my own age group, that separated me from my peer group.

Only children recognise that what may once have felt normal to them was certainly not the norm for others, and that many more activities or responsibilities could be shared in a sibling family:

I often get a sense of there being no one to turn to if I've got a problem. If there's a disagreement with Keith, say, over money, there's no one I can go to who can say I'm being unreasonable or he's being reasonable. Or if we have a problem together I feel there's no one there I can turn to.

I have been through bad patches, as in all marriages, and I've felt I've no one to turn to except possibly Jessica, but she's never lived near me. 'I'll sort it out' – there was no one whose shoulder I felt I could cry on, not even my parents'. I could never turn to them. Talking to someone is very difficult.

It's a disadvantage not having siblings to confide in, for a problem or for a second opinion – like when buying a dress for a special occasion. I've never felt able to do that, apart from my wedding dress, when another only-child schoolfriend came with me.

As the roles reverse and the only child begins to feel a responsibility towards the parents, this triggered the sense of aloneness for several:

But you're just alone. I feel it as far as decisions go with my parents – they had no one else to advise them when they considered taking out a home income plan. It would help to have them living nearer, so I could get there fairly quickly, because there is no one else to do it. It would help to have someone else to share problems.

When Dad was ill I had to go up – felt obliged to go up. Mother needed me – to talk to, take charge. I wished she was as practical in a crisis as I was.

I'd like someone now to talk to about our *parents, not* my *parents.*

The burden of being alone and feeling solely responsible for two parents merits its own chapter later (Chapter 10, THE ONLY CHILD AS CARER). The death of a parent greatly intensifies the sense of loneness:

When Mum died three years ago I went through the whole thing on my own – Dad was with someone else then. I would love to have had a brother or sister there for support. We don't necessarily have to get on – because you are brother and sister doesn't mean you have to be best friends – but at a time like that I just think, 'Oh God, I wish there was someone else to share that.' But I went through it. 'It makes you stronger' . . . They call it character-building, which I'm sick of doing.

I have never felt more alone than at my mother's graveside, thinking, 'There is no one else now.'

If parents do divorce or die, with siblings you can share that experience with someone. Blood is thicker than water and it is someone to share with, especially as I've moved around a lot. I don't have friends going back a long way.

Parental mortality emphasised the tiny size of the only-child family, especially for those of our interviewees unmarried or living alone:

You are ultimately alone, especially when your parents die. That's it. You are alone. Rather sad, when you think.

My lack of family gives me a permanent feeling of emptiness, as if something which should be there is missing.

Relations are roots. You know they are always there.

I increasingly consider death. Chances are that I'll outlive Gerry – what am I going to do? There's no one who'll look out for me

– I'll have to make decisions now, while I'm in possession of my faculties.

It was this family size in itself that brought comment from others:

There is no real extended family if you are an only child or two only children. You may not necessarily want an extended family, but it would be useful to call on if need be.

No shared recollections

During our interview, a woman overheard her husband recalling the details of playing on his own, and remarked how unusual that seemed to her. All her memories were of her sisters and family, and were also all mixed up, strewn among memories of so many other people. These were memories of events that could be recalled or jogged into being by siblings. For the only child, memories are inevitably more self-centred, with only their parents having seen events from outside:

I have a lack of self-knowledge, even in simple things – I have a scar on my chest that I have no recollection of getting.

It all adds to the sense of being alone.

*   *   *

I do feel alone, and as a child I spent a great deal of my time playing alone. I therefore developed an imagination and had to find ways to amuse myself. I read a great deal, and also mixed more with adults than probably children from larger families do. I feel this has made me less prone to boredom, and always able to amuse myself throughout my life. However, I don't think it helped me with peer-group relationships – I always found them difficult – and being honest, I don't think as a child I was very good at playing with other children.

This is a clear summary of a typical only-child childhood. Of the several key phrases, 'imagination', 'amuse myself', 'read' and 'mixed more with adults' indicate some of the variety of ways in which only children respond to the feeling of being apart.

'I therefore developed an imagination,' said the interviewee above – this was a common thread amongst many of them:

> I think you have a lot of imagination as an only child. I played in my own little world an awful lot of the time. Because my parents were in business we never had friends round, didn't have time to entertain, so there were no children in the house. I have no cousins. Mainly I played with dolls up to the age of 11 and 12, which is horrendously old. I had lots of them and could talk to them. And I had a very close relationship with a dog, if that sounds sense! We had an Alsatian, and I poured out everything to that Alsatian. I'd walk for miles through the woods with the dog on my own – it makes me go cold now.

The sense of separateness can be both chicken and egg: it leads you in a certain way, but also makes you manipulate situations so that you do in the end retain this separateness.

Coping as a Child

RECOGNISING, OR DENYING, THE ONLY-CHILD SITUATION
However much their imagination may have compensated for the absence of siblings, only children usually continued to long for them. Where being alone was felt as being lonely, the natural response was to express the wish for a playmate in the form of a brother or sister, even while recognising that they would bring their own difficulties:

> I never really thought very much of being an only. I can remember now always saying I wanted four older brothers – always, the whole of my life. I went through life saying that. Now it's a bit late! And I probably wouldn't have liked it if I had had them. Of course, it's a lot simpler on your own.

The desire for a sibling was frequently recalled. A few had taken this a stage further:

I would keep telling the teachers that my mother was having a baby, which of course she wasn't, and they kept on congratulating my mother, and my mother kept saying, 'No, actually I'm not.' Because that's what I wanted, someone to play with at home, so I kept saying she was actually having one. That went on for a long time.

Apart from saying they wanted a brother or sister, explicit protest at being an only child was hardly mentioned. They appear to have accepted their situation and go on to adjust to or cope with it:

I can look back now and see what I couldn't see at a conscious level as a child – you were just in the middle of it all. The fact that it didn't seem to be the same for other children – it's not the sort of thing they would understand, because they were having what appeared to be quite a happy childhood with their brothers and sisters, and there were you in this sort of adult world and just somehow it was like being at a different level.

If there are other children around to play with, and if they are 'suitable material', they may get cast as sibling substitutes.

SIBLING SUBSTITUTES

There wasn't a constant supply of people around to play with, but there was another only child in the cul-de-sac and we spent quite a lot of time together. We used to pretend we were sisters or twins – we used to push dolls around. I always wanted a sister – so there was always someone there.

I had a fairly close friend for a lot of my childhood and we almost were like sisters, and we went on holiday together and we were pretty inseparable.

It may be for more than just companionship that such a friend is substituting as a sibling:

I imagine siblings together can challenge the power of the parents: a sort of balance against that relationship. I missed having a sibling to share ideas and say to parents, 'We want to do X.' As one child alone – no, I couldn't do that. But I can remember with Margaret at secondary school – we'd behave like sisters and we'd go to one set of parents together.

In several cases, first partners were recognised in retrospect to have been a sort of sibling substitute:

My first major boyfriend in the Lower Sixth was an only child – we spent a lot of time together out of friendship – a little like brother and sister. We did those things that they did.

Why stop at one sibling? A whole family can have an even greater attraction . . .

I loved joining Diane's family, and always have loved joining the big families of girlfriends.

My first boyfriend had three brothers and lovely liberal parents. My wanting to be with him was part of a whole package of wanting to be with them.

All our only children had to spend time when other children weren't available. Using their imagination was the way most replaced the missing companions. One of the most common forms this took was to create an imaginary friend or friends.

IMAGINARY FRIENDS
Many children from sibling families create imaginary friends too, of course, but only children appear to use them for longer, or with greater intensity. This interviewee, for example, remembered her playmate in considerable detail:

Petra, the imaginary friend who I could see, only disappeared when I went away to school at nine, but she existed in the time before school. Petra was a very pretty dark-haired girl with a little red and white check dress, and she was there most of the time. I'd talk to her an awful lot; we laid places for her at table; we'd take her on rides in buses or taxis or in the car. When we'd come in for tea we'd close the door and I'd go hysterical because

Petra wasn't in yet, and she wanted to wash her hands and come for tea too. One particular day Petra came in and Mum said, 'Is everyone here now?', and I went 'No, no, you've closed the door again', and she said, 'Well, what's the problem? Petra's here.' And I said, 'But the cow's not', and Mum said, 'Look, I've had Petra now for four years, but I'm not having a cow. Tell the cow to go away. We're not having a cow.' But Petra was very much part of my life.

Some imaginary friends served more basically as companions:

I had loads of imaginary friends, both girls and boys. They weren't so much to play with as to talk to, especially after I'd been told off or something, to find consolation and comfort.

I had an imaginary brother for years. I mean, for six or seven years. He was about four years older and modelled on the older brother of the boy next door, with whom I was friendly. I spent years having entirely private conversations with him. I've never told anyone this before.

They could also serve as an outlet for feelings that had no other place:

My friend was called Beadle. I used to blame everything on to him. I created a complete world around him.

The imaginary companion could be an animal:

I didn't have an imaginary friend but I had an animal, a monkey called Pepe. He took part in all my games.

I had an imaginary horse when I was about seven or eight. I used to ride the horse round the back of the school and tether it up during lessons at the back of the church by the oil tank.

I gave personalities to my teddy bears, so that they took on the characteristics of imaginary friends.

Pets

Many of the only children we interviewed had either been given, or had acquired or adopted, a tangible companion in the form of a pet. Pets are common to almost all children, but the significance of a pet's role in the lives of only children, and their reliance upon them, seems greater:

> *I was bought a dog at age six and had him until 19. I took this dog for walks on my own – round the grounds of an old house.*

> *I was allowed a rabbit by my father, and that became a sort of surrogate brother or sister.*

> *We were on a farm, way out in the country. I was very close to the dogs – I talked to them and sang to them. I remember once singing away in the middle of nowhere and someone suddenly sticking their head out, from behind a hedge or somewhere!*

> *At primary school I had some friends, but they were reserved with newcomers, and it wasn't always easy as they were suspicious of incomers. I had a lovely dog and did things with him. That's not meant to sound pathetic. We had good times together.*

This is a pattern easily retained into adulthood:

> *Certainly, when I'm in a group of only children or in a group which contains only children, we find ourselves laughing with recognition. We are self-sufficient. I've noticed how we have pets now – and, for example, how many of us had imaginary friends.*

Amusing themselves

Only children become skilled at amusing themselves through their imagination, from early on:

> *I don't remember feeling lonely, except for some frustration on wet days because I couldn't go out and play. I was never at a loss for things to do – I always read a lot – I also had my own patch of garden where I dug up things and planted them again. I played for hours on my own. I was always able to amuse myself . . . quite happy on my own.*

I had friends, but I lived quite a way from them, so I really played on my own – amused myself, basically.

One source of entertainment was reading:

I used to read all the time – I had stacks and stacks of books stored in the wardrobe, which fell out when you opened it: Enid Blytons, adventure, gipsy caravans – that sort of thing.

Another was drawing:

My main thing was drawing – I filled piles and piles of sketch-books. I'd draw stories, and loved it. It was something you could do on your own.

I wasn't a great reader – it was visual elements that involved me, and I drew a great deal.

Or it could just be games:

If I was on my own I'd have to devise games. I was a great 'Dr Who' fan and a big fantasy games player.

I made up loads of fantasy games, though.

I had a lot of games where I'd play schools, on my own, and be teacher, on my own, and hand out books and talk to people as if I was teaching.

Many girls played fantasy games of a strongly adventur-ous style:

As a child, I didn't read at all. I made camps and was adventur-ous. I sort of fantasised for real, challenging.

My fantasies were the adventure type. If I saw 'Tarzan and Jane', then I was Jane. So I'd build a treehouse and swing around in the trees and, as far as I was concerned, I was in the jungle. If I watched a film I would turn into the character in the film – it would be me. After Mum read me Swallows and Amazons *I took the baby bath down to the river, sat in it and went off with it, with no implements or oars to guide it – I was just off. I didn't think it out very well.*

I was always the one who imagined all the games – we used to play cowboys (not cowboys and Indians), off on horses, tearing round and climbing on things, using carts.

AT SCHOOL

In response to the common feeling of being an outsider at school, only children adopted their own survival strategies. One was having a few close friends:

At school I tended to have just one or two really close friends. I was never much of a one for being in a crowd. In the early years I had one particular friend. And then, getting into first or second year of junior school, my original friend was left behind and then I palled up with another only child who lived in the same street as I did, and we stayed very, very close friends until she went to Australia when I was about 16 or 17. At junior school I can't remember having any other close friends.

Our grammar school was all-girls. About six of us sat together and would go to each other's houses each Friday. Very strong bonds. Friendships still going on. I don't remember any of them having close siblings – three of the group were onlies. Surrogate sisters, perhaps?

Even without close friends, our only children found ways of coping with their sense of being alone:

I had some friends, but an ability to be isolated from others. The darkroom was the only room in the whole school where a certain number of pupils had a key, and I made sure I was one of them, so I always had this place I could retreat to – never consciously, but it fitted my needs.

We lived ten miles from where I went to secondary school, but I remember it was very important to me to go into the town on the bus every Saturday morning and just walk around. I don't recall I ever had much to buy or do. It just seemed essential to go and bump into other pupils – friends was too strong a word – doing their Saturday jobs in shops or . . . I was just desperate to start the weekend being in the town, where it felt something was happening or could happen, and not be at home in the country on my own with my parents, who would be out doing things most of the time, anyway.

For some, school offered the chance to join in and no longer be quite so apart:

I loved school and got on with everyone and had a brilliant time. I treated school as a social centre. I did my work but in the summer holidays I couldn't wait to get back to school.

I loved school – I was a schoolaholic and didn't leave until I was 19, in the end. Isn't that terrible? I suppose it was partly the companionship. I became head girl, and clearly there was something about the whole set-up I enjoyed very much.

Coping as an Adult

The sense of apartness is strongly felt by only children, and in childhood strategies are found to cope with it. But how does it influence their behaviour when they are adults? What effects does this sense of being always alone create? There are two very common responses. The first is a need for space and the second is a difficulty with commitment.

THE NEED FOR SPACE

The only child's need for space is predominant, and we refer to it in several contexts. In Chapter 2, ROUGH AND TUMBLE, we looked at the need for both physical and emotional space. As we said there, the child may not have sought the space she has always had, nor the lonely, alone and apart times, but the consequence of always having had these leads to space being central in her life.

Only children appear to need to satisfy their sense of apartness by finding ways, all their lives, of ensuring that they get the space that feels normal to them. They may not even be aware of how they do this, but somehow or another they engineer ways of doing it. They may have a special place to which they go, or they may choose working situations that give them a sense of space or independence.

They may find ways of cutting themselves off from their families and the world which allow them the breathing space they crave. This, in turn, may be an instinctive defence against unfamiliar close involvement:

> *I enjoy my own company, and get irritated if I don't get my own space. My car is a symbol of that space – it's the one place I can get into and be on my own – that's always represented freedom. That's why I'd be lost without the car: not because I wouldn't be able to travel around but because it's my little empire.*

> *I know you are supposed to hate driving down the motorway, but I like it – it gives me time alone.*

Perhaps many of those cars you encounter on motorways with only a driver are just only children seeking their much needed space!

The only child's need for space is important in the context of this chapter because it is one of the responses to the adult's feeling of apartness – but this feeling isn't the only contributing factor to the need for space. One reason space is so predominant a need for only children is that their upbringing has reinforced that need, by not obliging them to share.

DIFFICULTIES WITH COMMITMENT

In Chapter 4, SOCIAL MATURITY, we related difficulties with commitment to problems with making choices. Such difficulties relate to the sense of apartness, too:

> *Commitment scares me to death. The fear of being swallowed – but also it is again that not having any experience as being an equal. It is child–parent, or vice versa.*

A lack of commitment was seen by several partners and only children themselves as a serious problem in relationships. Only children worry about this sense of apartness, yet need to perpetuate it. It is fear of giving up that little separate place within themselves that means they find it difficult to make commitments. Why? What exactly is the link? This fear of commitment appears to have two sources.

First, only children may have a strong fantasy, culled from their observations of other families, that other people are always able to be more intimate than they are. To the only child, making a commitment to a person or a course of action apparently means giving up her independence. She has no experience of having both intimacy *and* independence. For her, parents were so powerful and so influential, their presence so unremitting, that she doesn't know that you can be interdependent with someone and still remain neither consumed by them nor totally dependent on them.

Second, the separateness of the only child can make commitment within a relationship difficult, and this then reinforces the original feeling of apartness. But the fear of commitment doesn't derive solely from feeling always alone. This second element comes with that very strong message that only children are brought up with, of having to 'get it right', as we saw under *All the Blame*, in Chapter 1. Naturally, the more you feel it is imperative to get it right, the more reluctant you are to take the plunge, because you can't commit until you know it *is* right. Unfortunately, we can rarely be sure at the outset that any relationship is absolutely right. There have to be elements of compromise, of give and take, of 'going for it anyway', of risk – all of which are probably unfamiliar to the only child.

These two responses to feeling apart were reported by many only children, but they aren't the only ones. Having a strong sense of apartness generated a number of other, although less widespread, behavioural patterns, which we now go on to discuss.

RETAINING IMAGINATION AND FANTASY

Many only children said that they keep their aloneness by retaining the skills of fantasy and imagination developed as a child:

Even today I fantasise – I can very easily fantasise and have scenarios in my head which I carry round with me as I'm doing things – it's all going on. This is so easy to do. It's just always there.

I've been a tremendous daydreamer all my life. It is daydreaming about men and occasionally about being successful in something.

Everyone needs to escape from the real world at times through entertainment, holidays and hobbies. Only children may just be more adept at retaining apartness, avoiding engagement in reality through retaining their fantasy skills:

I have a vivid imagination and am a great daydreamer. I can live in a world of fantasy and can exist in it a long time. I can, for example, read a book such as Lord of the Rings *and be in that world for three days until I have finished reading it, and everything else of the adult world is an interruption.*

As we suggested in Chapter 2, ROUGH AND TUMBLE, there may be a link between only children's susceptibility to illusion and their gullibility.

COMPENSATING

By the time they are adult, only children may be locked into several internal conflicts (suggested in Chapter 4, SOCIAL MATURITY). Wanting close involvement with a partner yet also wanting to retain detachment and independence is one example. Similarly, the wish to retain the sense of being apart appears so ingrained with many that they have no effective choice. All the same, they may consciously work against this.

They may try to create a situation in which they won't be alone, by choosing partners from large families:

I remember being thrilled when I found Terry was from a large family. I suppose I chose him partly for that reason.

or by marrying into a large family:

I know I made a lot of effort with my wife's family to make up for my own lack of numbers. It's always me who presses them to come for Christmas, for example. I remember feeling comforted and secure hearing someone say when I was a child, 'We always go to my brother's for Boxing Day.' I wanted to have an arrangement like that, and I suppose I've made sure that I have.

Or, as a partner sees it:

The only children I know all want big families and to be surrounded by children. They want lots of children, to create a family. My husband hasn't a family, except the family he has created. It is very strange. I have twenty first cousins. I think he needs that.

Some may welcome the family without seeking it:

I've never gone for a relationship because of the family, but with my last boyfriend I enjoyed the large family and they welcomed me. Also, my best friend's family have taken me under their wing.

And some feel that with hindsight they would have chosen differently:

I married an only child, but now I'd look for someone with brothers and sisters, so it was a larger family to get into.

A couple of the only-child parents of an only child were conscious of having bequeathed him too tiny a family.

A cautionary note: joining a large family may not always act as a satisfactory substitute. The feeling of being alone and apart often remains, and is sometimes exacerbated by being with other families:

[My wife's family] are always nice to me, but I feel always slightly on the edge of them – I feel slightly cut off. Not exactly as though I'm there on sufferance, not that, but somehow . . . I know . . . they are giving me the attention and the presents and that, but I have no right to it – that's the difference.

Although we've been together a long time, I still always feel slightly on the edge of the family; I don't really feel part of it. I know I am, but I still can't feel it – that feeling of being outside is still there. Like, all the children, I adore them – do anything for them – but at their christenings I felt out, on the edge.

Another form of compensating behaviour for being alone is a magnification of a trait found amongst many people: listening to other people's conversations. It is as though the only child is so eager to be part of a group that he is driven to eavesdrop:

I do listen to conversations – but doesn't everyone do it?

Yes – others may well do so, but many only children obviously felt they did this more:

I'm so keen to ensure that I'm part of things that I listen in to others' conversations, to the detriment of my own. I can't, somehow, commit myself to giving my complete attention to the people I'm with in case something better or more important is going on elsewhere.

When I started work as a secretary I was always fascinated by other people's conversations – so much so that I was always being told to get on with my work.

I am always listening to other people! And to their conversations, to the point of being rude. I do it all the time – there'll be someone talking to me and I'll be listening to a conversation behind me and my eyes sort of defocus. People would say that they could see my ears move, even! I am certainly aware of what's going on in the room – in a restaurant – I'll be picking up all the vibes from other people.

Some combine eavesdropping with their skills of imagination and fantasy:

Often in a room with lots of other people I'll pick up on lots of conversations, and I'll piece things together and make up stories. I do it a lot, sometimes without realising. I hear snippets and build up people's lives around it. I have always listened to other people's conversations.

STAYING RESERVED

If I'm honest, I'm not one of the girls. I don't rely on women for friendships. If I've a problem, I don't necessarily share that. In friendships I try and stay on my own two feet – try and solve the problem, work it through myself.

One way of keeping apart where you have to be closely involved with others is to keep your feelings to yourself. At school, for instance, it may also be for self-protection: a teacher interviewee remarked on only children's reluctance to expose their feelings. Not sharing them can be a deliberate or an instinctive pattern:

I didn't have to share, which is a problem. I don't remember it as such, but I've seen it in my daughter [also an only child]. We need to learn to share, including sharing feelings. It worries me for her now – it didn't worry me when she was young.

Peter has not been a very good parent, as an only child – he can't imagine what it's like to have a brother or sister, and he doesn't talk or share very well.

But the thoughts and feelings may be there to come out – as one partner discovered:

When we first met he stunned me by talking endlessly for three weeks, because he had never talked to anyone. He spilled out everything because, as he said, he had never talked to anyone in his life.

There may be strength to be derived from keeping some feelings to oneself, as one partner said of her husband:

He had cancer for four years, and immediately went into all the books on the subject and into mind over matter. He beat it by an attitude of mind. On his own. He wouldn't see a psychiatrist or counsellor. He did it totally alone – there was nothing anyone could do for him. The power to beat it he found on his own. I'd have gone to groups for support.

I think things through a lot, to myself. Rather than talk to a colleague I work it through for myself – I think too much, maybe.

Also, I take life and things more seriously, I think, perhaps. It's harder to define, but there is something about being serious.

Are only children too serious? We often gained the impression they felt they were:

I think only children are, maybe, a little more serious. Maybe a little more sensitive to other people's feelings, being conscious and aware of situations which some kids never see and step into flat-footed.

It might just be how only children come across – being so responsible – or they may really have been very earnest and intense in their youth. Certainly, we had several interviewees swearing by their frivolity in middle age!

* * *

These are some of the ways in which only children cope with their pervading sense of being alone. Exactly how that aloneness is perceived by the individual will vary. One can find great enjoyment in people, another will want to retain a sense of space. But both attitudes derive from the same experience of an early life without siblings.

Only children may respond to the sense of aloneness, and perhaps the need for space that it engenders, by just doing things on their own. It may seem perfectly normal to the only child to behave in this way, but, as we have learnt through researching and writing this book, such activities may be seen by most people as activities to be shared:

When I was a businessman meeting people all day, I was glad to have a meal on my own in the evening. The chance to do that was absolutely delightful. I didn't want to talk to anyone. My wife sees someone in a restaurant eating alone and wonders if we should talk to them.

I'm not drawn to going out to have a beer with mates – I get as much fun from going to a pub and having a drink on my own.

We are doing a lot of DIY on the house and Ruth moans that we don't do it together, but I've got the tendency to be a bit isolated. I identify the plumbing, for example, as a personal task.

This feeling that you are always alone is, as we said, a chicken and egg situation: you feel alone because of being an only child but you also need to be alone because you have no experience of sharing. Only children may feel frustrated with themselves for needing to repeat the pattern, and want to change the way they behave, yet at the same time their experience makes it most unlikely that they *can* do so . . . resulting in even more frustration. They deal with it best when they and their families learn to accept it as part of how they are, and when they are allowed their physical and mental space within a framework of love and understanding. However, though strong and ingrained, the feeling may not be unchangeable. Sharing physical space can be learned. Learning to share emotional space is much more difficult. The sense that only children have their own private world which no one else can enter can be off-putting and frustrating for friends and partners.

On a positive note, let's remember that as with other only-child characteristics, the key to coping with being alone is understanding and accepting the feeling. You gain strength from doing so:

At a late stage in my life I have come to the conclusion that I will persist with my ideals, regardless of popularity. Rightly or wrongly, it's all I can do, and I have decided that this feeling of being 'alone' is best accepted, as I don't know what else I can do.

And, of course, it has its advantages, which should be cherished:

It's true you are always alone, even in company; always that sense of isolation that makes you vulnerable. But it makes you more powerful, too. I have reserves I can draw on, a sense of self-reliance and independence which others don't have.

6 The Triangle: a Summary

We have spent some time analysing the experience of only children, and relating it to how they behave in later life. Part 2 aims to help you cope, with this knowledge, in certain key life situations. We do this by using the positives from your experience, rather than by letting the negatives become overwhelming.

But just what have we learned?

From the only children to whom we have talked, it is clear there is a set of pressures felt to a greater or lesser degree by all of them. Having had to be everything to their parents, they have carried a heavy burden of responsibility, expectation and blame. Because they lacked experience of what they called the 'rough and tumble' of emotional life, they had difficulties with their self-image and were inclined to be emotionally immature behind a confident, grown-up exterior. Most of them felt that, in the end, the only child is always alone.

We suggested some explanations for these characteristics, as they arose. But the characteristics are not isolated, and we end Part 1 of the book with some theory that may link them. The first key to many feelings that the only children described to us seems to lie in the nature of the interactions within the triangle that is the only child's family.

Family Interactions

Contrast the interactions between the members of only-child families with those between members of families with two or more children. Within the first, the pattern of possible interactions looks like this:

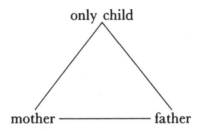

- — only three interactions are possible, and all involve at least one adult;
- — both the interactions in which the child can take part have an adult element;
- — the only interaction that the child can observe is an entirely adult one.

But in the multi-sibling family, the pattern looks like this:

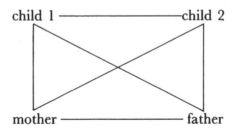

Here, the number of possible different interactions doubles instantly. Also, not all of them have an adult element. The one that is adult–adult may be balanced by the one that is child–child. Further, assuming that the fixed amount of time in a day does not allow the number of interactions within any family to increase indefinitely, then the addition of further children means that the number of interactions involving a child is likely to increase at the expense of adult–adult ones. Where the latter do take place, it may well be in the evening or outside the observation of children.

Additionally, in the multi-child family there will be child–child interactions in which each child takes part, and there will be child–adult interactions which the other child can observe and judge. This is not an experience available to the only child. With additional children, the number of interactions involving a child will increase, while those between any one child and an adult will decrease substantially.

Only children can observe adult–child interactions only in other families, and so have no perspective from which to assess their own. Because they are always involved, they are unable to judge how fair or right these interactions are. Only children have fewer interactions to observe in their families, but they take part in more of those that do happen than do sibling children in *their* families. Consequently, only children experience a much greater intensity in their relationships with their parents:

I do believe that single-child families tend to an intensity and an inward-looking tendency which are not really healthy. I think a lot depends on the parents' relationship. However, the child is too important in most cases and cannot possibly be that important outside the family, which does cause severe problems for the child.

The intensity of the only-child experience is key.

This intensity, remarked on frequently in our interviews, comes partly from the nature and number of family interactions and partly from the fact that the one child is the subject of all parental attention and activity:

I regret the over-possessiveness and claustrophobia of being just three of you, plus all the hidden agendas, some of which you knew and colluded with, some you didn't. I can look back now and see

what they were, but as a child I couldn't at a conscious level –
you were just in the middle of it, literally.

The second key to the many feelings that the only children described to us is to do with the distribution of power
within the family.

Where Is the Power?

Power in the sense of control rests initially, in most families,
with the two adults. Without sibling alliances or the wear-
ing down of parental resistance through sheer pressure of
numbers, the only child may find it difficult to break this
dominance. The parents of one child may more easily be
able to impose their ordered, adult values on that one child
than can the parents of larger families on all their children.
This control, together with unchallenged values, may have
contributed to the infrequency of teenage rebellion amongst
our interviewees. As we have also shown, within the triangle
of the family members the parents may each use the one
child to establish or maintain their own power in relation
to the partner:

I was a pawn in my parents' arguments. I was very aware of
being used as a pawn in their relationship.

I think I was used between my parents. I sensed that, certainly,
at times. At times I'm sure they both tried to use me as a weapon.
I don't think it was clear-cut – it would sometimes go one way
and sometimes the other.

'Two's company, but three's a crowd'

The third key to the triangle comes from this popular
saying.

With three people there frequently seems to be a stronger
bond between two of them, leaving the third as an outsider.
One parent using the child as a 'pawn' in arguments with
his or her partner may reflect a close bond with the child,

who may feel distanced from the other parent. Sometimes with older parents, who had developed a close relationship before the child was born, the bond between them remains the strongest:

> My mother was the type who supported my father whatever, and he was very strong and old-fashioned. They were very fond of each other and very close which I felt. They were the closest link of the three.

If the only child is either an ally of one parent against the other, or an observer of the close parental bond, the consequences of the triangle may contribute to his feeling of being an outsider.

*   *   *

The balance of interactions within the only-child family is thus very different from that in the multi-sibling family. The fact that the only child participates in more adult interactions and observes fewer child–adult ones has two, linked, consequences.

First, from the greater exposure to and involvement with adult actions and conversation comes the greater confidence shown by the only child in many social situations. With the constant opportunity to be observing adult reactions, he learns to recognise adult traits and social norms at an early stage of development, and naturally adopts many of them. He frequently becomes the 'little adult'. We and our interviewees recognise this as one of the bonuses for the only child. He is fortunate in starting on the ladder of life with the obvious advantages that greater self-confidence gives.

However – and this is our second consequence – the lack of close and extensive exposure to other children slows the only child's emotional development. Time and again we heard variations on the theme of the uncertainty felt in dealing with other children, from first days at school onwards – culminating thus in one case:

By adolescence I was able easily to relate to adults, but had nothing in the 'bank of experience' to help me deal with other teenagers at a time of naturally great uncertainty about feelings and personal confidence.

The uncertainty does not end with adolescence. The delayed emotional development has effects on partner and other relationships in adult life – but not necessarily for ever. One positive message we have is that many only children do 'catch up' on the skills they missed:

When I was training I had a Scottish friend who actually taught me to behave. I was very possessive with friends – they either were or they weren't, there was no in-between. And I remember her saying, 'You can have other friends, too', and I remember it as quite a learning experience, as I had to learn to share her with other people without getting jealous or angry. It was a great period of self-awareness. I'd gone right through childhood feeling on the periphery of everything, and she was the first person I really developed the sort of relationship with which children in families probably do much earlier.

Now, I love people. I am a totally different person to the person I was as the child and teenager. Totally. But the person I am now must have been there then, if only someone had opened the door, or turned the key.

Some of the differences between the only-child experience and that of other children arise from the *absence* of experiences that all other children would take for granted: not simply the absence of brothers or sisters themselves, but the consequent absence of the kind of personal growth that is brought about by the rough and tumble of sibling relationships; the absence of competition for time or space through which to learn the experience of sharing; and the absence of others to share parental expectations. These absences are at the heart of the only-child experience. Remember the one who said:

One thing I feel strongly: in families of several children, they learn how to 'live' – have relationships – not take arguments to heart too much. They do this in a 'safe' environment where the parents are referees. In a single-child environment, they have to learn these things in an 'unsafe' way – outside the family – and often they don't learn at all.

You have to accept that these absences are always with you – you can't change that. What you can do is learn to understand how they affect you. We hope you are further along that road of understanding now, and ready to move on to our SURVIVAL GUIDE.

Part 2

The Survival Guide

From the experiences of the only children we have interviewed, we've been able to build up an extensive picture of how their lives have been influenced by the absence of siblings. Our interviewees shared with us details about the difficulties they faced and the ways in which they experienced their distinctiveness. Many of them went on to analyse how these experiences both helped and hindered how they got on in the world. These people were not short on insight as to how they have learned to cope with their problems. Many felt they could have coped better if faced with the problems again now.

This part of the book is for *you*. (Your partners get their tune in Part 3.) Using the experiences and suggestions of our interviewees, we now turn to helping you make the most of your life as an only child. We examine relationships with partners and with friends. We deal with possible problems at work and with facing up to one of the greatest worries of only children – how best to look after elderly parents. Chapter 11, CELEBRATIONS, gathers up the many comments that our only children made about the difficulties experienced and the isolation felt at those family occasions when their aloneness could often seem magnified.

7   Relationships, and How to Survive Them

We now draw on the experiences of our interviewees to help you survive particular situations and life events. One of the most important of these is marriage or other intimate partner relationships. As we have seen, only children may have particular problems in this area. The lack of experience of sharing, of inter-sibling cut and thrust, and possible difficulties with commitment all mean that adjustment to family life can be more problematic for them than for others.

It is difficult to find statistics showing how successful or otherwise only children are at relationships. Counsellors to whom we have spoken suggest that there is a disproportionate number of only children within their client group. Yet, conversely, while the national figures for people having affairs within marriage are as high as 60 per cent, those for only children are only 30 per cent. Perhaps only children have more problems within their relationships, but have so many difficulties that they are unwilling to try again with another person! This may also fit with the picture of the only child as naturally cautious, as one who does not willingly take risks but prefers, if possible, to stick with the normal and the familiar.

The only child's experience in childhood may not be the best preparation for marriage. The patterns that she or he has learned may cause many problems, as the following experiences will show. The complexities of a relationship over time aren't easily conveyed in short quotes, so we use four longer case studies.

ROSEMARY AND MICHAEL

Rosemary married Michael when she was 21 and he was 24. She was an only child, and her parents' relationship was one of perfectionist standards – at least, on the surface:

> *There they were, always holding hands walking down the street and gazing into each other's eyes. That was how I thought married people should be. It's only later that I've come to understand that beneath that façade there was a bubbling cauldron of unresolved feelings and a great power struggle between them. But the illusion was there, and it meant I went into marriage without any realistic understanding of what relations between people were like. I had a bit of knowledge, an illusion, etc., but no realism. Take sex, for instance. My mother had told me a lot about it in one way – that it was something connected with love between men and women – and a bit about the physiology, but she stopped short of the real technicalities. She told me, for example, that men got 'all hard', and I had this vision of a totally rigid man!*
>
> *What I wanted was to get it* right. *It was as though I said to Michael, 'Tell me how to be and I'll be like that, and then you'll love me.' It also meant that I had no means of making judgements about his behaviour, either. I was so unsure about everything that I couldn't say anything about what he did.*

As it turned out this was a great problem, because Michael was a compulsive gambler. Rosemary ignored it for years, because she simply could not bring herself to confront the problem. When he got into debt she bailed him out, often borrowing money, on a pretext, from her parents. When she found membership cards from a casino in his pockets she ignored them. Of course, she did not ignore them without distress to herself. It caused her agonies emotionally, and enormous difficulties financially.

For instance, at one point she was doing two jobs in order to pay off the debts. Yet it was never discussed with Michael, still less with anyone else.

I suppose if I thought anything, which mostly I didn't, it was to be thankful that my rival in his affections was gambling and not another woman, but really the resentment was building up inside me, especially about the fact that he didn't share anything with me. And yet I didn't have any ways of coping with this. I just didn't know how to bring up the subject with him, and no notion of how his own background, so different from mine, was affecting him. All I knew was that somehow I was falling short of my 'Be perfect' aim, that somehow it was all my fault, and that somehow if I worked hard enough I could make it come right.

Eventually, Rosemary became so distressed that her doctor suggested she consulted Relate (formerly Marriage Guidance Council). Michael would not go at first, but Rosemary persisted and found it helpful to talk to her counsellor. Through the talking she came to understand the difference in the backgrounds of herself and her husband, and the way it was affecting their relationship.

In fact, Michael's gambling was his way of trying to maintain his independence from what he perceived as Rosemary's controlling of his life. He felt she was trying to fit him into the perfect image that she had got from her parents and that she felt was the only way of operating within a marriage. She had fallen into the only-child trap of trying to be perfect and expecting too much of others. Michael simply couldn't cope, and his reaction was to take up gambling – or rather, to increase his involvement with a habit he already had, which was accepted as the norm within his family.

Rosemary gradually came to understand that it was all right for her to feel resentment at Michael's behaviour, and that it was acceptable to believe that some of the problems in the relationship were his responsibility as well as hers. As she grew a little more confident and assertive, Michael noticed, and realised that the counselling had something to recommend it! He began to see a counsellor too, and then they began to have four-way sessions, each with their own counsellor.

Recovery for the relationship at first seemed impossible, but since there were two children involved each partner felt they should put effort into trying to repair it if they could. He had to learn to understand her 'Be perfect' compulsion, while she had to realise that this made him even more determined to show he was a free spirit, by gambling. Gradually they understood more about how they each reacted, and learned to talk about it rather than being driven by it. The marriage has grown stronger as a result. It has been helped, too, by the fact that Rosemary now sees more reality in her parents' marriage. In spite of the image they were at pains to project, theirs was not a perfect relationship. There were undercurrents, struggles and imperfections, as there are in any relationship. The problem for Rosemary was that this had never been admitted or acknowledged. This, of course, is the situation for many children, but the problem for onlies is that they are more vulnerable to it. In a sibling family there is the opportunity to gain other insights, other measures of relationships. The lone child has only the parents' relationship to judge and to measure by, and therefore is much more dependent on what that relationship is like in developing her own patterns of behaviour.

Rosemary and Michael repaired their marriage and now live together happily. The next couple had a very different experience.

ARTHUR AND YVONNE
Yvonne was an only child brought up in a parental relationship in which she was given every material advantage but which was devoid of expressions of affection:

Not only was there no love, but there wasn't much emotion of any

*sort. It wasn't considered right to let your feelings show, and we
didn't laugh or even smile much. Somehow I always sort of knew
that this was not the only way to live, and had a kind of envy
for the families I came into contact with who seemed to shout and
laugh a lot. I say sort of envy because I also felt a bit superior
to them when I heard about the rows they had, because I'd been
brought up to believe rows were not quite nice. So I felt better,
more good, I suppose, when I didn't have them. When I met
Arthur's family I thought they were wonderful because there were
five children and they always seemed to have a good time. They
also accepted me so well, and I loved that. It was the first time
I'd been accepted for myself. I really thought I could transform
myself by contact with this large family.*

Arthur and Yvonne reckoned without the influence that
family life has on character. For not only was Arthur from
a large family, he was also a twin, and had therefore been
accustomed all his life to sharing constantly, and also to
feeling responsible for another person. For him, marriage
and sharing his life with only one person was a relief, respite
from the ever-present family and his twin brother. For
Yvonne, on the other hand, being in the same room as
another person all the time, being expected to share time
and even thoughts with Arthur, was oppressive and almost
impossible. When she tried to spend time alone, Arthur felt
rejected and shut out. She then felt guilty, and as though
she were odd and unloving. They loved each other, but
neither was really equipped to give the other what their
backgrounds had taught each of them to need: for Arthur
– closeness; for Yvonne – space. Neither of them realised
this until one particular incident crystallised how they were
feeling:

*We were at a friend's house, and one of the other guests had just
been on one of these self-assessment courses – 'Know Yourself
Better', or some such thing. Anyway, he got us drawing this
picture. Each person had to draw four pictures: how you are, how
you'd like to be, what is stopping you? and what can you do about*

it? It was just a bit of fun, but when we all looked at them afterwards and the friend sort of analysed them I saw such a great difference between Arthur's and mine. In his pictures there were other people in every one, doing things to him or with him or him doing things to them. In my pictures no one appeared in any of the pictures but me. I don't think until then I'd ever realised just how self-sufficient I am. I simply don't need anyone else. That was the moment my marriage started to end, because instead of feeling guilty about it, I felt strong and terribly powerful. I was regretful that I couldn't need Arthur like he needed me, but resigned to it and not ashamed of it.

This story has a reasonably happy ending. Yvonne and Arthur ended their marriage amicably. Arthur later married the youngest of a family of four children, and he and his wife now have three of their own. Yvonne decided to make her new-found personal strength work for her, and has had a brilliant and successful career. She is a godmother to Arthur's second daughter.

Of course, marriages do not always end amicably, and couples learn insights and understanding at different rates. They may start off able to meet each other's needs, but then one of them may discover a different aspect of their life or personality.

PAUL AND TRICIA
Paul and Tricia, both only children, were married for twelve years. Paul tells their story:

On the very first Saturday night at university I met this girl. It turned out she was an only child, and she turned into my wife. We became glued to each other at university, probably because both of us needed a surrogate mother/father, or whatever. The other reason was I found in her a bit of a mission – certainly for the first six to eight months. She was the most insecure person about her own abilities. And the one thing I was secure about was my abilities. I spent endless hours telling her she could do it, that she was every bit the match for all the people around us,

'If anyone can get through this course you can' – and I almost became her counsellor. I don't think I was very emotionally mature, but she was so much worse that it made me feel very grown up.

A strange relationship, I have to say. We went through uni as a couple, really as a couple. Worked very hard – I was a very serious uni person – worked on the books night after night, almost always with Tricia the other side of the table. She lived there almost as much as you could in the rules, but all very proper, very proper, very proper – none of the intimacy you'd expect in the freedom that two students would suddenly have. 'Love' (in quotes) developed through companionship; there was sexual attraction, but both of us were unaware of some of those things. But again, very proper in that we never slept together – never, for the whole three years of university.

And yet always there was a clarity in our minds: I somehow always felt this was going to be my wife. I planned in great detail how I would propose to her – it was a great thing. I'm a great planner – I was more then than I am now. I was a list-maker, a planner. Probably it was much more to do with the doing than the emotion, though I look back and wonder if I ever really loved her. I probably loved her more like I loved my mother, in that she was the right sort of companion to be with. We did everything correctly; we asked her father's permission and did everything quite right. My mother was thrilled and proud of me. Here was a lovely daughter-in-law, I was becoming the perfect child, I had gone through university, I had never strayed, I had never slashed bus seats, never smoked cigarettes. So suddenly I'd found the perfect wife: she was professional, she was qualified, she was serious, pleasant – a very nice person – and I was set up for life.

We took separate flats in Birmingham – we didn't live together. We spent time almost universally in one flat, but at 11pm every night I would walk her back to her flat. We were quite formally engaged and we planned to get married after we had bought our first house. We did all the financial preparations. We chose and bought a house which I then went and lived in while she maintained her flat for four or five months, and then we got married and she moved in.

I remember so clearly the wedding because, you know, it had to be done right. And I remember this speech because I said things like 'I'd like to thank our respective parents because we had had a perfect upbringing – thank you so much for giving us the chance to go to university, where we had the chance to become qualified and meet each other and have a wonderful job and be on the road to the most delightful life, with our own wonderful house, and our lovely friends and relations around us at this perfect wedding' – that was the theme. It was like I was saying to my parents, 'Haven't I done my best?'

We had a very pleasant life. I did extraordinarily well in my job. I kept getting promoted and couldn't believe it. Tricia did quite well in her job, too. She had a number of crises of ability again – just like university all over again, saying she couldn't hack it, she wasn't really up to this – and I kept her going and ultimately she did get promoted like I did, only it took longer. But, you know, there was always the parallel.

And then with a fair degree of calculation we said, 'I think we should see if we would like some children.' And that also turned out to be a not terribly difficult thing to achieve. She left work and became a full-time mother. After the second child we decided we needed a bigger house and we moved to a nice four-bed detached house, and here I was, early thirties, with three lovely children and a house and a very good job.

But then a few things happened which started to change the way I was feeling. The job was very good for me in that it broadened my experience hugely. And I don't know whether it contributes, but I managed to get on to an international committee and I went all over Europe representing the company. I became a manager; I had people working for me, and I found that I could actually get on really well with people and, I think, develop some people skills. I can't remember whether I worked at it, but they seemed to come naturally. And they seemed to be quite a revelation: to find that I could work with people. Eventually, it built up so I felt like I was a complete person. Very, very strange sensations.

And, of course, you'll know what's coming. There was this woman I was working with, and you suddenly start saying to one another things like 'Life's a bit boring' and 'Maybe because my childhood was a bit unadventurous I don't think I've been an adolescent.' I can remember saying to her, 'You know, I think I sort of missed my adolescence. I'm sure there's lots of things I'd love to have done: travel and experience and girls and things.' And she was saying different sorts of things – like 'Oh, I had lots of fun. I was a typical girl. I was quite outrageous', and I was thinking to myself, 'Oh, this is an interesting person.' But she had other frustrations, in her life and her marriage. But inevitably (in retrospect) we ended up having an affair. And that seemed to mark the beginning of a whole set of changes in how I looked and behaved. Even my work – I ended up changing my job. I needed change, and thought maybe this change would fulfil my needs for change and leave me intact with the wife and family. But it wasn't to be. Once you set off down that path . . .

As Paul says: once you start on that path . . . But why did he? Partly it must have been because he had never had, or felt he had never had, an adolescence. This hunger for that change, that danger, that variety is something we have seen a lot with the only children we have interviewed. Asserting your own identity by breaking free from parental expectations is almost a human necessity. Yet the desire to conform that only children feel is stronger than the desire to rebel for many of them at the usual teenage rebellion stage. The need to make up for this later in life may be more pronounced with them because they have been more good than other children, from an earlier age. Paul had been good not only for his parents, but also for Tricia. On his own admission, he had been her counsellor and protector. At some stage in their lives only children must break the chains, and if they haven't done so in teenage, or through their work, it may well be the marriage that takes the strain. In that sense perhaps Paul's breakout was inevitable.

Yet his wife was also an only child, and she did not feel the need to break out, as far as we know. Perhaps she *had*

had a form of adolescence, in the sense of having moods, feeling very depressed, while she was with Paul in the early years. Or maybe for her the repression of her early childhood was so great that she simply could not allow it at all.

Far be it from us to suggest that two only children should never marry. Several of our interviewees were only children successfully married to another only child, and for them mutual understanding of needs for space, being alone and so on was an important component of the relationship. But when only children do marry each other they should be aware of the particular difficulties.

You both need to be aware of how your childhood experience has affected you. Are you, for example, really following your own path, or are you conforming to your parents' expectations? Can you talk about this? Paul and Tricia had a relationship which seemed mutually supportive, but in fact they were living in separate cocoons, not really sharing any feelings. This can be perfectly acceptable, but if one partner changes the other is left isolated, and the pattern they have established becomes destructive to their existing relationship. Certainly, there are very successful relationships between only children, but you'll have to be prepared to recognise each other's weaknesses. This may be especially difficult, because it means admitting some of your own!

For Paul and Tricia the end was a bitter divorce, with battles over the custody of the children which took a while to sort out. Paul is now happily married to the youngest child of a family of five, who, he says, allows him to be less than perfect and teases him so that he never loses touch with the fact that he is not perfect and that she doesn't want him to be. All only children need that from time to time.

KEN AND SYLVIA

Ken and Sylvia, unlike Paul and Tricia, did not divorce but certainly had their ups and downs in a marriage which has now lasted 24 years. Ken explains his side:

If it's my duty I do it, no question. In marriage certain things are my duty and I do them. This is what's held my marriage together through certain tempestuous and unhappy times. I've felt it to be my duty to stay, but not necessarily my desire. I've felt it impossible to say, 'Bugger off', even when my wife is impossible. In recent years I think the relationship has matured. It's only in the last two to four years that I've recognised that I need space. Before, I always fought against it, that feeling of needing it. I felt it, but it was my duty not to feel it. Now I spend less time with my wife, things are better – through hobbies, friends, etc., or just spending more time away.

For example, my job takes me to Germany a lot and I always tried to do the business in one day, so I didn't have to stay away. Or if it was a longer trip I'd always take my wife. Then I realised hurried trips were causing me too much stress, so I started to go the night before, have dinner with colleagues, practise the language, etc. Lo and behold my wife started to use those evenings to see friends, and enjoyed it, instead of being upset as I'd thought she would be. Then I found out that she didn't like going to Germany with me, really, as she always felt in the way. So now I stay away on those trips on my own, resent her less and we get on better. Resent? Yes, feeling it was my duty didn't stop me resenting that I had to do it!

Ken and Sylvia did not go for counselling, like Rosemary and Michael. In fact they did not even talk about what the problems were. They have never discussed the matter. Ken doubted if Sylvia had even considered what the difficulty was, though when she was asked she knew exactly what it was, and is only thankful that it has now been addressed so that she no longer has to go on trips she dislikes, where she knew that her presence was resented. Her feeling is that if they had 'made a big thing of it' the marriage would have been threatened, because Ken feels such a compulsion to behave dutifully that if they had discussed her problems openly he would have taken all the blame, and probably felt he should offer her a divorce. As Sylvia says:

He has such a feeling that he has to get it right, whatever right is, that he would not have been able to cope with the failure of getting it wrong.

For this couple the best way to deal with the problem was simply for one partner to change his behaviour – though not very radically. The result was a fairly radical change within the pattern of the marriage.

Counselling or talking it out is not always the way to survive marriage – either as, or with, an only child. However, some insights into what your need is, along with some acceptance of those needs, certainly help, and counselling can achieve these. Nor would we suggest that counselling will always help you to sustain a relationship, though sometimes it will help you to end one.

Thus far we have looked at marriages, but of course only children need to learn how to survive in other types of relationship too. Successful long-term relationships, of whatever nature, call for the ability to understand and relate to each other's needs.

MARTIN AND TIM

Martin was the only child of a prosperous middle-class family. When he was in the Sixth Form he developed an attachment to a schoolmaster and they had an intense emotional relationship which eventually developed into a sexual one. His parents were never aware of this because Martin always had friends of both sexes. At university he began to have girlfriends and had sexual relationships with them, though these were never very successful. When he graduated he went to New York:

I really threw myself into the gay scene there and had a lot of fleeting, though lovely, relationships. I realised when I was there that I was gay, and that all the messing about with women was really just trying to be something I was not. When I came home I determined to tell my parents, although I thought it would be a great shock and disappointment to them. After all, as an only child you do feel you've got a terrible responsibility to provide them with grandchildren, especially as my father was also an only child, so there was all that stuff about carrying on the family line. Anyway, that proved to be the hardest bit for my father to accept – that this was it for our bit of the family. Full stop. Apart from that, they were good about it. In fact my mother knew I was gay, she said, and so in a way it was a relief to have it in the open.

Shortly afterwards Martin met Tim. Martin was working for an advertising agency and Tim was a messenger who made deliveries to his office.

It's no exaggeration to say we fell in love at first sight, and he'd moved in with me within two weeks. When I discovered he was from this huge East End family who were always getting drunk together and rowing, and were constantly on the phone to each other about various family problems, it only added to his attraction for me. I'd always wanted brothers and sisters, and to be taken in and accepted by all these people as Tim's partner was wonderful. When they consulted me about their family problems I really felt that I belonged to them, and felt enclosed and warm in this strong, vibrant group of people. They saw me as a wise, sensible and intelligent person who could give them good advice – at least, that is how it seemed to me at the time.

The pattern that Martin and Tim had established within their relationship was of Martin as the responsible one, who took charge of all the finances, the bills, planning and so on – the perfect role for an only child. Tim's role, again entirely appropriate for the youngest child of a large family, was to provide the fun, the lightness, the affection. Martin's parents accepted him too. In fact, Martin said that his mother took to him as well as to the perfect daughter-in-law!

Two things then happened that called the pattern they had established into question. First, Martin lost his job. This meant that his role as the provider, the sensible one, was immediately threatened. Meanwhile, Tim was now the dispatch manager in his firm. While he was looking for another job and finding himself with lots of time on his hands, Martin spent more time than ever with Tim's family. In particular, he became caught up in the affairs of Nesta and George, Tim's sister and brother-in-law, who had recently become foster parents to two children. Their childlessness and attempts to adopt children had been the topic of endless family discussions, many of which had focused on their unsuitability to be parents, anyway. Nesta had a very quick temper and was often at the centre of family rows.

As he became more involved with them, Martin grew convinced that they were ill-treating the two foster children and discussed this with Tim. Somewhat to Martin's surprise, because he had intended to share this worry only with Tim, it soon became the main topic of conversation within the family:

> *The phone lines became hot every day, and everyone was constantly on to me asking my opinion as to what should be done, how it should be handled and so on. It made me feel so wanted and needed, and somehow made up for the loss of face I felt over my job. Everybody seemed to be thinking that I was the one who had to tackle the problem and, of course, I never questioned the fact that I was the right person to do so. After all, I was better educated – an intelligent bloke, as they kept telling me. I was used to taking charge and to being listened to, and somehow I felt I had to take responsibility.*

What Martin did was to report Nesta and George to the authorities. He believed this to be the responsible and right thing to do, and was astonished by the strength of the family reaction against him. They were shocked by his disloyalty and angry that he thought he had any right to interfere in family affairs:

> *Somehow, I had been completely duped. When they were going on*

about how dreadful Nesta was and how she ought to be reported, I believed that was what they meant. I didn't realise that this was just a part of their family culture. This month they were anti-Nesta, next month it might be another member of the family. I tried to interfere in their family, using the rules and norms I'd learned in mine. It can't work. Each family has its own rules and they can't mix. I mistook their acceptance of me for permission to do what seemed right and responsible to me, but was absolutely unacceptable to them.

The result of this unhappy incident was that Martin became alienated from Tim's family, which in turn led, though not for some months, to a breakdown in Martin and Tim's relationship.

Summary

We did not ask our only children to offer advice to others about relationships. We asked them only to share their experiences with us. The five we have quoted in this chapter have been deliberately chosen to represent extremes. The majority of only children do not experience such a clear development of understanding as Rosemary, or change as unexpectedly as Paul did. Few of them make such clear decisions to end a marriage as Yvonne did, or to to stay in one like Ken. But most are, like Martin, the victims of their only-child limitations, and they have to remember this. We have used these examples out of a wealth of long interviews because we believe they clearly illustrate the possible problems. What advice can we draw from their experiences, for other only children in their own relationships?

1   *Don't try to be perfect.* Everyone has their faults and their problems. If you fall short of perfection, it won't mean you are unlovable.

2   *Don't expect too much of your partners.* They are not perfect, either, and cannot meet all your needs. And don't try to control them.

3   *Try to understand yourself.* You need to accept your

insecurities and learn to love them. If you don't, how can anyone else?

4 *Don't be a rescuer.* You can't make everything right for your partner, and you are not responsible for everything that goes wrong.

5 *Don't be too self-centred.* Listen to your partner and learn from him or her.

6 *Don't think you can deny your only-child background.* It is what has shaped you. You can learn to cope with its effects, but you can't ignore them.

8   The Only Child and Friends

If you have an only child as a friend, you've got a loyal and faithful ally for life.

Only children as friends? Forget it. They have no sense of proportion. They're always wanting more from you.

Between these two statements – both from rational, intelligent people who have experience of only children as friends and acquaintances – lies the dilemma. In a sense, both can be true. This chapter follows the different journeys only children can take in learning about friendship and cultivating their own friends.

The Rules of Engagement

In Part 1 we reported some of the uncertainties that our interviewees felt in relationships. After intense exposure to adult modes of behaviour (without this being balanced by play with other children within the home), they often felt they just didn't know what one of them called 'the rules of engagement'. They felt they hadn't developed the skills to join in naturally when they had the chance, and they spent a great deal of time in fantasy or independent play:

Difficulties with sharing are natural, if you have not been brought up to do so.

I found it difficult to fit in with other children. You don't have to share as only children, so consequently I think it is a skill you take much longer to learn. At school I was always the third, always a trio or on my own – I was never a pair – I didn't have a special friend, actually. It was to do with being an only child and not knowing how to let go or not be possessive.

I don't think spending a great deal of time playing alone helped with peer-group relationships. I always found this difficult, and wasn't good at playing with other children. I now think that I expected too much from friendship. Let's face it, I read books by Enid Blyton, read Girl, School Friend *and* Girls' *Crystal every week, so my friendships never lived up to those depicted in those publications. (They've got a lot to answer for.)*

This doesn't make only children as irredeemably unable to make friends as might be expected, but it may leave them with a set of attitudes that gives them no kind of a head start in making friends. The main problems they seem to find are: expecting too much or being too intense, being over-possessive, finding conflict difficult, and trying to use friends as sibling substitutes.

But their background also gives them some advantages. The partners and friends we interviewed cited amongst other qualities: the loyalty of only children, their responsibility and reliability, their frequently encountered ability to keep up friendships and maintain a network. However, from what our interviewees said it appears that many only children don't achieve what they feel is a realistic attitude to, and understanding of, friendship until late in their twenties or thirties – sometimes even later:

It was only once I got into my thirties and early forties that I started to learn how to relate to people properly – to develop relationships with women friends, for instance, and all sorts of things. It's taken all those years to get to where, presumably, all those people who have siblings got a lot quicker.

So what are the journeys that only children make

in getting there? And what can we learn in the way of advice for others along the way? To go back again to the beginning . . .

Substitute Friends

For many only children and for some of our interviewees who were children just after the war and into the early fifties, nursery schools were non-existent. Friends were likely to be few in their early years. Although the world of pre-school education has greatly changed, early and close contact with other children may still have been infrequent for some only children. Imagination replaced companionship – perhaps in the form of an imaginary friend, as we saw in Chapter 5, ALWAYS ALONE. Some of these first friendships with imaginary friends could be pretty strong:

I was very, very lonely as a child and I was one of these quite sensitive children – horrible word. That meant I always had imaginary playfellows, and I used to spend hours sitting on the corner of the stairs, imagining and forming great scenarios with other people, and voices with imaginings. My imagination was very worrying to my mother at one point – she thought I was perhaps going to be schizophrenic. I was always play-acting, either in the head or having things lined up – bears, dolls. She says I used to stay there for hours, talking to them. We would go out for picnics and go out for this and that – whole scenarios of things. It must have been quite a pathetic sight, really! My eldest daughter had an imaginary friend and that was perfectly natural, but when a child goes on for hours on end on a regular basis, I'd be quite concerned.

And some of the friendships could last for a long time:

I was terribly lonely as a child and had two imaginary friends. One in particular I had – a boy – for years.

A lack of confidence with other children can push only children into such play:

I did have imaginary friends, and I disappeared into an imaginary world a lot of the time. I created an escapist world. I preferred it to the real world.

These friends were invented to fulfil a particular need. The good, or troublesome, aspect of imaginary friends – depending on your point of view – is that they have no mind of their own, have no being except what you impart to them. Does this reveal a need to control friends?

I did have an imaginary friend called Lally, but also – and I think I remember this, but my parents later reminded me, since they always assumed I would be a teacher – I used to hold conversations in the garden. The rows of flowers would always be told what to do – I would stand up and talk to them.

But sometimes the controlling mechanism doesn't work, because they aren't always successful playmates:

I had imaginary friends for a short while – Mr Bridger, who lived in the kitchen. I didn't get much joy out of him, I think. He wasn't very rewarding.

Don't mistake us. We know an awful lot of children have imaginary friends at some point in their childhood. All we are saying is that their frequency and role in single children's childhoods may be much greater – this is part of the distinctiveness of the only-child experience. Though imaginary companions may provide a learning experience, the time spent with them is not time spent learning the real life skills of interaction with real friends.

This doesn't apply across the board: many an only child has had access to groups of other young children such as cousins living nearby, or parents may have made great efforts to involve the child with other children. But for those who did not, the significance of imaginary friends for the developing behaviour of only children may be greater. Extensive play with imaginary friends may provide comfort and many other rewards, but it hardly equips you well for building real friendships, or for understanding the accompanying give and take.

Making Friends at School

Many only children that we spoke to remembered their difficulties and awkwardness with other children, and in making friends:

I always liked to have a special friend at school, and if I fell out with her I was devastated.

I didn't make friends easily. I was always a bit outside.

Once at school, many onlies felt at a disadvantage when it came to friendship, at least with people of their own age. Many felt happier with older children or adults, as we have seen.

School can be one of the only child's first experiences outside the parents' remit. Unlike children with siblings, who can gain experiences, experiment and get feedback from a brother or sister, the only child's first tentative trying-out of relationships with peers is likely to happen at school. Our interviewees varied in their reactions to this new experience:

I was not very good with others of my age. I didn't want to indulge in the playground rough and tumble. But I managed from quite early on to develop one or two good friends who were quite like me, so that I was part of a, you know, a small group of friends who were quite odd sort of kids. They were my protection, sort of, in the playground.

Even in infants' school I must have had a problem making friends. I always had one particular one, but when that friend wasn't there, I sort of didn't know what to do. I relied on that person and was lost if she wasn't there

I found it difficult to make friends, to be in a group. I still do. I suppose I'd hang about on the sidelines until I spotted one or two like me and then I'd make my move.

'One or two like me' proved to be a significant phrase. The strategy adopted by many only children seems to have been to find one, or perhaps two, particular allies:

I've always needed a best friend. Always been much more open with girlfriends and been very close to one particular girl. And I always need that bond with one.

One of the most likely allies is another only child, because each may instinctively recognise each other's needs and uncertainties:

It never occurred to me before now, but all my friends were only children.

Although she may be choosing special friends on the edge of the group, this is not to say, of course, that the only child does not want to join in – only that she may not know how:

You know that game – the farmer wants a wife? We used to play it on a Friday afternoon at my infants' school. I didn't mind the bit where you were all going round in a circle singing. But what was dreadful for me was that point where the singing stops and the one in the middle has to choose a wife or a child or a dog. I was so terrified they'd choose me, because I knew I'd look so foolish because I just didn't know how to behave in the way the others seemed to, clowning about and having fun. So I used to stand there with a smile on my face, praying no one would choose me, and breathe a sigh of relief when they didn't. At the same time, of course, there was this nagging disappointment that no one wanted me, just because they saw me, presumably, as someone a bit different.

She may be desperate to join in because she is lonely. She wants the company, and sets about getting it:

At my first school I was quite a good pupil in the fact that I participated, but I wasn't actually doing anything very much. It was the same again at secondary school – I was very active and always up to something, but not concentrating in class because I think I wanted all the children to all be my friends.

Or, in a teacher's perception:

> *Only children see school as a place to socialise and chat – it is the only place they've got. Only children in my class are like that. They are also much more sensitive to break-ups of friendships.*

> *In the summer hols I couldn't wait to get back to school.*

This enthusiasm could be obsessive, and sometimes led to extremes:

> *I bought friendship. I'd give them things to make sure they were my friends. I once gave away something precious of my mother's.*

> *I played on my own a lot and was obsessive about trying to get friends at school – would do anything to get friendship 'cos I was lonely, I think. But I didn't know this till I was about thirty – extraordinary. As a schoolboy I used to go home with other kids. Age eight, I'd say, 'If you take me home for tea my mother won't mind', and she was always having to come and rescue me from someone's house. As a child I didn't know why I was doing these things, but I was desperate to be friends with someone who I could relate to.*

A Certain Isolation

But anxious as only children mostly are to join in, they don't enter this social arena on quite the same basis as the other children there. Because the only-child experience has been so much with adults, the image of the 'little adult' often comes across to friends in childhood, and our interviewees often reported to us that they felt isolated from their peers:

> *I knew from an early age that I wasn't exactly 'one of the lads'. Because I was good at reading, the teachers liked me, but not the other boys.*

Or, worse, they might be punished:

> *As a child I didn't have other kids to play with, really. I was born in a council house in Liverpool – Dad was in a factory and*

my mother taught shorthand. They had bourgeois pretensions and my mother didn't like me playing in the street. The consequence was the kids used to gang up on this snotty-nosed little shit on the corner and try and beat me up. That was all a bit grim.

Or they might be bullied or ostracised because of their lack of understanding of the 'rules of engagement':

Only children haven't had the chance to get streetwise.

Not knowing how to get involved with others doesn't usually lead to popularity. So only children are able from a very early age to be extremely self-protective. They have an instinct for situations that are possibly threatening. Their desire to calculate, to be an observer before you get involved, to ensure that your way of retreat is ready before you commit yourself, contrasts sharply with other children's ways of reacting. As a nursery school teacher put it:

The one who hangs back, who finds it difficult to join in and who does so only gradually, that's the only child.

As they get older, the memory of the treatment they received can direct them strongly against bullying and into protecting the underdog, as we showed in Chapter 1, under *All the Responsibility*. The protectiveness, sometimes overprotectiveness, of their parents may lessen their opportunities for playing with their contemporaries. Some of our interviewees grew up in a period when most city children were allowed, even expected, to play outside, but as we have seen several times our only children were often prevented from doing so:

I would not ever have been allowed to play outside with other children.

This may have been because the parents were over-anxious – or because of their rising social aspirations, as mentioned above.

Of course, it may also be the case that the only child remembers feeling uncomfortable with the rough and tumble of such play, and was more at ease in the seclusion of his own home:

It seemed safer at home. I was always glad to get there, and relieved when the holidays came.

or because, having been the centre of attention, he had difficulty making the break from his mother:

School was terrible. I had a strong bond with my mother, and the separation was dreadful. Also, she didn't handle it well. She hung around.

At playtime my mother used to bring me buttered scones to the school gate. So I always had an excuse to hang about by the gate and not play with the others. Silly idea . . . no wonder I was a fat child.

The fact that the only children we spoke to had often been grown up in their behaviour and attitudes had often helped them get on with teachers:

I think at 14 I got on better with adults. At secondary school I had better relationships with the teachers than anyone else. I found the school discos boring. I wanted to go out with boys, but found them boring. I have always gone out with older men, and at school I was good friends with the teachers – I went to the theatre with the English teacher, for example.

This made them popular with adults, but it did not necessarily endear them much to their peers:

I didn't always share the adult expectation that I should play with other children. I was happy with my own company, so that must have seemed odd.

We should modify this rather gloomy picture by emphasising that many only children did have happy and positive memories of early friendships, some of which endured into adulthood:

Friends have been the joy of my life. It was a revelation to me to find someone I could lark about with and share games with. I cherish them all, and especially the support they've been to me in troubled times.

Stratagems and Tactics

By the time they reached secondary school many only children had honed their friendship skills quite finely and had learned quite a lot about the rules of engagement. They knew by then what sort of friends they needed, to get something of what they were missing at home:

I used this boy as a substitute family. I used to go there all the time and play snooker with his Dad and his brothers. His mother was fantastic. She always was happy about people being in the house, and never minded the noise or the mess. My own mum would have gone mad – not that she minded the friends coming, but there were so many rules about times and noise and no coffee in the bedrooms that I didn't bother.

The Bostons, they were my escape. Because there were four children there was lots of activity and they were better off then we were. At my house I'd have to be quiet and dutiful. At theirs I was able to giggle and lark about. Yet I obviously still came over as a responsible, sober type of chap because Mrs B always sort of left me in charge when she went out, and as time went on she even let me drive her car, which often she wouldn't let Greg, her own son, do.

I felt a need to get a mate early on, and got into that – getting a little circle of friends together. I did meet a girl on the first day, and we are still in touch.

Just as significantly, the only children we spoke to had begun to learn how to use friends to protect themselves:

There was this girl called Sandy who was very tough, but thick. She would protect me in the dinner hour from teasing if I gave her the answers in the mental arithmetic tests. As I was clever and always knew the answers, that wasn't a problem to me as long as the teacher didn't find out. Then she did. She asked me why I did it, and I remember clearly knowing that I could not tell her the reason because she wouldn't understand and would tell me off. So I told her it was because I felt sorry for Sandy. She was then very sympathetic to me, and told me what a charming girl I was, though misguided. The only child finds ways of coping, you see! I made her agree not to punish Sandy. In her view this further showed how kind-hearted I was, whereas it was actually just about protecting myself! I knew that if she had known this she would have said something to me that I didn't want to hear. It would have been about fighting my own battles. People always said that: 'Fight your own battles.' Didn't they know I had no idea how to fight my own battles? I'd never learned.

The absence of squabbling and rowing with a sibling in the family, which we referred to in Chapter 2, ROUGH AND TUMBLE, certainly puts only children at a disadvantage. Like the one quoted here, they often simply do not know how to fight. So they learn to develop friendships that will protect them:

I was never very popular at secondary school – I realise now it was partly my obsessive need to be good and to try and get others to be good. Also, I was bright, but without the social skills to offset it. I could get through the school day, mostly, but the bus journey home – it was eight or nine miles – was hard: a lot of mocking and teasing. I used to stay late for clubs the first year or so. But then I found a girlfriend at the end of the second year who also travelled on the bus, and that allowed me to sit downstairs with her and avoid the rowdiness upstairs. We stayed together through into the Sixth Form, and though I don't think I was conscious of what I was doing then I now think it was a pretty good way of avoiding those problems.

Achieving a Balance

Even where most of their early experience *had* been negative, the majority of the only children we spoke to seemed to have redressed this balance as they grew older, and had developed deep and long-lasting relationships with friends. They found, though, that there were certain tendencies that they always had to guard against. Many of them felt that they had found it hard to learn a sense of proportion in friendship; felt they were not sufficiently relaxed, or that they expected too much of friends:

I always found it difficult to share friends. I had two good friends at school, but I really needed each of them to be my best friend and to be loyal, first and foremost, to me. I liked to do things with each of them, but separately, not shared time. I suppose I couldn't cope with sharing the attention and the anxiety that they might like each other better than they liked me. You will know what's coming, of course. In the end they ganged up against me and became each other's best friend! What I did then was to bow out and look for another best friend. It didn't occur to me, either, to hang about and be in a threesome – which both of them would have been happy with – or to wait until they got fed up with each other again. I didn't know how to do anything but withdraw, and I think I barely spoke to them again. Interestingly, I am now very close to one of them again because we happened to meet in the street and took to each other immediately. She is a lovely person, and I feel sad for all the years we wasted.

It was in the teenage years that the only-child propensity to expect too much in relationships first began to show, especially in relationships with the opposite sex. Those who went to single-sex schools, especially, often felt completely unfamiliar with the other sex – seeing them as an alien species, almost. The normal teenage uncertainties were compounded by the only child's lack of proportion or over-intensity:

I was at an all-girls school, and my father had a very odd idea of boys too. I was not allowed near them. So I found it very difficult to relate.

I went to an all-girls school, and I really didn't know what these other strange people were!

It wasn't until I was in a stable relationship that I had men as casual friends – but that could as much be to do with all-female household and girls' school as only child. I wasn't used to making the right noises – when you are attached, that's OK, but when you are not then it is the wrong signals.

Where contact was established, several of the only children reported that they frightened away girls of the opposite sex by being too intense:

I scared her witless.

With Marjorie I had no sense of proportion. I fell for her totally, and scared her off pretty smartly.

Many, as we have noted earlier, were aware that they had no sense of proportion in their relationships with friends. We also talked earlier about their inability to judge themselves, to measure themselves accurately in relation to other people. It comes from that absence of cut and thrust, the lack of experience of squabbles and criticism and making up. Even if siblings don't especially like each other, they learn tolerance and acceptance in the relationship. They have to. The fact that only children don't have these possibilities results in their misjudging other people's intentions or their commitment to friendships.

This inexperience of sibling conflict means that they are often not comfortable with conflict in general. The significance of this for friendships is twofold. First, only children may find it difficult to survive any of the normal contretemps that are inevitable in any relationship:

We had this stupid row about politics – something to do with the Health Service, and I just didn't know how to make it up. I don't know if he took it seriously. I suspect not, but I was too scared to ring up in case he had really meant it.

Second, only children may not make the best types of friends when it comes to sticking up for you in an argument or a fight. That feeling of 'being in the same team' is something that sibling children usually experience within their own families, but onlies don't know what it means, of course:

> You have to stick together if you are the same family, I know – I've seen others do it even when one is in the wrong. I'm not sure how, though.

> You can never tell people to f*** off because you are frightened they will. Siblings can always tell them to because they know they won't.

Another problem that only children perceive themselves to have is difficulty in achieving a balance between not giving enough in a friendship and yet being too easily put off, too easily rejected. Again, this refers back to that absence of cut-and-thrust relationships in the early years. On the one hand, lone children have no measure of what is the appropriate level of demand to make in a relationship – they haven't checked it out, they have no yardstick. We are not suggesting for a minute that sibling children always get it right, but they at least have formed some sort of map of the area from their own family relationships and from observing their siblings' relationships with their own friends:

> I keep a bit aloof, and I've no really close friends now. I'm good company, and I have a sense of humour, but I've no drinking mates and I'd have a job to find someone outside the family to talk to.

> Some of my friends have commented that I'm insular. Even on holiday with friends, I'll potter on my own. There is an inner bit that I keep to myself. I tend not to be forthcoming.

Only children can also be misguided when it comes to judging when withdrawal is right and necessary. They are often so afraid of being too pushy or demanding that they remove themselves in order to save running the risk of being rejected – long before the risk of rejection is real, as did the person quoted on p. 189.

The tendency to regard friends as sibling substitutes, and the need to be on their guard against this, was something that our interviewees were well aware of – though it could have its advantages:

> *I had a friend called Pauline at secondary school – we'd act like sisters and play one set of parents off against the other when we wanted to do something we weren't really allowed to do.*

But more frequently the sibling expectation is doomed to disappointment in the end:

> *I'd always thought of her as the nearest thing to a sister I'd ever had. We had always been there for each other at fraught stages of our lives. I'd rung her in the middle of the night and she once turned up on my doorstep at three in the morning. But when the chips were really down one time and I needed her very badly, it was her brother's wedding or graduation or something and of course she couldn't be with me in preference to him. I understood entirely, but felt bereft all the same.*

Summary

In spite of all their disadvantages and the difficulties they encounter, most of the only children we spoke to managed to develop successful friendships eventually. One of the things we have to learn at any stage in life is how to make sure that we learn from other people and use their experience to enrich and extend our own. Only children must make sure they do this with their friends. You may not know the rules of engagement, but your friends probably will. There is nothing wrong with making up for your own lack of experience by learning from them.

Let's remember too that only children offer advantages as friends, as well as disadvantages, and those advantages can be pretty substantial. Only children are loyal, reliable and responsible. In fact, as they are responsible to a fault, they will probably be the last to let their friends down. And many are wonderful at staying in touch. Mind you, what they perceive as frequent contact may not exactly coincide with other people's idea of it!

With most of my friends I expect a phone call once a week or so. With my friend who is an only child I don't expect anything . . . I just know I'll hear when it's right for her.

I have one or two friends where I maintain the friendship, and if perhaps we meet once or twice a year for a drink then for us that's the friendship maintained. One is an only child from school, and when I see him there is nothing lost. There is no doubt in my mind that he is a friend for life. For my wife, a friend with whom you don't renew acquaintance at least once a week is a friendship lost.

And they won't be the ones to drop you from their Christmas card list, either. Indeed, they will go on sending you a card for at least two years after you dropped them from yours, since they are so afraid of not being liked!

I've been lucky and have been all over the world, and I deliberately keep the friends I met then. They are important to me, and I make more of an effort. Also, I like people and I bother with them. I can go most places in the world and have friends there, and that's important to me. It's very important to me.

If you as an only child want to be a good friend and benefit from friendships, we suggest the following guide:

1 Keep a sense of proportion.
2 Don't expect too much.
3 Remember friendships can and do survive rows.
4 Use your friends' experience to extend yours.
5 Relax a bit more.
6 Remember you are a valued, trusted and reliable person.

9   The Only Child at Work

At work, only children live up to their reputation as high achievers. As a result of parental expectations, attention and resources, very many have had a good education or training and acquired 'good' jobs. The social maturity of the only child, combined with his many other assets, means that work settings often suit him best, and allow him to shine. We don't want to dispute this success story.

But only children have to make considerable adjustments in the world of work. Judging by our interviewees, their achievement may not be quite the straightforward success story it appears. In a work setting, the only child can probably gloss over the uncertainties that may confront him. His difficulties being less under the spotlight than when he is with a partner, they may be less obvious to the outsider.

Given what we already know about only children – their obsession with the need to 'be everything', feeling they must carry all the responsibility and all the blame, being very hard on themselves and setting themselves high expectations – what are they like in a work situation? Although we'll look at *what* the only child does as a job or occupation, we are more concerned with *how* she does it. What kind of colleague is she? What kind of boss? What sort of work should only children seek? What do they have to watch out for?

The High Achiever

Some of those we talked to were typical of the image that the world has of an only child – ambitious high achievers:

I'm incredibly ambitious. I agonise about whether I've reached my zenith. It may not be as important to me as it once was, but it's still bloody important. My image of myself is conditioned by my success at work – though it is by no means always tied up with earning money.

I had just been promoted to the point where I was the most senior person of my age. Nobody else at my age had got to that level. Now I'm a managing director, but quite insecure about having that role. Yet motivated to go on – with ambition to want to be that.

What we do do is to use our time at work very well.

The skills of organisation, liking order, making lists, getting it right – all those adult messages imparted early suit the adult element of work. The ability to achieve the task, to get the job done, are very useful indeed in the workplace:

I like a certain kind of order – I take pride in my belongings, in presentation. I like to put on . . . er . . . well, . . . if I'm doing something, presentation is important – it's a certain pride, really.

He likes things to be orderly, but doesn't need to assert himself on to other people at all – that self-confidence. He doesn't need it for self-aggrandisement.

He works very well on his own.

Sometimes it's that sense of separation that is appreciated by others:

If someone's got a client or personal problem, a hell of a lot of these people gravitate to me, and I've only been here a year.

He is always the negotiator and could be a counsellor – everyone wants to talk to him; he's everyone's counsellor.

Certainly, their reliability – remember they always feel

they carry all the responsibility – makes only children dependable colleagues. You can rely on them to get things done and to achieve the targets they are set:

> *I'm good at getting myself motivated – you've got to sort out activities for yourself as a kid, and this carries through into adulthood.*

> *If I do something I have to do it, and really do it. I'm one-track-minded – it's got me where I am in work. I sold my soul to it and I chose one of the diciest professions to start in. It was a challenge. I enjoy, adore, the work and it is all-consuming, which is something I need – I'm a personality that needs extremes.*

But achieving the task is not to be seen in isolation. It's usually achieved through co-operation and contact with others. Relationships are important at work, too, and the only child may have less success in getting on with colleagues. Aspects of his background and experience can prove problematic in the workplace, and he may lack some of the necessary skills.

Criticism and Competition

In most jobs criticism and competition – we referred to both in Chapter 3, SELF-IMAGE – are natural to the environment: either explicit, in that constructive criticism contributes to successful completion of the work; or implicit, as part of what we loosely term 'office politics' (although it doesn't need an office to flourish!). We doubt that many people positively enjoy criticism but, as we've shown before, lacking the experience of rough and tumble, only children tend to feel particularly ill adapted to cope with it.

The attitudes that our respondents had to competition and to criticism were significant in how they progressed in their working lives:

> *I take failure hard and I'm a bit of perfectionist – I set myself high targets and don't like it if I don't meet them.*

I am extremely sensitive to criticism. We do find it hard because we are so hard on ourselves. Therefore when someone else is hard on you it is especially difficult. We have been so used to taking the blame that we always think everything is our fault.

I can't cope with criticism at a personal level, and find it hard at a professional level. Until recently I'd sulk for hours, and only recently have I just begun to be able to see that it is helpful sometimes.

I set myself too high expectations – always too high. It means you're always striving to do something. The excitement is in the hunt, not the result. I judge myself very harshly, I'm more lenient to others. And I don't cope with criticism very well. I'll take it from people I respect but I don't respect very many people. I'm pig-headed, so I won't listen to many people.

Because only children have not usually experienced being teased, brought down and undermined as part of daily living, they find it difficult to keep a sense of proportion in the workplace. They tend to be set back and over-depressed by criticism. They may find it difficult to accept that they are in the wrong, to admit mistakes, because they have such a heavy 'Be perfect' message laid on them early in life:

When I first started work it was quite a big shock to the system. As a child I was loved and adored and didn't have to do anything to earn it. At school I was Miss Goody-goody and won prizes, etc. I felt happy and comfortable – all I had to do for that to continue was to be good and work hard.

I can't take criticism, of course. Because you have no experience of sharing criticism with other people, you always feel it is cataclysmic . . . Everything is absolute and everything is terribly personal, and it becomes terribly important to avoid criticism.

As far as competition is concerned, we felt that our only children fell into two extremes. Either they described themselves as intensely competitive:

I'm extremely competitive in the job market. I want to be the most wanted person in my field. If there is no one else to compete with I'll compete with myself. Interestingly, I don't like team games, but I'll go to the gym and compete with myself about weights or time to go round the circuit.

Or they had decided to opt out of competition entirely. This may well have been because they did not wish to enter into a situation unless they were sure of being the best!

I simply never compete. I always withdraw. I'll tell you it is because I don't care about winning, but I suspect it is more because I fear I won't.

Only children compete with themselves as much as with others. And since they are hard taskmasters on themselves, it is not surprising that they set high standards for other people to follow as well. They have to be very careful about this or they will be impossible, especially as bosses:

My own work rate is incredibly high. I shift a lot of work in a very short time. I've worked hard at not expecting the same output from my colleagues, and we've put into place all the mechanisms . . . you know, like targets and work plans agreed together, etc. What I can't do much about, though, is the fact that they still feel pretty inadequate because I can't hide the speed at which I feel compelled to work, or my output. Nor, if I'm really honest, can I get away from the fact that I do feel cross when they miss a deadline, however understanding I try to be. To me, missing a deadline is impossible. I would never do it, no matter what the cost to myself.

Having to be Everything

One of the things that can help only children not to become too exacting as a boss is, of course, their need to be popular. Though their tendency is to want to be in charge, to control, this is tempered by their need to be needed, liked and reassured:

With male bosses I have a pattern where I can very much act the little girl, if I'm not careful, and offer to do lots of things instead of being a rational adult and saying, 'Well, why don't we do etc., etc.' – because I want them to like me.

What you're seeking always is approval – it hasn't worked through from childhood. Plus you want to make everyone happy, and you can't, but you have a bloody good try. Now I am getting harder – maybe it takes getting to my age to do it.

. . . at work there were other things I had to do. When I first worked I wanted what I was used to – praise and adoration. I was too eager to please. It took me time to adjust to the fact that work wasn't about that. I threw myself too much into the first job – I wanted to be loved and adored and be indispensable. I have a better sense of proportion now.

It may also be that only children manipulate their work situation so as to make up for their lack of family. They may 'create' a substitute family right there in the workplace:

I'm aware that I've found myself a working situation in which I'm central – I'm everything to my staff here. A little substitute family of long standing. I want to know everything, too, because that makes me feel involved. Yet, of course, I don't want them to know everything about me because I am alone inside, held back, observing rather than participating.

This can make for cosy working situations, but on the other hand it can make such people even more prone to have too high an expectation of their colleagues. Not only do colleagues have to adhere to high standards professionally, but they must be willing to provide personal support too. Like the example above, these only children may want to know everything and expect their colleagues to act like their family:

I get resentful if they won't stay to have a drink with me when I'm depressed, and I know I make it hard for them to refuse.

Of course, the only child's saving grace is that he is never any harder on other people than on himself. That old feeling of having to 'be everything' is as prevalent in the workplace as in the home – sometimes with disastrous results:

> *When I had my first job outside the school system I felt I had to be everything to everybody. I'd work from seven in the morning until eleven at night, never allowing myself any time off and always feeling I had to support everybody. And I don't just mean support them in the workplace. I was taking on all their personal problems as well. Things went badly wrong and I had a break-down. One morning I just couldn't get up and go to work, just couldn't get out of bed. I ended up being off for three months. My doctor referred me to a psychologist and I learned a lot, which has helped me and also helped me to help others. I still tend to overwork but now I test anything I want to do against my acronym*
> FAIR:
>
> — *Is it* Fundamental *to me? Does it absolutely have to be done?*
> — *Is it* Achievable? *Am I setting myself a reasonable aim or target, or am I setting myself up to fail?*
> — *Is it* Independent? *Is it going to lead to other demands which I won't be able to cope with?*
> — *Is it* Realistic? *Am I being honest about all my other commitments and the amount of time I have available?*
>
> *This is something which has worked for me, and I'd recommend any only child to try to get a similar testing system.*

Wise words, and ones that any only child might do well to take note of, lest she end up like this one:

> *Five years ago I had a heart attack. I brought it on myself by driving myself too hard. I know that sounds like a typical only child, always ready to take the blame, but really I know I did. Anyway, I went on a diet, gave up meat, started to take regular exercise and generally take care of myself. I vowed I'd never work as hard again. But honestly, look at me now – I'm back in the old routine. I don't seem to be able to do anything other than drive myself. It is what fulfils the expectations I have of myself, even*

though the result is that I'm now waiting for my next heart attack to strike.

Not all only children are as pessimistic or as fatalistic as this, but a common pattern is not to want to admit that they don't know something, or to ask for help in their working lives. All those early messages about getting it right and carrying all the blame if they get it wrong have had their effect:

We're very hesitant about asking for help. You expect people to turn round and ask if you want help.

We apportion the blame to ourselves. 'I'm not doing enough' – I hate that feeling. I recognise but can't do anything about it.

Some of them manipulate their working situations so that too great a demand, too great a responsibility, is *not* placed on them. The lack of commitment that they tend to show in personal relationships, as we saw in Chapter 4, SOCIAL MATURITY, works to give them a self-protecting mechanism in their working lives. Some choose to work on short-term contracts:

I'll tell you my greatest fear in life – it's a contract that goes on for a year, because it means that my life is f***ing well predestined; I've got no control over it. I can handle relatively short contracts because I can grasp the end.

Supply teaching suits me fine . . . no long-term commitments.

Or they find themselves a job or a career where they can be in control of situations themselves:

I work as a decorator, self-employed for the sole reason that I can manage my own time.

That's why I work at home – it's a positive, being able to do things on my own. I prefer not having the restrictions of someone else!

I work freelance and sometimes I wonder if there's something about working alone that means I don't want to be part of a team or be dependent. I was brought up to be dependent and never want to be dependent again.

Working on their own, or as a freelancer, may be appropriate for some only children, as we note below.

Office Politics

One 'team' aspect of many work situations is what is usually referred to as 'office politics'. For only children this is analogous to the group situation at school, which they usually dislike or avoid:

I can't cope with office politics – I find honest people far easier to work with rather than covert answers which are supposed to tell me something, but I can't work out the message for the life of me. That unnerves me because it's unwritten. The parallel is with teasing – playing games which we've never come across. We don't experience children playing off versus each other, like those with brothers and sisters do. Things are black and white, not shades of grey and purple and brown. I actually do not understand office politics – you either have it or you don't. You can't learn it.

The two companies merged and I couldn't stand the larger office – I can't stand all the office politics. I can't be bothered and want to get out, and I only spend a couple of afternoons a week there. I can see the value of groups, but I can't stand it all the time.

I didn't do enough sparring as a child, so I can't walk away from such situations at work. I hate to spar. I'm not good at it and can't easily deal with office politics.

A way of coping with this is the not-unexpected one of opting out, creating your own space:

I work at Didsbury, but Cheadle is my bolt-hole. I need to get out, and it's my way of doing it. When we combined sites I negotiated my second office here, for my self-preservation. Perhaps that's what you get from being an only child – being a good negotiator.

But rather than opting out in *this* way, some only children prefer not to work in group situations at all, choosing, as we saw earlier, to work on their own:

> *He chose in his job to be totally, totally alone, and if he could he would be preferably without a telephone.*

Fitting into the Group

Does what we have said so far in this chapter imply that only children do not make good team players? Not necessarily, but they do have to realise that they may have more difficulty fitting into a team than do children with the experience of adjustment and negotiation within the family that they themselves lack:

> *I always preferred sports where it was me against them, not team games, so I liked tennis and swimming. If I had to play a team game I wanted to be centre forward, right in the middle, to be leading or attacking.*

> *In my work I have sometimes had to use a shared computer, and then I go mad. If I have planned to do work and I go in and find I can't because someone else is on the machine, I get mad. I'll even book time months ahead in order to guarantee my space. Not being able to get on them when I want – well, I'll go berserk if I can't use them. Woe betide them if someone else is on the machine.*

In order to fit into a team, only children have to understand and cope with their natural tendency to expect to be the centre of attention – that tendency to judge every situation by how it affects them:

> *I'll never forget what happened at the first office I worked in. I decided that I didn't like my desk in the place it was in. I felt it would be easier to reach the things I needed if I changed the angle at which it was placed. One morning I went in early and shifted it around. I was absolutely unprepared for the bollocking I got from my colleagues when they came in. I had simply not taken into account that by moving my desk I had impeded access for*

others. It had honestly never occurred to me. I was mortified when they called me selfish and inconsiderate, but of course they were right.

Being an only child makes you independent; you work very independently. Every now and then I think I may be difficult to work with. You have very independent thoughts and ways of doing things. I don't find sharing things easy. The pluses are that you observe a lot and therefore think things through. There's a rational explanation for everything.

Once having recognised this, they must then guard against going to the other extreme and taking on too much responsibility for the actions of others:

He is terribly over-responsible. I kept telling him – you cannot solve everyone's problems. If that is a trait of only children, then Charles is that 100 per cent . . . He totally feels responsible for keeping the whole world happy.

There's a lack of responsibility, too – you have none to siblings. But we move that responsible feeling on to other people – my clients, for example. I feel responsible for them.

They also have to realise that working with other people means conflict sometimes, and the only child's tendency to shy away from conflict may make this difficult for her to accept:

It really upsets me if I see two people going at each other. I find conflict very difficult, and I find it difficult to stand up for myself. I work in a male-orientated job. On one job people were riding roughshod over me: had a meeting about my work and brought forward my schedule, then did it again, and I had to finish the work even sooner. Looking back, I should have immediately stopped this and demanded to be at the first meeting. Instead, I boiled inwardly, did the work faster, and they became more and more demanding. I wasn't standing up for myself – I was nervous of my position. I should have dealt with it at the early stages.

He works very well on his own. He didn't like the rat race. He didn't learn to push for himself. He's far too nice – couldn't take the cut and thrust of business, and withdrew. Now he works as a specialist consultant and it suits him perfectly. He has no ability to push and shove in the dirty way that's needed to get on. But he is totally dependable, my Rock of Gibraltar.

Finding the appropriate level for relationships can also be difficult:

I missed out on the equal-to-equal relationships: i.e., child–child or adult–adult. So now I tend to adopt child–parent or parent–child. At my last job I was being trained and put myself into the child role and got horribly victimised by someone. Now that I am training other people I find myself taking on an inappropriate parent role.

Colleagues can find only children too serious, too responsible. Certainly, they can be seen as lacking flexibility, too concerned about things which to others are not important:

I remember I used to get teased about how I never liked anyone to interfere with my desk. Perhaps no one likes other people going through their things, but for me, I used to get upset if someone had borrowed my stapler or changed the position of my phone. It was a joke at first, but when I saw it really irritated them I managed not to show that I minded. I suppose like most only children I'd been able to go out and leave things and then come back to find them untouched.

It's an idea to try to become more spontaneous, to have a little fun, to kick over the traces once in a while. This allows colleagues to see that you are not always perfect, that you have your irresponsible moments as well:

I know the importance of being gregarious and can do it happily when required – play the party games and so on.

It will make them less resistant to acknowledging your undoubted advantages as a colleague. Who is it who can always put his hands on the file that's needed? Who is the most organised person around? Who makes the lists? Never leaves the lights on or forgets to buy the coffee? The only child, of course. What you have to do is be pleased and proud about these qualities, and foster them, as long as you don't put down those who don't have them or regard them as inferior. They are not – they are just different.

Summary
1 Think about the job you choose, and why. Is it because of parental expectations, about fulfilling their ambitions rather than your own? There may be nothing wrong with this, but it is as well to be aware of it. Similarly, there is no point in taking up a job just because you want to rebel against what your parents want. It must be because you want it for yourself.
2 Because you may have less opportunity than other children to discuss your chosen path with others of a similar age, try to seek the opinions and advice of those outside the family.

If I wasn't an only child I believe I would have made career choices and decisions a little earlier, because I might have talked them out with someone else. I might have articulated some thoughts that stayed shut away.

This will also help you to check out the old issue of family expectations. Are they reasonable? Do you really want to follow in your father's footsteps? Or are you planning to do so because there is no one else who will?

3 Be aware of how your only-child experience has affected you. Do you like to be alone more than with others? How strong is your need for personal space?
4 From the experiences of our interviewees, we would say it is an idea to try to find yourself either a job in which you are the boss – it's OK to be a high achiever, you know – or one in which you can exert some control by working on your own or in a special-

ised area. This can also satisfy feelings of needing to be special.

5   Be aware of your tendency to be a bit solitary, and try not to become too involved with jobs that depend for their interest on machines rather than people. You can fall too easily into a situation where you withdraw from contact with others and spend too much time with your objects because you find them easier!

My training was to do with the landscape, and I really enjoyed the contact with the environment, being outdoors, etc. But my first job was working with people and environmental issues and gave me a lot of freedom. Looking back, I realise I rapidly concentrated on working with people not because of any aversion to the landscape but because I needed that contact with people and enjoyed it. I enjoyed the organisational elements and being helpful to them – you don't get quite the same response from a tree. There were enough clues before – I should have realised that 'people' jobs would always suit me better. But I suppose at the time there was no one close to me who would simply say, 'Don't be stupid! What are you doing that course for? You'll never be happy with that.'

6   Don't be ashamed of your organisational abilities and tendency to want everything in its place. These are valuable skills.

7   Set reasonable limits. Don't take on the world.

8   Don't judge others by your high standards.

9   And don't ask too much of them, either. You can't expect your workmates to be your family.

10   Guard against the besetting sin of the only child – solipsism. The workplace does not revolve around you. Keep (or develop) a sense of humour – even the most serious job has its lighter side, and there is nothing wrong with a little fun now and then.

10   The Only Child as Carer

Caring for them – God, I dread it.

As an only child, of course, there was absolutely no alternative – when my mother needed care I had to provide it.

The awful dread of them being ill – I am going to fall apart when it happens. How will I manage, cope with that and work, etc.?

This chapter is about caring for elderly parents, about coping with the time when they can't manage any longer without some help. It is the subject on which our interviewees expressed the greatest dread – the fear of having to take on this responsibility on their own. In this they had some justification, in that many of them had relatively older parents who were likely to need care at an early stage in their children's adult life.

Most of this chapter consists of advice about coping with caring, but we start with some only children's views on the subject:

My own parents worry me enormously. There is no one else.

I dread caring. The good news is that Dad died first, or I don't know what I'd have done, because he was absolutely hopeless on his own. But mother had had her life ruined by her mother-in-law, and vowed never to repeat this, so when Dad died she went and got a warden-controlled flat. So I've come out lightly, but the notion of having to look after them, especially as I have so little regard for her . . .

I don't find it terribly easy to spend long periods with her because she has lost her short-term memory, and you know the kinds of repetitive conversations one has. Sometimes, if she is tired or has been excited by something like her ninetieth birthday, which was on Monday, she gets stuck in a groove, and after everyone else had gone there was myself and my two sons there and she kept asking us if we wanted a drink. And we would only have just got to the end of saying 'No', we didn't, when she was asking us if we wanted a drink again. And I know it sounds quite trivial, but it's the sort of thing I'm not terribly good at – eventually I do have to say, 'Mum, you've said that ten times – stop it.' And for a little while the boys both look at me disapprovingly. But what you can do for a parent and what you can put up with from a grandparent are entirely different. It is not nearly so threatening, though goodness knows why, since the blood line is still pretty near, but they clearly don't find anything she does nearly as threatening as I do. I am extremely fortunate – she is a very happy person and content with what she has, and doesn't worry (at least not publicly) about what she can't do or have. I expect she has her moments, but she keeps them to herself.

I notice that with my husband, who is one of four, whenever there's a family problem they have a case conference on the phone or whatever. It's not that they are terribly close – they don't see each other that often – but as soon as there's something that needs discussion they all check it out and come to a decision. Whereas I can't actually check it out like that.

For only children, caring is a double anxiety. Being worried about, or positively dreading becoming responsible for, the care of elderly parents is coupled with feelings of strong moral obligation that they have to provide that care. It's some burden – and hardly surprising if it's an ocean that only children dread having to swim in.

Of course, these two emotions aren't exclusive to onlies.

But only children feel the obligations and the lack of alternatives more strongly than offspring with siblings simply because there is no one who can share these obligations to the same degree – or even just share the discussion, if not the caring. Though it is well established that one person in a family habitually finds herself (or, less often, himself) in the carer role, at least those with siblings have the chance to 'talk about what we should do with *our* mother', as one put it. Having to carry all the responsibility comes naturally to the only child, as we have seen, but carrying it alone at this time is hard:

> *When I was caring for my mother when she was dying, it wasn't just that you can't share what's going on, but also you don't feel you can ask anybody to help, whether they be a very good friend or not. I had to take the decision whether to up the morphine or not, which is an awful decision to have to make. The one person who did help was an older acquaintance who gave up a couple of days a week. She was an only child and knew what to do – she understood the immediacy of need.*

Few will relish the prospect of full-time caring:

> *I think about caring, and then straight away I don't – don't want to think about it. I'd make sure they were comfortable and cared for, but I wouldn't be invaded.*

On the other hand, few will shirk the responsibility when faced with it:

> *Caring is an immediate issue, with Dad. The responsibility is huge – you are the focus of making it OK for them. If there is one thing I have always felt, it is that I should be able to make everything all right. But with Dad, who has Parkinson's, there's a complete helplessness because there is absolutely nothing I can do, and I'm the only person Mum can turn to. It leaves me feeling guilty because I can't do anything at all; trapped because I can't go abroad or don't feel able to, and very frustrated by the whole situation, although I don't begrudge the time or care.*

Those old feelings of having to make it right and feeling guilty if you can't are particularly prevalent at this time. And for some who are married to only children, the responsibility is doubled:

> *I'd view it as a burden if I had to have Mum to live with me. We are in a difficult situation as we each have a set of parents, and of course we have a duty to both of them.*

Despite the widespread and heartfelt fears of our interviewees, it *is* possible to survive life as an only-child carer. More than that – it is possible to develop a new and fulfilled relationship with the cared-for parent or parents. Drawing on the experience of onlies and other carers, this chapter sets out advice that we hope you will find useful. The keys are (1) *preparation*, (2) *communication*, (3) *negotiation* and (4) *expectation*. These are the successful survival strategies for the only-child carer, which we'll now look at more closely.

YOU ARE NOT ALONE
A word first on caring generally. Caring for relatives is now very widespread in our society – one in seven of the population is a carer. So the first step in survival for the only child is to recognise that you are not alone! We know only too much about your only-child perception that you *are* alone, but in this instance you are not. You are one of a vast band of six or seven million people, and many of these will tell you that it is possible to survive the experience of caring for your parents *without* being entirely swamped by it.

1   Preparation

Does this sound like you?

> *I daren't think about what will happen when Mum and Dad get older. They phone me every Sunday, and each week when I get*

*that call and they are all right, I think to myself, 'Thank God –
I've got another week's reprieve.'*

But one day the phone call will tell you they are not all
right, and then you will have to react – and it might then
be too late for proper planning. That won't do. *Start planning
now.* There are three aspects to think about when preparing
for caring: *financial, practical* and *psychological*.

(a) FINANCIAL PLANNING

First of all, it is necessary to understand the current situation, and not to harbour any false impressions. Many
people still believe that the state will provide residential
care for an older person who is in need. This is no longer
the case. Even if your parent* has no income other than
state benefit, there is no longer any obligation for care to
be provided free of charge in a residential home. The situation will vary from area to area, but basically an assessment will always be needed before decisions are made. This
will be carried out by the local Social Services department.
They *may* assess your parent as needing residential care,
but equally they may decide that he or she should remain
at home, with care being provided to support him or her
there. It may well be expected that this care will be 'topped
up' by a family member. If you cannot provide this care
yourself, you will need to know what assets are available
in order to buy it in. So be sure that you know the answers
to the following questions:

— What assets do you have? What assets does your
  parent have?
— How can these assets be realised?
— Can property be transferred?
— Is there any insurance to mature?

* For simplicity, we refer from now on to 'the parent', but, of
course, everything we say applies equally to the person with the
prospect of caring for both parents.

— How can you best combine paid work with caring?
— Do you want to consider residential-care
alternatives?
    or sheltered housing?
    or buying in care?

Once you've sorted out what money is available, move on to the practical aspects of providing care.

(b) PRACTICAL PLANNING
Start by answering these questions:

— What sort of help is, or will be, needed?
— What is available in your area in the way of
    statutory help – e.g., from Social Services or
    Health Service?
    voluntary help – e.g., from the Red Cross or Age
    Concern?
    informal help – e.g., from friends?
— What is transport like locally?
— Is a move to a more accessible or better serviced
    area practicable?
— Can you build a walk-in shower?
— What kind of health care now would prevent future
    problems – e.g., attention to exercise or diet?

(c) PSYCHOLOGICAL PLANNING
Yes, this does sound off-putting, but we simply mean the adjustments the only child may have to make to survive the caring experience. It is likely that there will be things unsaid and unspoken expectations, on both your side and your parent's, that can get in the way of making these essential preparations. Did your parent care for his parents? What has been discussed in the past?
    You'll need also to make some kind of guess about what *kind* of old person your parent is going to be. It is not usually difficult to see in late middle age whether it is his mental

or his physical health that will give out first. Start looking
for signs:

1 If your parents are still together, which partner is
   more dependent? How will the one manage without
   the other?
2 Are there lapses of memory?
3 What is your parent's interest in current affairs? The
   popular test of asking who the Prime Minister is isn't
   foolproof in assessing dementia.
4 It is more relevant to note whether your parent stays
   active and interested in events *outside* his immediate
   experience and circle. If he does, the likelihood is
   he'll remain more alert and independent as he gets
   older.
5 On the other hand, if he is finding it difficult to get
   up out of his chair, or you notice he is walking more
   slowly or that he tires more easily, then it may be his
   physical health that will fail first.

You can't say which scenario is preferable – each brings
its own difficulties. The key is to be prepared, not to be
caught unawares.

2 Communication

We know it is difficult, but you must talk to your parent
about preparation and plans for the caring situation. Most
people avoid doing this – which is entirely understandable,
because it is certainly difficult. But sense must prevail. Lack
of advance communication about how the situation is to be
dealt with when a parent can no longer look after herself
grows out of lack of communication about other things. Of
course, you are not going to be able to establish intimate
communication patterns with an ageing parent where such
closeness has been absent in the past. *But* beginning to
make comments like 'Have you thought of what you would
do if one of you is left alone?', and tentative inquiries about

finances, may be possible. You'll probably find that your parent has been worrying about it too, and is relieved to have the opportunity to talk about it.

Most families are not used to communicating about their emotions, and we've learnt that the families of only children are worse than most! So you will probably be wise to stick to practicalities at first. The experience of Judith, for example, may be helpful:

> *Of course, as an only daughter living a hundred miles away, my first thought when Dad died was complete horror that my mother might think I should offer her a home with me. I simply couldn't cope, not because I don't love her – I do rather a lot, in fact – but because my lifestyle [as an air stewardess on long-haul flights] just doesn't allow me to have a mother waiting at home. I like to be free to do as I please when I'm off, and of course there is a man, or sometimes men, around from time to time. I just didn't feel I could discuss all this, but I knew it ought to be brought into the open. One weekend when I was there I mentioned that I thought she should get a downstairs loo put in as there was only one in the bathroom. We talked about this and eventually decided that it shouldn't just be a loo but a shower as well, so that if Mum became infirm she could have a bed downstairs and still be independent. It sort of came out that she had been thinking about this too for months, and I realised that she had no more desire to live with me than I had to have her, yet we had been unable to say it. My mistake was in assuming she wanted to muscle in on my life when, as she said, the thought of my irregular hours and not being able to keep to her routine was horrifying to her.*

Many only children will have been unable to share feelings with their parents, and can't expect to start immediately. But remember that you are entitled to your own views about caring, just as your parent is. This brings us to point 3 in our survival strategy.

3 Negotiation

In most relationships some measure of compromise, or negotiation, exists – even if it is not made explicit. We usually have some notion of what is or is not acceptable behaviour, and tend to moderate our own accordingly. The child usually knows just how far to go to annoy a parent, and when to stop. The lover usually knows how far a partner can be pushed and when persuasion is necessary. Only children, however, have particular difficulties about learning the 'rules' of relationships, as we have seen.

This is particularly a problem when it comes to caring. In a caring relationship these negotiating rights are often difficult to establish, anyway, because one or other of the participants has tacitly abandoned them. The carer may do so in the interests of a quiet life; the person in need of care may feel over-grateful or beholden to the carer. In some circumstances it may be impossible to negotiate because the cared-for person is suffering from some sort of dementia which makes communication extremely difficult.

Such a scenario can lead to guilt and resentment – two of the commonest emotions associated with caring, and ones to which the only child is especially prone. It is vital to come to terms with these emotions. What you must remember is that *however* grateful you are to your parents for giving you life, and *however* obliged you feel to them, YOU HAVE NEEDS TOO. It is fine to want things for yourself: time off, privacy, opportunities to see friends; the right to be tired, or to be angry. Learn to understand this at an early stage, and it will serve you well in the future:

> *I have always known that Father would need to be near me at some stage. For a 77-year-old with considerable problems, he is quite amazingly undemanding now. He lives in his own flat just down the road, and we manage quite well with the sort of daily contact one has with him. He isn't afraid of staying in his own flat and in fact he much prefers it. I hope that he will be able to die in his own place. I would be perfectly prepared to look after*

him for a sort of acute phase myself, with what help there could be.

Remember, too, that if you are to be effective *and* survive as a carer, you must take account of our fourth point.

4 Expectation

We have already reported the difficulties that only children have with unrealistic expectations. It is vital to be realistic about what the caring situation can and cannot offer.

The caring that you, as an only child, do for your parent cannot happen separately from the context of your previous relationship with her. It is through that relationship that you have become her carer. If this has been difficult in the past, it will not suddenly become all sweetness and light now. If your mother has always been awkward, she will not change and become sweet-tempered and grateful because she now needs to be cared for. If you have always resented the way your father treated you, do not imagine you will suddenly stop doing so when he needs your help with walking or dressing.

The caring relationship is inevitably affected by what has gone before. You have to cope with it as it is, not as you would like it to be. Don't imagine, either, that by taking on the caring role you will be able to undo the past and resolve all previous difficulties. You can't. But it need not be all gloom. Many only children will have shared the experience of Renée:

I had always been frightened of my mother, though I only came to realise this later in life. She dominated me and tried to control me and my father through her strong personality and quick temper. 'Not doing anything to upset mother' was a strong theme through my life. When she had her stroke and moved in with us I was still frightened of her, I think, but gradually I came to see her as a frail old lady. More importantly, I see now that there has always been a frail old lady inside her, and that's probably why she has over-compensated by shouting and being angry. The other side is that she sees me now as someone who is capable instead of weak and helpless, which is how she always seemed to treat me before. We've grown to understand each other a bit more, and I'm glad we've had the opportunity, otherwise I'd feel a lot of unfinished business around when she dies.

Lastly, there is the issue of your parent's death. Only children have reported to us that they believe this to be particularly difficult for them to cope with because they have no siblings to share with:

I think the period following the death of my mother was the loneliest of my life. I know it is a terrible time for many people, but for the only child, remember, there is no one to think or share the words 'our mother'. No one who is feeling what you are feeling, no one to share reminiscences with. The isolation I felt was dreadful.

Summary

If you can follow our survival guide to caring, if you can prepare for, communicate and negotiate about the present or potential caring situation, and if you can set expectations on both sides at the right level, you will stand every chance of being able to deal as painlessly as possible with what is an inevitable situation for many only children. You might even, like these people, gain something:

When Mum was ill we said we'd like her to come and live with us, and for me it was quite a decision because it's not something I'd ever envisaged – that I'd offer to share my home with Mum or Dad – although I knew something would happen at some point. I suppose I always hoped they'd die before it happened, because you don't particularly think about it. But Mum had changed a lot and so had I, and it was extremely important to me that she actually did stay with us for those last six months. That time I valued a lot.

I think one of the pluses of being an only child and a carer is that, provided you can work your way through the problems, you can actually end up with a more balanced relationship with your parent than you've had before. At least they have to see you as a grown-up, at long last.

11   Celebrations

Christmas this year was a crippler. See, I've got my old mum who is 84 and my Aunt Martha who is 89. They hate each other because Martha is my mother's sister, and there is a family feud which goes back to God knows when. They are both crippled with arthritis, and I can't leave them on their own on Christmas Day, can I? So me and Louise are stuck with them every Christmas until they pop their clogs. So we go up to Leeds and take them out for Christmas dinner at the best place we can afford, and then we come straight home afterwards, go to bed and then pretend that Boxing Day is our Christmas. We get to this hotel and it was f***ing awful – it was a big, bleak room and it was draughty, unwelcoming and £50 a head. So we get to the meal, I'm sitting there and halfway through a woman dies at the next table. I looked at her and thought 'She's gone.' She was completely rigid and staring straight ahead, and her eyes had gone like marbles. I thought, 'She's dead.' Some waiters came and moved her chair out with her on it, upright. I couldn't believe it and said to Louise, 'That woman's just died at the next table.' Then the soup was a disaster, the pâté was terrible. Two people at the next table turned their plates upside down and refused to eat anything. Then when the pudding came they ran out of the alternative to Christmas pudding. There was no custard for my Aunt Martha. My mother refused to speak to Aunt Martha, so she was crying. Meanwhile, my mother was being friendly and gracious to everyone else so we couldn't accuse her of being horrid – building her defences all the *time and cruelly hurting Martha at the same time. Then a fire broke out and the alarms went off . . . that was the cherry on the cake. We had to get out fast because the place was on fire, and of course we couldn't use the ramps. We had to go down steps, which was a problem for the arthritics. In fact, it nearly killed my mother, I thought she was going to make death number two. Then the fire engines came and we abandoned the day. That was my Christmas Day, and what's worse it was Louise's too.*

Many people have Christmas horror stories. Family members who exchange a few phone calls a year find themselves cooped up in one house for three or four days, with few outside distractions but a strong pressure to enjoy themselves. Mingling with the excitement and anticipation, there's some sense of dread for many people as the end of December approaches. For our only children just the mention of the word brought near-universal groans. For many of them the dread, guilt and pressure and the responsibilities they felt outweighed any enjoyment. It soon became clear that it wasn't Christmas itself that appalled them, as much as the expectations they felt about any family occasion. Since they alone made up the family, such times were generally more difficult than for those with siblings. A sense of celebration was rarely what they felt.

Our first example may be extreme, but celebrations of all kinds – birthdays, anniversaries, Christmas or any other festivities – caused our interviewees particular difficulties. It was yet again that feeling of 'having to be everything':

When the girls are home and we're all here, and special times like Christmas or celebrations, I feel I must be all things to all people, which now I find intensely irritating. If I'm not well there's dreadful consternation all round. Is it because of years of always being intensely capable and always being there? Always coping, etc., being efficient? But oneness does encourage, along with the responsibility, this feeling of compensation for what the one parent has lost, so you've got to play daughter and carer and stimulator . . . Absolutely when I've come the entertainment has arrived. I notice it now with Mum older – this past Christmas I felt all the family were looking at me and saying, 'Right, it's Christmas. This is your responsibility – you've got to be on the ball from the moment you get up.' The minute I was quiet they were asking, 'Are you all right? Are you in a mood?' And I was saying, 'I'm absolutely fine. There's nothing wrong – I've just been quiet for ten mins.' For some reason there's this demand element that comes in. You have got all the right food in; you have got to have the games, etc. You feel drained because you daren't flicker an eye muscle or someone's going to jump on it. Once I used to worry that they weren't having an excellent time, or happy. At my parties I wasn't allowed to feel this or feel that, was always holding something in check – always something, whether it was my anger or wanting to have a damn good cry or whatever. There was always the controlling element, having to control something inside you very often. Always something you were pushing down for someone else's sake.

There was some sense of 'being everything', even as a child:

It's a dilemma. You get the biggest pillow-case and that, but then you sort of have to provide the response. You have to be pleased with your presents all day. You can't sort of take a little rest while someone else is in the spotlight.

Mostly it was the sense of getting all the goodies, in childhood, tempered by the lack of company or of anyone to share with, that explained the absence of affectionate memories:

Oh, I loathed Christmas. Don't mention Christmas – it was horrible. There was nobody to open presents with, nobody to open your stocking with. There were your parents, but it's not quite the same. And then because of the hotel they were worn out after lunch – Christmas afternoon was like all the other Sunday afternoons. It was 'Play with your new toys quietly behind the settee.' I always remember Christmas was me behind the settee! There were no cousins or anyone else coming into the house at all at Christmas.

It wasn't that our respondents all looked back on Christmases with loathing – more that such occasions were just

*a bit boring, really. There was only you, so I must admit it was
something to be got through, really.*

*Christmas was always a bit tedious and always has been. I just
used to wish I had lots more people around. Mum would say to
Dad and Grandad, 'Entertain Jane while we cook', but they'd
drink and sleep, and one year I went off through the French
windows. I used to think, 'I've got all these toys and I just want
to show everybody, and I've got no one to play with. They could
come round to my house.' But of course they were busy with their
own families. It was a bit lonely because it was a family time.
That was a bit of a bore. I always had good birthday parties,
but they only had me so they were able to put more effort in.*

Many interviewees expressed the view that there were
always too few people to make a celebration real:

*What family? You can't play Trivial Pursuit with three because
it's really boring with three of you – it's horrific. And birthdays
– you don't really get them. It's no fun with birthdays – never
really anything special. You think, 'So this is it, is it?'*

*My pleasurable anticipation was always followed by disappoint-
ment. There just weren't enough of us.*

*There wasn't anyone to share with or play with on times like
bank holidays or birthdays, so I've never enjoyed them.*

*With such a tiny family I feel very much that we are a dying
breed. Each Christmas it's a bit like that Agatha Christie –
people keep disappearing. There were two sets of grandparents,
then one, now just my parents – soon it will be just Mum and
me. I'd like to have a family with lots of buzziness.*

There were, of course, some only children who enjoyed
celebrations:

*Christmas was brilliant. All the presents. One present from every
aunt and uncle. A mass of stuff there in the morning, which you
could have immediate access to. You got more – I did, anyway –*

and enjoyed it as a kid should. Same at Easter. I woke up with 12 eggs and only me and mother and father to eat them. It went on for ever with the eggs!

But Christmas seems to be especially difficult for the only children of families that celebrate it. Because Christmas is seen as a family time it is expected that you will be with family – and there's less acceptance of looking elsewhere for company. Also, for the only child there's a clear conclusion to be drawn: all those families that have many more people around *must* be having fun – or they imagine they are, as a result of seeing all the Christmas images on TV.

Various Christmases I've had people around. Others when there's been Mum and I, I'd go to start clearing my room on Christmas Day. Once I wrote all my thank-you letters on Christmas Day, or did work. Last year with Kevin, he came to me in the morning and in the afternoon I went over to all their family, and we were a bit late and there was this huge pile of presents I had to open while they all watched. But I was in my element – it was nice to be in a family environment and be one of a crowd, and do what you want without anyone watching you or having any expectations – everyone is there as friends, not trying to be the happy family.

Once you've opened the presents, that's the day. You're expected to get on with it. I used to write the thank-you letters on Christmas Day – Christmas is a bad time. I always long for big parties of people – oh wow – what a wonderful experience.

It's the clash between image and reality that may be stronger in the only-child families:

Christmas is, of course, not what it was because it never was. All those Dickensian images. It's like that for most people, but for only children the not being what it was is more obvious because there is no dilution.

When we consider the mythology based on larger families, which is still propounded, no wonder the much smaller families find life difficult. The whole ethos of Christmas and family gathering:

how can two only children, when married, be at both parents on Christmas Day? Which means guilt and problems. It may be a trivial point, but it's a useful example of only children attempting to conform to norms which are impossible.

When everyone else is busy with their own family, the isolation of the single child is more keenly felt. It is the 'guilt and problems' experienced as adults that particularly struck home for these only children too:

Christmas? It's war! Not a time to look forward to but a time of stress and tension.

Oh, the guilt of Christmas! If you ever think of not going . . . I dread Christmas. I was elated this year – I got my first speeding conviction on the way back. I was so keen to get away.

The problem is compounded when only children marry each other:

Because I married another only child, there were awful problems about Christmas. Many a time we've had two Christmas dinners in one day. Christmas is just hell . . . it is a constant struggle about who we are going to be with: who to spend Christmas Day with, how many days and meals with each, how long we see each. We did once get to counting the number of days spent with each family . . . and did morning coffee count as a meal?

It isn't usually Christmas itself that is the problem, but it being a national holiday that is projected as a family celebration. Families that do not celebrate Christmas have similar problems:

Of course Christmas isn't a problem for us – as a child I was quite happy – it is now they've become a big deal. If I don't go and see my parents within 24 hours of my birthday, it's a big deal. If I don't go to lunch on New Year's Day, it's a big deal. The importance to them is enormous – it is marking off time for them. As a child, my parents did include other children on birthdays, etc., so those were all right. I go home now and there's just the four of us, and we have to blow out candles and Mother wheels out the fairy-cake decoration she made when I was 12, and the four of us are sitting there.

And, of course, celebrations are a problem for partners too, as the only child in the first example (p. 220) reminds us . . . it's Louise's Christmas too:

As a child it was brilliant because we used to go to the Lake District with lots of other relatives. Now I feel under tremendous pressure to go home, because otherwise they'll be alone. It's immensely difficult because my new chap wants to spend it with me, but if I don't go to my parents it will be bad news.

The only child's sense of obligation is particularly strong at festive times:

It's the same with birthdays. I find them hard . . . either yours or your parents – it's hard to say that you are not going to be there.

I notice with other families with several teenagers (who naturally can tend to be a bit selfish), one would just be off – to watch a video for example. They go. They don't feel they have to be downstairs entertaining or anything – they just go and disappear without even saying anything. That wonderful freedom to just think, 'I want to do something', and then go and do it. Amazing. I can't remember ever feeling like that. I can remember feeling 'I'd love to go and do so and so but I can't – I have to still be here doing what's expected of me.'

The feeling of having to be what one interviewee called 'the floorshow' was common:

On a Sunday I go over there, and it is as though the entertainment has arrived. I feel I have to make them laugh, bring a bit of life into the place.

Not unnaturally, this feeling of being pressurised to show that you are enjoying yourself, or to be the cabaret, leads to resentment and anger. Nor is the resentment confined to the only children. It is felt keenly by their partners too.

A FEW GROUND RULES

If celebrations are not to become battlegrounds, there are a few rules to be established:

1 First, remember that the pressure you are feeling about celebrations probably has its roots in that familiar imperative: 'Get it right.' Give yourself permission to feel that you cannot make Christmas or that birthday or special anniversary perfect for *everyone* concerned. If you are meeting your mother's need you are probably upsetting your partner, and so on.

2 At an early stage decide on your limits. If, like our first example, you can bear to spend a dreadful Christmas Day and then laugh about it and start your own Christmas on Boxing Day, fine, do that. If you can't, for goodness' sake don't force yourself.

3 Don't make decisions by default. Only children are good at planning, so plan. Tell everyone, consult everyone, and do it early enough not to be driven into decisions because there is no time to think of alternatives.

4 If necessary, establish rotas: 'I'll come this Christmas but not next', and so on. Make it clear to parents that they are not the only people to be considered. You have other calls on your time.

Above all, let yourself off the guilt trip. We know it is hard for you to believe but it is, you know, quite all right to spend your birthday or Christmas, or even your mother's birthday, in the way that suits you. A celebration should be just that – not an endurance test.

A TEN-POINT SURVIVAL PLAN

We've looked at how the only child behaves in certain key activities and situations, tried to show the effects of his early experience on his behaviour, and given advice on how to avoid the worst of the pitfalls that our interviewees pointed out to us. To sum up, our survival plan might go like this:

1 *Don't try to be perfect – there is no* right *way.* Whatever message you got from your parents, there are many different ways of being, and not one of them is exactly right. You can make mistakes and still be lovable.

2 *Be kind to yourself, not so hard on yourself.* We know you had to carry all the blame, or felt that you did, but other people won't be as hard on you as you are yourself . . . honestly.

3 *Lighten up. A little humour never hurt anyone.* It is really important to see the funny side of things. You won't be thought irresponsible if you fall about laughing now and then.

4 *Don't expect so much of people. Be realistic, not over-critical.* Yes, we know all about the expectations that were imposed on you when you were a child, but that's no excuse to do it to others. You get further with people by example and reward than by making them feel guilty.

5 *Remember the positives of being an only child. No one is more organised and more reliable.* On the whole, we are pretty good types to be around in a crisis. We are loyal, dependable and – that old standby – responsible, so rejoice in it!

6 *Don't get too hooked into achievement.* Try to measure success via other things. Remember the lilies of the field, that toiled not? There are other things to judge people by, and you'll have a more relaxed life if you do.

7 *Learn to say 'No'. Not always – but more often, and without guilt.* Maybe you do feel that no one else can do things as well as you, but that doesn't mean you have to do *everything*. People will respect and even like you more if you refuse now and then.

8 *It's OK to be vulnerable. Admit your insecurities and learn to love them.* In fact, it is more appealing to be vulnerable than you may realise. Weaknesses and insecurities can be endearing qualities, especially if they are unexpected.

9 *Don't be a rescuer – you are not responsible for other people.* You can't change other people, either. The individual only makes changes when he or she wants to. You can't do it for them, and you can't protect them from their own weakness. Don't try.

10 *Avoid solipsism. Don't be too self-centred.* You know all those remarks about only children being selfish and self-centred? Prove them wrong. Prove that we can be as considerate of others as anyone else.

Part 3

For Partners and New Parents

If you are not an only child, we would not be surprised if by now you are thinking, 'This is so typical of only children. It's all self – all from *their* point of view. What about how other people see you, to add a touch of down-to-earth realism?'

This is just what we are going to do now, starting with the views and experiences of those closest to only children – their partners. We then go on to give advice to those who have, or are planning to have, an only child. It is not *our* advice: it comes from our interviewees themselves, and we hope it will be useful to parents.

12 Partners

We have taken our time in getting to the views of people other than only children. This is not because what they have to say is any less important, but because we felt it essential to define first the only-child experience from the only-child viewpoint.

Remember, if you are the partner of an only child, that only children haven't had the benefit you may have had of growing up with an annoying sibling or two to remind them unfailingly of their peculiarities. What we have tried to do is to provide points of recognition for only children, by which they can identify some of the features they have in common with other onlies and which until now they probably thought were their own personal foibles. Through this recognition they have the opportunity, if they wish, to see themselves as part of a distinct group – even if it is one with widely divergent characteristics – with a defining common experience from which many of these patterns have developed.

So where do *partners* come into this? Well, if only children do have common behaviour patterns arising from their distinct upbringing, then the people likely to be most exposed to such behaviour are their partners. Our first message of reassurance – we hope – for partners is that those irritating quirks that you have had to live with may not all be the personal idiosyncrasies of your beloved – some of them may stem from his or her being an only child.

From what many partners have told us, we have been able to identify quite a few of these peculiarities below. You may still find such behaviour strange, but at least you'll have an idea of why he or she may be doing it! We offer suggestions on how best to respond to annoying behaviour, and how to make life easier for yourself in living with your special only child! We wouldn't want you to think we are expecting you always to adjust to fit these strange creatures, only children.

So now we let the partners speak.

I don't know how I can have been so foolish, but I have actually married two only children! I've no doubt at all that they are a breed apart. Bless their hearts – it is that they somehow are not quite as aware of other people as the rest of us. Both my husbands, as only sons, are used to thinking that the world revolves around them and their needs. I don't think this is just because of doting mothers, because actually number one had rather an indifferent mother. It is just that you've never been used to having to take on board the needs and wishes of a group, or have any experience of adjusting your needs to fit in. It really isn't that he is selfish – when reminded he is the most thoughtful and considerate of men. It is simply that thoughts of considering others are not, as it were, endemic . . . he has to be reminded. However busy and stressed I am, he thinks of himself first.

The partners we have talked to have identified some problem areas, which we examine in the following pages. Those that occurred most frequently were only children's

difficulties with sharing;
fear of emotional closeness;
emotional immaturity;
problems as parents;
tendency to put self first;
problems with anger and conflict; and

being over-responsible, as well as too serious.

Of course, difficulties in relationships are not confined to only children, as we noted earlier. But we want to identify those elements that may arise directly from the early experience of the only child. And although this chapter concentrates on the difficulties of living with only children, they do have their strengths too – indeed, it was probably those that attracted their partners to them in the first place. Remember that only children are responsible, willing to work on their shortcomings, reliable, loyal and often successful. Being a partner of an only child is not all bad!

It does sound as though I'm complaining, and really I'm not. I believe, actually, that only children can be more considerate. It is as though once they've recognised their faults they are much more willing than other people to make up for them. Perhaps that's why I've married two of them!

Before looking in more detail at the particular problem areas, we make four observations:

1 Most obviously, living with someone is about being close to an individual of equivalent power (that is, a peer as distinct from a parent). And it is the absence of that experience that is almost the very definition of only children.

2 But although they may have no experience of close relationships, that doesn't mean they don't want them. Indeed, they may have a great need for them. For a partner, the odd behaviour of an only child doesn't mean she doesn't love you or care about you – just that she isn't used to having someone living so close to her.

3 Expectations of a relationship can have a significant effect upon its progress. And what partners find – if they have a sibling-family background, once they are living with an only child, may be very different from what they expected. Of course, we all have a public

persona that differs from our private one behind closed doors, but the contrast between these personae may, for only children, be greater than for most. The shock of this contrast may throw some partners, who find the only-child behaviour difficult to deal with. Prospective partners may be taken in by the exceptional confidence, reliability or leadership that only children show in public, and be unprepared, once within domestic confines, for the uncertainty and lack of interpersonal skills they find there.

4   Conversely, just as we have said before that only children may be unduly idealistic about the benefits of having siblings, so in having no practical experience from which to assess relationships they may have unrealistic expectations of cohabitation, based upon a fantasised image. One possible consequence is that, like this interviewee, they set themselves up for failure:

A real dilemma – I perceived my parents as being happy together. I wanted to be with my new husband how my parents were – holding hands down the street, obviously in love, etc. – but I had no skills to get there, except to do what my mother told me and it would happen.

So what have the partners' views given us? Most obviously, they have contributed a description of only children that centres on their difficulties in relationships, and confirms their problems with space, closeness, anger and commitment.

Overwhelmingly, the most important element of successful living with a partner is a set of skills and qualities in which the only child tends to be deficient. These are the skills of SHARING: sharing time, space, emotions and resources. They are skills in which only children, lacking that immensely shaping childhood experience of rough and tumble, have not been trained. Of course, through other life experiences they may have acquired some sharing skills.

However, remember our earlier analysis, which suggested that their social maturity might have been gained at the expense of their emotional maturity. So when you start out on a life with an only child, you could at worst find yourself taking on the equivalent of a learner driver who, however well versed in the highway code of relationships, lacks all practical knowledge of the fundamentals of cohabitation.

The important thing for you to remember, as the partner or friend of an only child, is that when it comes to sharing they are very late starters in the game of cohabitation. Let's now look at how this lack of experience in the sharing business affects people, and how *you* as partner can deal with it.

Their Own Space

Time and again the partners of only children, and indeed they themselves, have pointed out to us the need to find some separate space of their own, whether it be a room, a desk or even a shed:

> *Definitely, he physically takes himself away, either to the study or to the garden, or to the shed if it is raining. Somehow, he always manages that!*

Most only children have been used to having some space – often just their own bedroom, however small – which is their own. They may have been used to living communally, in the way that most families do, but doing so out of their own personal space. What they have lacked is the experience of sharing space with a peer, and when they *have* shared it has mostly been with people who were more powerful than they – notably, their own parents. Having no idea of how to share space on an equal footing, they may not comprehend that it is possible to stake your own claim to, or to negotiate for your part of, your bit of attention.

The only child may resent changes being made to any living space without prior negotiation, since he is used to being able to leave things, then to come back and find them exactly as he left them. To those who have been brought up in a large family, this may seem a quirky notion that smacks of being stick-in-the-mud, too rigid and so on. Only children may be acutely conscious of this and therefore reluctant to make too much fuss, but the failure of others to recognise this need for private and untouched space may result in them becoming frustrated and intolerant, often without their recognising the reason for it:

I respect her need for space absolutely. But what I find difficult is that she spreads her things everywhere, all over my space. How is this? How can her need be so exclusive? Why does she need to make such a point of needing her own space so much that she takes over mine as well?

Cohabitation should be about sharing power, as well as sharing space, time, resources and responsibility. The early living situation of only children involved people of superior power – their parents – so that they are unused to having the same rights as a partner. Sharing in their early years happened only when the parents permitted it. They may fear losing whatever power they now have if they are too close to someone else.

When you live with people, and share all the space with them, it may mean that others will do things to your space or to your things in that space – what you leave won't necessarily be there unchanged when you return. This is especially the case when there are children around. Unless some agreement has been arrived at, the only child can easily feel affronted or imposed on if she finds that changes have been made.

Sharing Time

It was absolutely extraordinary to me that Roger would not think there was anything odd about him going off to the sailing club at the weekends. He would do it every other weekend, even when the children were tiny and I really needed him at home. Well, no, I didn't need him, exactly. I could manage without him, but I wanted him there. He never understood. To him, he was part of the sailing club, and he had to go there no matter what I wanted.

The only child grew up being able to make his own timetable, and often thinking that the world revolved round him. The result, for some partners, is that they find themselves and their needs coming a poor second:

I can never do anything spontaneously because the message I always get from him is 'If you disturb my timetable there will be big shit – you'll really have to pay for it.' He has a lack of respect for other people around. Everything is mapped out by him and for him.

It can leave partners feeling peripheral, unwanted, not an essential part of the only child's life:

It is the norm to an only child to be on his own. Company can be a great and much wanted addition. But it is the addition, not the norm.

Of course, sharing time and space and resources extends to sharing your families too. Mostly the experience of our interviewees was that they welcomed partners or close friends who came from large families, and leapt at the chance to join in the communal activity they had missed. A word of caution, though. As we've already hinted, the only child may well live in something of a fantasy world as far as what living together should be like. As we have seen, it is not unusual for the only to marry into a large family *because* she is conscious of all that has been lacking in her family life hitherto. It is as though she hopes at one fell swoop to make up for not having had the opportunity to share time and space thus far. Be warned. It will be a rare only child who possesses the skills that allow her to do this immediately. It is likely that friction will occur because the need for space reasserts itself, over and above her desire to change:

> *My friend and I both married only children, and both of them have had problems with our siblings and see them as a threat, in part for the control they have over us. It's because it's something only children never had and can't understand. So they can't under-stand how siblings can have apparent power over you – but they're just brother and sister, so they do. My partner can't understand how they have the right to be judgemental. I feel because they give me unconditional love they do have the right to be judgemental. At a subliminal level, for only children it is denying that right to a sibling's attention because they don't have siblings. If they can't have them, why should we?*

Or, at worst, this is expressed as:

> *There's the feeling from only children that 'It's all right for you, you've got those relations you can turn to, those relations to help you, but I've only got aged parents – so why do we have to be involved with your family?'*

How to cope
Somehow or another, try to ensure that your particular only child has some of that precious space that he covets so much. It needn't be much – a cupboard or even a drawer may suffice – but it must be private and it must be left untouched at all times by everyone else. Also – crucially important – don't start imagining that the need to get away from others and spend time alone is anything to do with rejecting you and your relationship. It isn't! Most onlies will so much appreciate the opportunity to be alone for a short time that they will return with greatly renewed energy and pleasure to the communal scene.

> *On holiday or when out with a group, it's worse keeping an eye on him than on the kids. It's a nightmare, for example, if you go to a new town or, say, a French market with him. He always wanders off. He has no awareness of being part of a group. He won't say where he is going, he just goes, and if I tax him with it he just says, 'Well, I knew where you were.'*

I'm conscious of being alone and like it, and need to spend time alone. It's a largish house, so I'm never crowded. I don't like anyone knowing what I'm doing all the time. I like time for myself to do what I want. If we go on holiday together we both make a break for a couple of hours in an afternoon – it's never been discussed, it just happens.

When you go on holiday, build in a little time for him to go off on his own. Encourage the expectation that this is inevitable and normal, that everyone will accept it, and that he need not feel guilty about it. We are not suggesting that partners should be martyrs about this – when the only child comes back from his solitary walk, make sure he minds the kids. But building this kind of time and space into your lives will be helpful to everyone – and, not least of all, to you. He will not want to spend every hour of your life together with you, so you may both benefit from the space.

Remember how important planning is to the only child? This is a big help when it comes to organising the sharing of your space and time, and can extend to resources too. Sit your only-child partner down with a diary, a map, a year-planner and a list of plans, and he'll be happy to organise it all for both of you. He'll be loyal about keeping to it, too – another of his good characteristics. Then, as long as you don't depart from the plans too much (or don't let him notice that you do), you should get on famously!

Fear of Closeness

The only child's need for space is not confined to the physical. It may well be that he has a strong need, also, for emotional space:

I always felt that he had this little room in his head where he would retreat to and close the door whenever the emotional going got tough.

When he is directly involved, he can't seem to cope. For example, his best friend's marriage is breaking up and he can't bring himself to phone him, to get himself really in there getting his hands dirty with the emotions. Now if Terry asked him to do something practical, he'd be marvellous. I suppose it's fear of inadequacy. He forces himself to do what he sees as the right thing, but would sooner do it at a distance.

The experience of the only child brought up in a two-parent family may be of always being on the outside of the central, key relationship. Even where there was only one parent, the reaction may be the same, because the relationship with the single parent may have been *too* intense, *too* close, in a way that the lone child then reacts against.

A lack of experience of emotional closeness may be observed by others as a lack of commitment, of passion, of intensity or of devotion. But it is not usually any such thing. On the contrary, the only child may be desperate to make a strong commitment, but because of past experiences may feel that this would result in her as an individual being swallowed up. The only people with whom she has lived before, her parents, both had power over her.

One of the experiences that the only child will not have had is that of a relationship that's intense one minute, cool the next; loving and easy one minute, then suddenly angry and difficult. What is lacking here is the ability, usually learned in families, to understand that you can be both close to someone *and* free of them. The only child may fear disproportionately the closeness because she may see that her own power, perhaps even her very identity, may be lost:

I've never lived with anyone – that scares me. I have a penchant for married men, which relieves me of the responsibility. I had one partner who was an only child – self-contained. His ideal relationship would be two adjoining flats with a door between. That makes sense – I'd always make sure I had a room that was mine, and they'd have to knock.

There are many only children who might echo that!

Of course, their fear of closeness doesn't exist in isolation. In particular, contrary feelings of longing for, and fear of, closeness seem to be closely linked to only children's need for personal space:

> *But I did, and do, like sharing or physical closeness. I remember with great joy sharing a room when I first went to college, being able to chat at night with the light out – I'd never had that before. I still very much enjoy sharing a room, even though I work hard to create some space for me – like having my own wardrobe and chest of drawers. I like the sharing but am scared of losing my privacy, I suppose.*

Although they may be reluctant to commit themselves, only children can be possessive and demanding of their partners, as one only-child interviewee describes:

> *Only children can take years to come to terms with sharing, and in some cases never come to grips at all. In a relationship they are much more possessive of the person – 'You're my other half' – and you feel you yourself have to be the beginning, middle and end for the other person, you have to be sufficient for all that other person's needs. The feeling is 'I'm not enough' – you've got to supply the whole works, have got to be everything for the other person. With my last relationship I left feeling I wasn't enough for him. If someone leaves me, the feeling is that there wasn't enough to hold them, because at the end of the day you were enough for your parents because they didn't want any more children.*

How to cope

Go slowly and steadily. Always be aware of the possibility of overwhelming only children. Remember, again, that their retreat need not mean in any way rejection. It is not usually that they don't *want* to be close. Nor should you even assume that they *can't* – only that they will need to practise more than people from multi-child families would, because they have a whole big area to make up. Once they learn how fulfilling a close relationship can be, they can be loyal

246 FOR PARTNERS AND NEW PARENTS

partners. Take heart. They can also be quick learners.

Emotional Immaturity

As we said in Chapter 4, SOCIAL MATURITY, only children often present as more mature socially than their peers. This is because they have had more experience of adult company, they have had to 'be everything', and they have often had more responsibility placed on them than children from sibling families. Partners can be deceived by this façade, and assume that it implies a similar emotional maturity. Often, nothing could be further from the truth! Once again, we believe this has most probably arisen because only children have been deprived of what so many of our respondents have called 'the rough and tumble' of life:

> *She was so easy in company, so good at the chitchat and small talk, that I didn't realise that when it came to her emotions she was a complete novice. She never seemed to be able to talk things out or to deal with things in a spontaneous way. I found it especially difficult that she never seemed to shout at me, because I often shouted at her and it made me feel so guilty. That kind of reaction was right in work or in our social life, but it didn't feel real to me when it came to our personal life.*

Several of our respondents have reported that only children are good at coping with the practicalities when a crisis occurs, but less reliable if the reaction called for is an emotional one:

> *When our daughter was injured in an accident, he was marvellous at keeping calm, doing the practical things. What I wanted, though, was to see him scream and shout, to be reassured that he felt as badly as I did. I knew he did, but you'd never have known from his behaviour. I suppose you can't have it all ways.*

Indeed you can't, and you may have to accept this with your only-child partner.

This emotional immaturity may lead onlies to have unrealistic expectations of their partners:

I don't ask for help – 'You should know how I'm feeling,' I say to my husband!

As only children we seek unqualified love in our relationships.

As they do tend to be late developers in the emotions department, it is perhaps not surprising that many of the only children we spoke to had sought love with partners of different ages from their own. It seems natural to many of them to relate to people either considerably older or, occasionally, younger than themselves. Indeed, when we came to write *Age Gap Relationships* we found that a disproportionate number of only children were in such relationships.

Being attracted to men a fair bit older than me is out of a natural expectation that I would be around that age group, plus it links with needing my own space, so someone older will have a well developed sense of their own space, which is consequently better for me.

Audrey is 19 years older than me, although I can't say I was consciously looking for an older partner or someone with a family.

My partner's 57, and I [mid-twenties] have just thrown a massive party for sixty people for him. I was getting on wonderfully with the fifty-to-sixty age group. There's a sort of security thing with them – I don't feel secure with someone younger.

Many of my partners have been older, clever men. I've always had a definite pattern of being looked after than looking after.

It is easier relating to older people. You've always got an insecurity with people your own age. You are an outsider with them.

One only child offered an explanation:

Whatever they are, only children are not risk-takers. They are cautious and responsible. They don't want to say they'll do something if they don't think they can accomplish it, and this natural caution is never more apparent than in their relationships. Add to

*that the fact that they have usually had the experience of being
more at ease with older people than those of their own age, because
the skills they learned at home of being socially mature led them
to find it easier to relate to people older than themselves than with
their peers.*

How to cope

First of all, realise that emotional maturity can be acquired.
It is going to be very important that you and your partner
understand that talking about and sharing your feelings
can be enormously helpful. If you come from a multi-child
family, you may have learned more about expressing your
feelings than you know, and certainly it is likely that you
will be more adept at it than the only child.

Emotional maturity can be acquired in all sorts of ways:
through experience, through example – even, perhaps,
through a planned programme of counselling. Only children, like other people, can learn to recognise what they
need to do to bring their emotional reactions in line with
their social ones. As they grow more confident in their
emotions, so they become less anxious about their in-
adequacies. It is not the lack of maturity in itself that is
the real problem. Many second, third and fourth children
are immature in the emotions department, and everyone
learns to live with them. The problem for onlies is that
there is this mismatch between how they appear and how
they are. Consequently, as we have noted, partners and
others have unreasonable expectations of them. Finding
that the only child is vulnerable like everyone else can be
a very reassuring discovery for a partner:

*I suppose I was always in awe of her, really, because she always
seemed in control, and inwardly I think I resented that because it
made me feel inadequate. When I found she, too, was a gibbering
wreck inside, it helped our relationship no end, and we were able
to be closer because I found she needed me much more than I had
realised.*

Self, Self, Self

I've no proof of this, but I always think that only children must be over-represented in the world of acting. I know that my husband is transformed when the spotlight is on him, whether he's speaking at a meeting, giving a speech or in some other way being the centre of attention.

Seeing yourself at the centre of the universe and as having the right to be at the centre of the universe is an occupational hazard for the only child, and consequently a hazard for his partner. Remember what we said about the only child who takes the last slice of cake? You will have to live with that. You will probably be able to teach your particular only child that he shouldn't do so, but it is more difficult to deal with the feeling he will have that he has a *right* to take it:

Dave wouldn't take the last slice of cake because he has learned that it is not polite to do so. But he has no natural embarrassment about doing so. There is nothing wrong, for him, in thinking that the last slice is his, whereas in my house the last slice would naturally have been cut into four so we all had a share.

On holidays, Brian just used to go off without a care in the world, he just went off. I think there's a risk that without siblings only children aren't brought up to respect other people's wishes. If they are not trained to respect these they can turn out horrible people. If you have had a detached relationship with your parents, as he had, it can be especially difficult. A 'Why should I consider you in my actions?' feeling.

Indeed, the partner of the only child may have to be constantly reminding him that he has to consider other people. On the whole, those we talked to were reasonably tolerant about this, if only because they found that their only-child partners were usually apologetic or even remorseful when their self-centredness was pointed out:

I can't be angry with him for too long, really, because he doesn't mean to be selfish. He is just programmed that way. He's mortified when he realises how it seems to others.

As a partner, though, you will have to train yourself to understand that it *may* be an unending task.

Children?

One of the consequences of putting themselves first may be, for only children, that they have difficulties with the idea of having children. So you must check this out carefully. In fact, a surprising number of our interviewees expressed rather strong feelings about *not* wanting children:

I honestly never considered having a family of my own – I always told my husband so. I had a very strong preference not to. I suppose I felt I'd had the experience of parenting my own parents, and didn't want to repeat it.

For many, it was because of a dislike of children:

I can't stand children – they revolt me. Nappies and that . . . I can't see the point and I wouldn't have the patience.

I hate kids. I have a real problem with kids – the younger they are, the worse the problem. I don't want kids and really worry about it. I'm used to being on my own, not used to being responsible for someone else – the whole thing scares me witless. I do have motherly instincts, but towards men. That's what happens. It worries me that I can't face the idea of kids.

I absolutely can't stand kids. I absolutely recoil when they come near me in the supermarket. I can't bear kids a million miles near me. I think that's quite unusual?

I absolutely don't want any children, and have had the snip. Luckily my wife doesn't want any either, so we're a committed childless pair. I don't like children, really. I don't dislike them (because they are human beings) but I don't like them in the house. The irony is that they like me and crawl all over me, and I sit there inwardly seething but making them laugh. And I'm on the edge of screaming!

There is often a lack of any previous contact with babies:

I've no nieces and nephews – I'm not used to being with small children, and don't really like them. With young children I have to sit on my hands because I am motivated by an overwhelming desire to slap them. I have never thought about babies, apart from fleetingly for five seconds in 1972. Now, the more I see of small children, the more I think I've made the right decision.

After school – and, more significantly, perhaps, after primary school – only children may never have spent any time in contact with young children. If they have no nieces or nephews, for example, their whole experience may have been with adults, and kids can then seem very frightening because they are so unpredictable. Children, after all, don't usually play by the 'rules', and they can make it difficult to plan things out – something, as we have seen, that onlies like to do. And with their lack of experience in playing with others when they themselves were young, only children may feel inadequate and inexperienced in playing with small children now.

How to cope
Don't be afraid to point out to your partner times when he is being self-centred. (Most only children are very worried about this, and keen to correct it if they can.) Don't let him get away with it. Point it out and the chances are he will learn, if not to eliminate it at least to stifle his self-centredness fifty per cent of the time!

As to the question of having children, you'll have to proceed with caution. It is absolutely vital, though, that you don't take anything for granted. Don't assume your only-child partner will want children, or be able to cope if you have them. Talk about it. Don't ignore it. Be sure you know how important it is to you to have children, and don't assume that the only child will change his mind as time goes by. Remember that they are strong-minded and don't easily take risks. Because unfamiliarity has a lot to do with it, any introductions to young children you can make may help him to change. You'll need to do this, as well as build up his confidence about how he can relate to them.

Anger

As we saw in Chapter 4, SOCIAL MATURITY, only children tend to have problems with anger, and the fact that they don't show anger can be absolutely infuriating for their partners:

> *I can't stand the way he never loses his rag. Because he always seems calm and doesn't get in a tizz, it makes me feel a fool if I lose my temper. Somehow, it leaves him in control.*

Yes, of course it does – that's *why* he never loses his temper, . because he wants to remain in control. The only child may see that being placatory and remaining calm is a strength, but for the partner it can undoubtedly be pretty riling. Once you realise that the reason he doesn't get angry is not that he is superman but because he doesn't know how to cope and is ill at ease, then you understand. As one partner said:

> *He buries conflict instead of resolving it. I have to force him to bring it into the open.*

As we have seen, many only children do lack the skills to resolve conflict. Set this alongside their above-average ability as a mediator, and you often have a tendency to skate around the edge of family conflicts rather than be directly involved. Perhaps the key is this:

> *When the only child is directly involved she can't be objective – it comes from all that concentration on self and lack of emotional maturity. She prefers to be one step removed. But, of course, a feature of family life is that you are always directly involved.*

How to cope

It hasn't been easy, but I've made him get involved in rows and upsets. He even gets cross quite often now. Of course, he always did . . . he can just show it more now. When he really blew his top with me the first time, I think he was quite surprised to find I was still here when he came back after storming out of the house. I'd had a monopoly on storming out before!

Don't assume you are in the wrong because you get cross. Remember that the only child is not superior because he does not lose his temper – it's that he's just an amateur when it comes to squabbling. Teach him that you can be cross with someone and still love them, that someone can shout at you one minute and laugh with you the next.

An Overdeveloped Sense of Responsibility

Let's face it – only children can be dull, too conscientious, over-responsible, lacking in a sense of fun and altogether a bit of a pain. Life to them is a serious business, and they are not the most relaxed of people when it comes to how the family presents to the world. Remember all the 'Be perfect' messages they received – those aren't easy to ignore. Remember too how, from an early age, they felt the weight of all the responsibility:

Alwin is very concerned indeed about how other people see us. He wouldn't want the boys to go out looking scruffy, for example, and if they behave badly he gets uptight because he thinks it is a reflection on him. He feels responsible for all of us.

Jim is so serious all the time. When the kids and I are larking about and making a noise, there he'll be, shushing us. We were all in the pictures recently, and Jo and I got the giggles about something extremely silly. I was helpless with laughter, but he kept telling me to pull myself together. I feel sad, really, because I know it is only that he never learned that irresponsible stuff, like I did as the youngest of a big family.

How to cope

Try to be patient and to understand that your only child may be longing to be irresponsible, but doesn't know how. He can learn, bit by bit, and will probably love doing so. He also has to learn that other people can be responsible too:

> *Only children as parents have to fit into what's an unfamiliar situation, including that of other people taking responsibility.*

If you ever get too fed up, remember how useful it is to be with someone who does see that the bills are paid on time, who orders more fuel before it runs out, and who can be relied on to have the right documents to hand at the airport. He hasn't been used to sharing responsibility, only to taking it *all* on. And he may welcome sharing responsibility for the upkeep of a house or car, for example. It can be a great relief not to have to battle on on your own.

They may not be a bundle of fun, but they do have their good points, these only children. When you have taught them to laugh at themselves a bit, they make perfect mates!

Family Life

> *No one should be allowed to have only one child. Being an only makes it virtually impossible to fit in with family life.*

Strong words, spoken by the wife of an only child, but time and again the only children and their partners have expressed to us their difficulties about fitting into family life:

> *Remember, there is a whole area of family life that they know nothing at all about, a whole area of experience which you can never make up. It's about rivalry, about competing for attention, rowing, making up, roughing it in relationships, which only children have never had and can never have. I know I enjoyed a very privileged position as the youngest child of three, but I always felt so sorry for Jim [husband]. He used to look so forlorn when*

the children and I were being silly and having fun. Somehow, for him, being close in a family was serious and full of effort, whereas I know it should be fun.

The rules of family life are another area where only children may not be very knowledgeable or experienced. Unwritten and never discussed, these rules exist none the less, and they tell you just how far you can go with teasing someone, what the limits of baiting a person are, when you have to stop playing up. With siblings the rules are learned, either through their reactions or through others' reactions to them. Only children never have the opportunity to see these transactions – which explains their reactions, or over-reactions, to what they perceive as 'fairness'. They have learned to judge by adult rules, not in the cut-and-thrust world of siblings. Therefore, while having a great need to participate in family life, they are often inadequate when it comes to it:

Dave's problem is that he likes to be involved with the children's fighting and their rough games, but doesn't know the rules. I'm one of four so I think I know how far to go, know when things are getting out of hand. I know the line between teasing and hurting. Dave doesn't know this. I watch and I listen and I can tell what's happening. I think, 'Here we go, that's over the top, he should have stopped one stage earlier.' Then I hear the tears and screams and think to myself, 'If he knew the rules we wouldn't have had this trouble.'

How to cope

As the partner of an only child, you are going to have to help him make up for this lack of experience. You will have to understand that things you take for granted, like people coming in when you are in the bathroom, other people moving your things, noisy siblings, teasing and family jokes may not be what he is used to. He may have to learn to adapt slowly, and be helped to do so. The good thing about only children is that they may wish very much to make these adaptations and to become involved with the rough and tumble. We stress again that what they lack is not the will, but the skills, to do it. They will often make a lot of effort with their partner's family in order to make up for their lack of experience. Many only children we have spoken to have told us how important that family was to them. They often welcome the opportunity to fit into a larger family:

> *I remember being so delighted when I found that Giles was one of four. I felt that I'd suddenly got the chance to be one of a family group. My parents were so much older that I'd always been lonely, so my brother- and sisters-in-law were like a comfort blanket to me.*

13 Hints for New Parents of an Only Child

No one is born a parent. Everyone has to learn how to be one, and perhaps the best anyone can hope for is that our children will one day say, 'They did the best they could.' We asked all the only children we interviewed what advice they would give to parents who were planning to have only one child. Many had an instant reply, often expressed very firmly: 'Don't'.

Oh God – have another one, or two – that's the first advice.

Don't have any if you can only have one. Think about how the child will feel. You can't observe your parents being parents to another. You can't judge or keep a sense of proportion. It's too much responsibility for one person.

Well, this is probably too late, but don't *do it.* DON'T!

Not one of our interviewees advised having only one child:

In the sense of whether I would ever advise anyone to have an only child because the pay-off might justify it, I would say no, there are no real advantages. Of course, you find positive things in any experience – people who came out of Belsen said they learned positive things.

and, less seriously, from one husband of an only child:
'Don't do it!'

In spite of this heartfelt advice, we know that through
either choice or circumstance some parents will have just
one child. Those we interviewed gave thoughtful advice to
parents on how to minimise the difficulties, drawing on
their own experience. Our theme throughout has been that
while being an only child is a special experience and can
certainly have its problems, it is understanding that experience that is the key to coping with the situation. Only
children *can* be happy, relaxed and well adjusted indi-
viduals. Parents who choose to have only one, or who have
the choice forced upon them, have no need to feel guilty
about it. Indeed, it is vital that they do not do so. There
is the risk that such guilt may, as we have seen in several
cases, be offloaded on to the child.

None the less, in an apparently family-centred society,
the parent of an only child may be misunderstood and feel
resentful about the assumptions made by other people:

*The concept is that to have only one child is selfish, and to have
none is even more so. 'Lovely people have lots of children', goes
the mythology.*

*I feel that I've always had to defend myself about having only
one. People are always asking you when you are going to have
another, and when you say, 'Never', they start wagging their
fingers at you and warning you about the perils of spoilt onlies
and all that. In fact, I wasn't able to have any more after Harry,
for medical reasons, and I really resent the lack of understanding
shown about that. There is no more reason to assume I'm selfish
than there is to assume Harry is spoilt.*

We have already noted that being an only child has
advantages as well as disadvantages. Successful parenting
means capitalising on the good and minimising the bad.
Our interviews indicated four main pointers for the parents
of an only child:

1 *Cherish the childhood of your only child.* Don't make him or her into a little adult too early.

2 *Compensate for him being an only child* . . . but not too much!

3 *Don't make an ally of him* in your relationship with his other parent . . . the triangle.

4 Remember, *he cannot be everything.* Get your own life in order.

For the only child, parents do play a greater role in her life because the parental influence is undiluted by siblings. Parents are likely to be much stronger models for the only child than for sibling children, and it is this which contributes to her advanced adult behaviour. There may also be little scope for evaluation by the lone child of her own or parental behaviour. What you as parents say and do *must* be right in her judgement – she can't see your different interaction with a sibling, and thereby realise how fallible you are!

But first, a word about parenting in general. There is no such thing as a perfect parent. What you can be as a parent, what you can give, is largely determined by your own experience of being parented. If you yourself were an only child with some of the 'absences' that we have identified, there is no magic formula by which you will be able to overcome all that and become a totally different kind of person in your role as a parent. What you have to aim for – all you can aim for – is to improve a little on the experience you had, and to smooth out some of the rough edges for your own child. If you can do that, and above all if you can establish sufficiently good communication with your only child to enable you to discuss important issues, share feelings with her and enable her to share hers, then you will have done pretty well.

Cherish the Childhood

I hesitate to give advice – if parents felt there were good enough reasons that they only wanted one, I'd obviously say, 'Think carefully', but the choice is theirs. Have other children in the house, keep that relationship with children their own ages as much as possible so they can relate to their own peer groups, and keep a very free and easy atmosphere.

Remember what we said in Chapter 4, SOCIAL MATURITY. Being surrounded by adult company, the only child may rapidly become the little adult and bypass childhood.

It is important to let the child have a full childhood. Because only children tend to be very stimulated, with two adults tending to them, they seem older to the parents than they are -- because of their vocabulary, etc. – and then the parents may expect and demand more of the child than the stage of development they are at.

There is a real risk of integrating them so much into your adult life that it's quite late before they start getting a life of their own.

Several interviewees we quoted in Chapter 4 felt that they had missed out on childhood:

I went straight into being an adult.

Of course, every parent wants their child to be the most advanced, to be capable beyond her years. This is natural. The dangers for the child are that

1   she has no sibling interactions to compensate;
2   she becomes over-influenced by adult standards and expectations.

So you must be prepared for these dangers, and ensure that there is plenty of children's company for her. Our interviewees had lots of suggestions about this:

If they are going to grow up socially normal they need other kids – they need as much contact with kids their own age as possible, so they don't end up isolated.

Have your children mixing with children of their own age early. Like Angela – we've been friends since I was five – I've got really strong bonding with her because we are the same age. We have only not been best buddies when there have been boyfriends around.

Have your house as an open house, where there could always be children staying or they could play, a very relaxed house where they would want to come. And I'd have bunk beds in rooms – a sense of belonging. At Christmas I would try and get together with other families, and, say, rent a house if I could. I would always make it not just the three of us, if possible. I would try and make all celebrations a sense of occasion and bring others together, so we felt part of a whole big gang. Then everyone's around and the only child wouldn't notice being just one.

And one recalled

. . . the pleasure of hearing my two children playing together – something I was unable to experience in my own lonely childhood.

But remember that the play is for the child's benefit:

I noticed that when other children came to play at my house my parents tended to expect us to play near them, almost to participate, whereas if I went to their houses it was different – the parents would just send us off to play. My parents seemed almost to want us to entertain them.

And remember, too, that she may find it difficult or confusing being a child with friends, while being a small adult with you:

Don't split the roles. I was expected to play different roles. When other kids were around I had to be a normal child with them. It was different when there were adults about. It was one hell of a shock to play with hooligans you don't want to be with, when you are used to adult company.

Several interviewees agreed on the value of staying overnight with friends, and vice versa:

Find as many opportunities as possible to mix and meet with other kids, especially having friends to stay overnight.

And always try to remember that underneath the mature exterior of your charming 'little adult' there is a small and very uncertain child. So:

Make your only child feel wanted. Make sure the only child has plenty of company of the same age. And don't pin all your hopes and expectations on one person or let too much weigh down on them – they are more sensitive, and there's only them to take the burden.

Compensate, But Not Too Much

Parents of one child undoubtedly face a dilemma about how indulgent they should be. On the one hand, this child is their one chance, their precious jewel. On the other, they are haunted by that most familiar of charges against the only child – the 'spoilt brat' tag. Of course, we believe you should try to achieve some kind of middle way between these two extremes, but we recognise that it may be easier said than done. We feel that at least we can be reassuring about the latter.

The most frequent comment made either to only children or about them is that they are 'spoilt'. Unsurprisingly, this is also the one comment that infuriates only children most, by its constant repetition (and, to them – or most of them – its irrelevance):

It annoys me when people will say, 'Oh you're so lucky you don't have to share with brothers and sisters, and all these things you can do which other people can't because they can't afford it', and the assumption that you'd always be spoilt – it is so irritating. I think there are times when you are very young that you are a bit precocious because you tend to be more adult than the other children of that age. That's an assumption people make – if you are a bit like that they say, 'Oh, you are spoilt', because they can't handle it.

There *are* some spoilt only children, and some recognise it:

> *I was terribly spoilt, terribly – I never did anything in the house – washing or hoovering or anything. I've been spoilt rotten, and as a consequence I am totally incapable of sharing anything.*

When they say 'spoilt', most people mean in one of two ways. Either they mean the child is materially spoilt – too many possessions, or insufficient awareness of their value or meaning – or they mean that the child's behaviour reveals insufficient awareness of other people's need for space or attention. Both come together in the popular description of the 'spoilt brat'.

But in general, only children are no more or less 'spoilt' than any other children. Being over-indulged is a consequence of parental attitudes, not of the family structure. Parents of siblings so inclined will be as likely to spoil their children as any parent of an only child. Spoiling can happen irrespective of resources: it is more about letting a child have all he wants, whether what's available is a little or a lot. It is more about not involving a child in a share of the household chores and not teaching him to suppress his own needs in favour of those of others when appropriate, than it is about there being only one child to make use of those resources. And being spoilt is not necessarily the same as being self-centred. Certainly, only children may have a self-centred outlook on the world, as both they and their parents realise.

Only children can be spoilt in the amount of parental attention they receive (see under *All the Attention* in Chapter 1), but the consequences of this are not generally considered indicative of a spoilt child.

These children certainly have their share of human failings. But because everyone thinks of the terms 'spoilt child' and 'only child' as synonymous, many parents seem to have been so aware of the risk that they went in the opposite direction, to avoid spoiling the child:

My parents were so worried about me being seen as a spoilt only child that they went the other way and never recognised anything. So they ignored a lot of things, including the cries for help.

Far from being irredeemably selfish, only children's greater exposure to adults and adult behaviour often instils 'correct' manners and behaviour very early:

I think we are overly polite. I think I'm so conscious of possible selfishness I've gone the other way.

As one partner reminded us:

It really isn't that he is self-centred by design. When I remind him, he can be hugely generous and considerate. He has to be reminded, but then if anything he is over-conscious of others' feelings.

Don't let the risk of producing a spoilt only child put you off giving instinctive attention to your child.

Our interviewees were, needless to say, very aware of the 'spoilt' tag, and offered various suggestions:

Strike a balance between being overly restrictive and totally lax.

You've got to be very careful of the balance. Don't over-indulge, because it's bad if the child always gets what it wants. On the other hand, you don't want to over-cosset the child. There's a danger of the parent putting absolutely everything into that child – won't let it walk down the road on its own. It's got to be allowed a certain amount of freedom.

Allowing the child to make its own mistakes – not smothering it. Try not to inhibit them by being overprotective – that was my problem. Give them as much freedom as you can bear to do.

It is important to consider the particular needs of your only child when thinking about schooling. A sibling of the opposite sex introduces early familiarity of this other species. Our only children who had been to single-sex schools felt singularly ill equipped to deal with the opposite sex when they met them later in life, as they recognised:

I don't think I had much idea how to relate to the opposite sex for ages. I only met them once I left home, and although I really enjoyed hearing men's views on things, as far as sexual relationships were concerned it took me a long time to work out how to forge them successfully!

There is something about being an only child and being isolated from the opposite sex that is very different, even from two siblings of the same sex.

Their partners were aware of this difficulty too:

He went to boys' schools, and lacks understanding of women. If he walks into a room full of women he is totally pole-axed, and doesn't know what to say.

It may be a helpful compensation to ensure they have co-educational schooling:

Don't send only children to a single-sex school. It is good for girls in that they learn better in that environment, but you have to relate to boys and it's important to do it early.

Boarding school may seem a natural substitute for the lack of siblings, but it should be clear from the nature of sibling relationships (described in Chapter 2, ROUGH AND TUMBLE) that it offers a very different experience. Competing with unrelated children, without blood ties, on foreign territory, minus the supervising influence of a loving parent, is not a substitute for the sibling experience. Far from compensating for only-child 'deprivation', it could be worsening it, as a counsellor explained:

Boarding schools are a disaster. They remember the fear of going, and of being dragged there, and then of suppressing everything and feeling afterwards that they survived. They often say now that they are survivors and will get through anything, but I'm sure it is at the price of further repressed feelings.

This is not to say that for some only children the experience was not enjoyable – indeed, for some the joys of being

with a ready-made set of playmates overcame any difficulties. For them, the holidays were worse:

> *It was lovely to see my parents but I got bored very quickly, being
> back in a place where I'd lost all my friends. I didn't really know
> anybody there.*

For not only had they lost contact with any former local
friends, there was no sibling to be with at this time.

If you are thinking of sending your only away to school,
be sure it is for his benefit and not yours:

> *My parents had been used in the UK to having time to themselves.
> Once we moved and were in Canada, they didn't get that time,
> so they sent me away to boarding school in the UK, to get that
> again. I was a couple of years behind everyone by then. I played
> truant a lot. The headmistress wrote to my parents that I was
> homesick and to take me back, and they did. They told me later
> it was the worst mistake they ever made.*

A teacher commented:

> *I have a feeling that boarding school is for the parents – by sending
> the child away to us, they won't actually have to see the child
> having other relationships, and they can resume their own intense
> one-to-one marriage relationship. Yet when the child returns home
> they can become the centre of the parents' attention again.*

So our advice is to think carefully about boarding school,
and only to go ahead if you are sure that is what your child
wants:

> *If the child wants to go to boarding school, fine, but don't push
> it. But make it co-ed. Learning to be with people is most important.*

We know that you will want to do the very best for your
child, and that everything that concerns her is likely to be
a big deal to you, but beware of

> *. . . trying to organise the life of the only child. It's easy to feel
> it is a test of you, the parent. You feel it's a huge responsibility,
> and it affects you as you feel the child reflects the parents, so you*

want it to talk properly, behave well, etc. With several children, you stand back and become interested in how they all are – although a first child can suffer a bit the same as an only.

In compensating for lack of sibling company, don't forget to bear in mind what is appropriate for your child:

It's important not to force only children to be sociable, just for the sake of it. Parents mustn't make only children do something like going to a party for the sake of it, because they think the child needs to. Parents could make being an only child a positive thing by recognising a child can sometimes be happy with their own company and by not spoiling them. There is the risk of over-compensating, by flooding the house with kids.

What parents *can* usefully do is provide an outlet or support for their child, especially once he has started school:

Parents must be able to give the children back-up. I cannot imagine living away from my parents. All the traumas faced at school or Scouts – there were no siblings to relate these to, so I related it to my parents and they gave you the business there and then. Not in the holidays or at the weekend, but when you needed it.

If you yourself are an only child or come from a small family, while you may be able to replace your child's missing siblings with other young company, there may be less you can do in the way of providing substitute aunts and uncles. This can be particularly acute for two married only children:

There is no real extended family if you are the only child of two only children, as I am. You may not necessarily want an extended family, but it would be useful to call on if need be.

One suggestion made by several of the only children we spoke to is to use godparents (or their cultural equivalent) to widen the range of adult relations.

Don't Make an Ally of Your Child

In Chapter 6 we talked about the power triangle in family relationships. The result of the alliance between the parents is that the only child often feels excluded and apart. But it may be that the strength of the triangle works another way, and that one of the parents forms an alliance with the child against the other parent. This is not a comfortable situation for the child:

He was always jealous of me. I got the feeling that after I was born my father never got a look in.

I was used in disputes and rows. I was always manipulated by Mother into being on her side. My father was scapegoated and blamed, and I was invited to recognise this and on occasion to say so.

Mum and I sort of colluded, and that affected the whole parental relationship. It was always a matter of side-taking – you'd be supported by Mum against Dad.

Another type of dependency is where a parent lives some of her life through the one child. Several of our interviewees remember this, although suspected it may just have been true of their generation:

Both parents tend to have their own lives now, don't they? My mother didn't have a life of her own – it was mine and my father's by proxy. So perhaps some of that pressure is dissipated now.

They felt lucky to have me, and stopped. But the consequence was that I definitely don't have a dominant mother, but a possessive one. We moved twice before school and I didn't go to nursery. I was very isolated, smothered by a mother who didn't want to let me out of sight. I imagine I was very precious to her, but I remember all childhood feeling smothered.

The child must have his own life, or at a later stage the problems of separation may be difficult for both parties to handle. We showed in Chapter 3, SELF-IMAGE, that teenage rebellion seems difficult, for only children. And they may need some parental help in separating:

It must be easier being a parent of more than one child – also, that would enforce parent–child separation. Parents can go away for a weekend and leave two children. How do you justify not taking one away with you?

My Mum has told Kate [this interviewee's wife] more of childhood incidents than she's ever told me! When she faced the separation of me going to uni, I think actually there was true heartache for my Mum, but for some reason she could never bring herself to tell me that she needed more communication, and so on.

Separation has its heartache for all parents, but those of only children are especially liable to try to keep the child tied to them, either to delay the pain of separation or to compensate for their own lack of company. This connects with the last of our hints in this chapter – about getting your own life in order – because this business of making an ally of the child may have its roots in unresolved conflicts in your own life.

They Can't Be Everything

Without doubt, EVERYTHING ABOUT ONLY CHILDREN IS WRIT LARGE FOR THEIR PARENTS. But it is vital that you keep a sense of proportion about what you are expecting of your child. A teacher commented:

Only children's parents expect so much more of their child – they focus all their expectations and hope on the one. All is channelled into that child. Parents expect the best of that child and for that child, and they are very protective of that child. They want teachers to be aware almost by telepathy that amongst several hundred children something may be wrong with theirs! It is hard for parents to understand why that isn't possible – they are used to that level of detail in their relationship with the child.

And our only children had equally strong opinions:

Yes, you're everything to your parents. You're their reason for being. And I think it's very easy for parents of only children to exploit that with the guilt trip.

I would say that you need to try not to focus on the only child too much. If there is a couple, it is easier. The husband and wife need to take time out for themselves and go off for an evening, have a special life and try to make the child feel they do have a life of their own, so that this focus is spread a little – so the focus doesn't come to be a burden. We have a nephew with one child. He is away a lot, and the child has to be companion for the mother – it is very hard for him. As a parent, make sure you are secure in yourself, so you are not projecting too much on to your child.

Be aware of the child's needs for its own space, that it is going to feel pressure from you to get everything right, and don't burden the child with it. Don't make them feel they are your one hope in hell.

It is easy for grown-up only children to give this advice, much harder for parents to follow it, perhaps – especially when your child appears so grown up and responsible. But remember not to be fooled by adult appearances, and don't give responsibility without dealing with the emotional needs too.

Given the number of only children we talked to, you might expect that there would be one or two among them who had been sexually abused in childhood. This was indeed the case. Two suggested that being an only child was of itself a factor in the abuse, since the only child is more likely to be alone with an adult potential abuser and because he or she is likely to want to please and to feel an obligation to fulfil the norms of the family, whatever form they may take.

Some of our interviewees felt that their parents had moved from one place to another to meet their own needs, with too little regard for how this would affect their child:

Don't move around the country a lot, or the only child will have no friends at all. It can be very traumatic, with the constant uprooting.

Whatever their circumstances – not just those of the only-child set-up – parents must make every effort not to expect a child, either by its very arrival or by its continual presence within the family, to make up for the family's shortcomings. As parents, you must be prepared to sort yourselves out, to address your own problems and difficulties, and must not expect your child to compensate for them. Don't pin all your hopes and expectations on this one child, or let too much weigh down on him or her. Only children are pretty sensitive, probably more vulnerable than they show, and there's only them to take the burden.

Summary
> *Oh heck . . . lordy . . . lordy . . . : Ask, 'Do you want to nurture the only-child experience or flatten it?'*

What most parents would wish to do is to nurture the good bits of the only-child experience, and flatten the less good bits. We believe that the advice we have offered, deriving as it does from the experience of the only children we have talked to, will enable you to do just that. And always remember the wise words of this only child:

> *I think you can expect too much of [only children]. They'll absorb everything that's going on, without throwing it down their throats all the time. A lot of people who choose only one child today put enormous pressure on that one child. I think a lot are choosing now to have one child who is going to be exceptionally bright and they can put everything into it; and those also having late children, because the parents are both professional. I would say not ever to forget that a child is a child – they must have a childhood. It's a wonderful age – enjoy it. It just goes too quickly. And let the child enjoy it. It's a time to be enjoyed.*

Conclusion

This book is a start – a first dip into the uncharted waters of the only child's personal experiences. We know that there are many issues that we haven't explored enough, and probably others of which we aren't even yet aware.

So what do we know now that we didn't when we set out to write this book?

At the start we believed that there were distinct components to the only-child experience that separated it from that of people brought up in a multi-sibling family, and that these traits had gone relatively unreported. We guessed that many single children might be well aware of many of them, but would believe them to be purely personal rather than arising, at least in part, from their upbringing. The views of our interviewees have certainly confirmed our belief in the existence of distinct only-child characteristics, but they have extended that belief in two ways.

First, there has proved to be a much more extensive range of traits than we anticipated – some we would never have dreamed of, even within our own fertile only-child imaginations. But it wasn't just the range.

Second, as our selection of quotations has shown, we were surprised by the intensity of feeling – and eloquence – expressed in describing these characteristics. We feel privileged to have been given so much of our interviewees' time, and to have shared such depth of personal insight.

On occasion, the frankness and openness of some of our respondents revealed feelings and pain so deep and intimate that we have not felt able to report them fully.

It is clear that there is still a lot more to be learned about only children. We would still welcome the reactions of only children and their partners to what we have written, and indeed to what we have not written. It has been an unexpectedly fruitful learning experience for us – one that we would be happy to continue.

*   *   *

Obviously, we have learnt a great deal about the adult lives of only children and about the nature of the upbringing that contributed to the adult outlook. This, we hope, has been reflected in the preceding pages. One feeling stands out, evident time and again in our interviewees' responses, and this is to do with the role of siblings. It does not seem to us greatly relevant whether an individual loves or hates his sibling(s), whether they get along well or fight from dawn till dusk; whether they share thoughts and feelings, or despise each other. What is significant is that they have had to adjust to the presence of siblings within the family. What they have been forced to learn through these adjustments are skills and attitudes that contribute to a healthy emotional life.

If children are nature's way of ensuring the survival of the human species, then siblings must surely furnish the natural training for social survival. Without a sibling in your upbringing, you are missing a vital social tool. The accommodation you have to make to siblings, and the shared focus this means for your parents, provide a social training for life. Of course, only children get round not having the skills that sibling experience brings; they cope without these skills initially, and learn many of them later, thus 'catching up'. Of course, they have enormous compensations, in terms of parental attention and resources. But if the compensations were *so* great, we would have expected more than just a bare handful of our interviewees to say that they were happy being only children. Clearly, onlies do feel they are missing something vital, that there is an important gap. We hope this book may help fill some of that gap.

We think we have identified the only-child experience and the behaviour that results. We want to reach people who feel that that experience may be relevant to them, and whom it may help to understand themselves better. We know, for example, that talking about their experiences has been useful to our interviewees, and that it has helped them to gain insight and understanding:

> *I responded to your request for an interview with great enthusiasm, as I have very strong and deep feelings on the subject of only children. But after we had talked, I also began to think. My marriage had recently failed and my life was in turmoil. I'd always been very aware of my husband's failings and thought I was aware and interested in understanding my own difficulties and problems. But it was only when I started to think more clearly about things, following the interview, that I was confronted with the realisation that so many of our difficulties in the marriage actually related back to my own situation as an only child and what I hadn't learned in my early life. I now realise that I have spent so much of my life trying to be 'as expected' because I had to fulfil all my parents' expectations. There was no one to share the burden. At long last I am now trying to be 'me', whoever that is. I shall never be perfect, but I think I'm OK.*

We want to help only children understand themselves a bit better, help them laugh at themselves a little, give them a few more insights – help them feel that they are OK.

Index

Websites which feature Only Children

In the United Kingdom

www.BeingAnOnly.com

A not-for-profit company that offers resources and information for only children of all ages. The website aims to become a network of only children and affiliated professionals worldwide to create a wider family of 'surrogate siblings' who understand the needs and potential of only children.

They host an annual conference, regular workshops and social events and a directory of services.

www.onlychild.org.uk

Contains stories and poetry written by adult only children about their experiences and how it has affected them. Also provides details of workshops for adult onlies in the UK.

In the United States of America

www.onlychild.com

They work with only children of all ages, their parents, relatives, friends, community organisations and educational institutions and publish a quarterly magazine, 'Only Child', which constructively addresses the concerns and interests of only children.